Solidarity Across Divides

Promoting the Moral Point of View

George Vasilev

EDINBURGH
University Press

Edinburgh University Press Ltd
13 Infirmary Street, Edinburgh, EH1 1LT
www.euppublishing.com

First published in hardback by Edinburgh University Press 2015

Typeset in 11/14 Sabon by
Servis Filmsetting Ltd, Stockport, Cheshire

A CIP record for this book is available from the British Library

ISBN 978 0 7486 9730 4 (hardback)
ISBN 978 1 3995 7097 8 (paperback)
ISBN 978 0 7486 9731 1 (webready PDF)
ISBN 978 1 4744 0510 2 (epub)

For Vasko and Petkana

Contents

Acknowledgements

This book is a product of several years' work done at various institutions. I am indebted to a long list of people who have lent their support and shown me a great deal of patience during this lengthy period.

The original incarnation of this book was my PhD thesis, written at the University of Melbourne. I owe a great deal of gratitude to Robyn Eckersley, my principle supervisor, for the devoted mentorship she provided in this period, and for the great interest she has shown in ensuring I find my feet in the academic world since. Robyn facilitated my encounter with the book's key theoretical works, inspired my passion for them, and taught me the skills necessary for their analysis. I could not imagine writing this book without her involvement, and it is therefore to her I owe the greatest intellectual debt.

I would also like to acknowledge the crucial contribution made by Les Holmes during this period as my associate supervisor. His astute observations and input from a comparative perspective helped hone some of the unwieldy segments of the book and brought its empirical component into closer alignment with its theoretical one. I am most fortunate for the positive intellectual influence he has had over me, first as my lecturer, then as supervisor, and now as colleague.

Will Kymlicka and Matthew Festenstein were the examiners of my PhD thesis. I am grateful for their careful reading of my work and their generous feedback. This proved extremely beneficial in guiding me with my book revisions.

In 2011–12, I was a postdoctoral fellow at the University of Melbourne and the European University Institute in Florence,

Italy. A significant overhaul of the book manuscript was carried out during this period. I would like to express my gratitude to the sponsors of these fellowships – the Australian European University Institute Fellowships Association and the University of Melbourne. The fellowships were an opportunity to make writing and research my sole academic pursuits for a brief period, and I am grateful to have profited from this indulgence in the beautiful surrounds of each institution. In particular, I would like to thank Rainer Bauböck for his exceptional mentorship and incisive feedback on various aspects of the book during my stay at the European University Institute.

I would also like to express my gratitude to the Centre for Balkan Studies, University of Bologna, Italy, where I spent several weeks as a visiting researcher. Stefano Bianchini and Francesco Privitera, along with Sara Barbieri, Camilla Bruschi, Sonia Geromino and Federica Gorni went above and beyond the call of duty to make me feel at home and to ensure my stay was productive. I was provided with a hefty collection of books from the Centre as a going away gift, to which I have returned time and again to build on my knowledge of Balkan politics.

I began working at La Trobe University in 2013 as a lecturer in politics and have benefited greatly from many conversations and friendships there. I would like to thank the following colleagues in particular for their company and advice in the course of writing the book: Dennis Altman, Miriam Bankovsky, Nicholas Barry, Nick Bisley, Daniel Bray, Carolyn D'Cruz, Ben Habib, Jim Leibold, Margaret Mayhew, Michael O'Keefe, Tarryn Phillips, Chris Roche, Raul Sanchez-Urribari, Jon Symons, Gwenda Tavan, Dirk Tomsa and Jasmine Westendorf.

Other colleagues who have been generous with their time and criticism during conversations, seminars, reading groups and peer reviews in the course of writing the book include: Karin de Vries, Camille La Brooy, Mark Chou, John Dryzek, Kingsley Edney, Selen Ercan, Jean-Paul Gagnon, Xabier Itçaina, Joseph Lacey, Adrian Little, Claire Loughnan, Anita Manatschal, Philomena Murray, Jacinta O'Hagan, Vesco Paskalev, Avery Poole, Chris Reus-Smit, Andrew Schaap, Jon Symons, Bosko Tripković, Alexander Trechsel, Ines Valdez and David Walker. In particular,

I would like to thank Selen Ercan for carefully reading the full book manuscript and offering valuable comments.

I wish to acknowledge the professionalism of the staff at Edinburgh University Press. In particular, I would like to thank Jenny Daly and Michelle Houston for their enthusiastic support of the book, Eliza Wright for her attentive desk editing and stoic patience during my many requests and queries, and the anonymous referees, whose feedback was highly beneficial in the redrafting process.

Daniel Bray and Sana Nakata have been incredibly supportive friends and colleagues. I would like to thank them for their encouragement and companionship over the years, not to mention all the 'free supervision' they have provided by reading over many drafts and offering sound advice on matters scholarly or otherwise. Their fantastic dinners and fine wines provided the sustenance and high spirits required for the serious business of writing a research monograph.

Other friends have also left their mark on this book in positive ways. In particular, I would like to thank Vicky Jardim, Jenny Nahal, Allen Petkovski, Dragi Ristevski and Stephen Tang for their warmth and loyal friendship.

The Rogers family merits special thanks. Tony, Carol, Anna, Gaby, Alice, Jimmy, along with the 'little mongrels', Lily, Matthew, Bonnie, Zahra and Camilla, have been the source of so much fun, generosity and hospitality. Spending time with them always energised me to return to my work.

I owe immense gratitude to my family for the understanding and limitless love they have shown me. My sister Lena and her husband Nick always took a caring interest in the book's progress. Seeing their little wonder, Nevenka, has become one of my most cherished weekly treats. My parents, Vasko and Petkana, provided a loving family environment and unconditional support without which this book, and so much else in my life, would not have been possible. Their success in a new country despite unfavourable odds, and the opportunities they have provided their children when having had so little in their own lives is an example that touches me and fills me with admiration. For all they have done for me, I dedicate this book to them.

My most important debt is to Kate Rogers. She was there with me through the most foreboding and the most triumphant moments of this intellectual endeavour. She only ever offered tender companionship and immeasurable patience when I offered so little in return. I am most fortunate for her understanding, thoughtfulness and good humour. Seeing her smile at the beginning and end of each day brings me joy and strength. I thank her for all she has done.

Several chapters in the book are revised and expanded versions of journal articles I previously published. This includes: Chapter 4, which appeared in *Policy Studies*, 2015 as 'Minority rights activism beyond borders: The synergies between deliberation and strategic action'; Chapter 5 in *Critical Review of Social and Political Philosophy*, 2013 as 'Preaching to the choir or converting the uninitiated? The integrative potential of in-group deliberations'; Chapter 6 in *Review of Politics*, 2015 as 'The uneasy alliance between consensus and democracy' and *Democratic Theory*, 2015 as 'On Mouffe's agonism: Why it is not a refutation of consensus'.

Introduction

Consider the following items of news:

Mark Boyd, an 18-year-old Protestant youth, is knocked down by a hit-and-run driver on 'the Shankill', the notorious stretch of road running through West Belfast's Loyalist heartland. Laying in agony with a broken leg, two men approach him to offer assistance. But before doing so, they summon him to sing the Sash, the sectarian song popular among Northern Ireland's Protestant population. Unfortunately, Mark does not know its words. In spite of all his assertions that he is Protestant and not Catholic, he is set upon by the would-be good Samaritans, only escaping a potentially worse fate at their hands by fleeing to a nearby take-away store. (Summarised from McAleese 2007)

On the outskirts of Skopje, Macedonia, five men on a fishing trip are shot dead in cold blood. As people are arrested, interethnic tensions simmer. Rumours have spread that the suspects are ethnic Albanian and that the murder of their victims, all ethnic Macedonian, was politically motivated. It is not long before tensions erupt. Ten thousand frenzied Albanians gather in front of Skopje's Jaja-Pasha mosque after mid-day prayer. Their indignation has been roused by activists using social media to spread accusations that the police framed the suspects and that the government is vilifying Albanians as terrorists. The crowd marches towards the government building, hurling stones at police and burning dumpsters. They chant 'Allah is great!' and 'Gruevski [the Prime Minister] is a terrorist!' (Summarised from Marusic 2012)

The enchanting Bosnian town of Mostar has a public water company run by two directors. One is a Croat who has an office in the western Croat side of the town, and manages the Croat staff and water supply there. Another is a Bosniak, who has an office on the eastern Bosniak side, and supervises the predominantly Bosniak staff and customers there. 'Only the water itself is common', says one of the directors, everything else is separate. The comment is an ironic reference to the duplication and division running through his company. But it is also an allegory of Mostar more generally. The town languishes at the hands of a bloated and corrupt bureaucracy, parodied by international observers for having 'at least two of everything': one administrative structure for Croats and another for Bosniaks. (Summarised from ICG 2009: 11–12)

A domestic football game is underway at Beirut's Camille Chamoun Sports City Stadium. Football is Lebanon's most popular sport. However, the terraces of the 48,000-seat stadium are empty. The government has imposed a ban on attendance, fearing that sectarian violence between fans might reignite a civil war. Not dissuaded by the ban, leaders of each community continue to fund competing teams, using them to generate support and spread sectarian messages among their constituencies outside the stadiums. (Summarised from Montague 2009)

Belgium sets a new world record. It takes 541 days for a government to be formed after an election, eclipsing the 353-day record previously set by Cambodia. The reason for this history-making delay? The linguistically divided parties cannot agree on the future direction of the country. The Dutch speaking parties would like to see power further devolved to the regions and eventually, the emergence of an independent Flemish state. The French speaking parties would like the status quo to remain. Against the backdrop of the impasse, the communities trade insults. Dutch speakers are referred to as 'tetchy, right-wing nationalist extremists', and Francophones as 'work-shy scroungers'. (Summarised from Chrisafis 2011)

What unites all of these events is their depiction of behaviour that is an expression and outcome of collapsed solidarity. As an ideal, solidarity concerns the simple but powerful normative intuition that moral obligations should extend beyond particularistic affinities to encompass all who are potentially exposed to the harms and benefits of our actions. It is an aspiration present in the idealisations of democrats of all stripes, who have referred to it variously as: a preparedness of 'taking responsibility' for one who 'has formed his identity under completely different circumstances' (Habermas 1998: 29); a disposition of 'mutual respect and caring that presumes distance' (Young 2000: 22); a commitment by groups to deal justly with others (Miller 2000: 157); the inclination to view all human lives as equally grievable (Butler 2004: 19–49); a sense of duty among 'the powerful to listen and respond' (Tully 2004: 99); the sharing of affiliations and bonds across ethnic lines in the form of 'cross-cutting cleavages' (Lijphart 1969); the readiness to come to the aid of another, even if this goes against one's immediate interests (Putnam 2000: 20–1); the expectation to interact 'on an equal basis with people with whom we might harbour prejudice' (Kymlicka 2001: 299); or the recognition of the legitimacy of another's position, even if one disagrees on its merits (Mouffe 2000: 101–2).

This orientation of attentiveness across difference is absent in the above interactions, as people are conceiving obligations of justice to begin and end strictly at the boundaries of their own group identity. The duty to care for and respect another is being ranked on the basis of arbitrary distinctions pertaining to ethnicity and religion, representing a breach of solidarity's universalist requirement that it extends equally to individuals of all backgrounds, regardless of the circumstances under which they have formed their identities. In one or more of these situations, people are harbouring dehumanising images of those on opposing ends of a group divide, wish to inhabit homogenous spaces defined exclusively by their own group identity, have a desire to marginalise their competitors from political decisions, want to see their rivals remain vulnerable to their own caprices, maintain disparaging attitudes and stereotypes of other ways of life, are calculating and strategising, are reluctant to admit culpability for wrongs committed in the name of their community, and are quick to interpret evidence in a manner that one-sidedly portrays themselves as victims. Under such circumstances, group contours define the limits of proper human conduct and serve to justify behaviour that leaves certain citizens treated as less than equal.

The presence of this kind of group centrism is morally questionable and has a number of functional repercussions that combine to undermine the success of multicultural democracy. In the absence of ties of solidarity, the commitment to notions of impartiality and equal moral worth will be weak or entirely absent from public life. Instead, joint problems will be approached in terms of 'what is good for me or my group', and not 'what is good for all who have to bear the consequences of my preferences'. That the realisation of one's interests might impact negatively on others will be of marginal concern, or worse still, might be an end in itself where another is regarded as some kind of threat to be controlled or overcome.

Apart from being questionable in its own right, such parochialism and strategising: contributes to legislative stalemates by leaving political actors less willing to compromise and more inclined to pursue committed agendas; takes away from the rational soundness of public policies by rendering collective decision making less informed, less reflective, and therefore prone to straying from what best serves citizens' interests; lays the ground for ethnic outbidding, as opportunist politicians will have an impressionable audience in their depiction of moderate opponents as weak or traitorous; heightens the propensity for identity-blaming, as people will be drawn to blame not an individual or set of individuals for their transgressions, but all members of the opposing identity associated with those individuals; and nurtures legitimacy deficits around the state insofar as people will find it difficult to accept legally binding directives that go the way of their opponents instead of their own.

In short, a society characterised by a breakdown in solidarity cannot flourish. People will care about the fate of their group ahead of the fate of their society, leaving prosperity and security unevenly distributed and incompletely realised, and the practice of governance increasingly strained as citizens resist, rather than consent to, political authority in the face of their disagreements. Where this is an ingrained feature of social life, the spectre of violent conflict is never too far away, while the interactions characterising inter-group encounters are anything but emblematic of healthy and vibrant multiculturalism.

Given the moral and functional imperatives served by solidarity, it comes as no surprise that governments, social scientists and philosophers devote considerable attention to understanding and promoting the phenomenon. Indeed, as far back as the nineteenth century, John Stuart Mill, Emile Durkheim, Karl Marx and others were seeking to grasp the nature of social attachments under conditions of conflicting values and interests. These scholars were responding to the rapid changes European societies had undergone as they shifted from authority based on religious sources of legitimation and more localised affiliations founded on village, town or regional ties towards mass and anonymous nation-states ordered through secular government, rational public moralities and capitalist modes of production. In recent times, this line of investigation has acquired renewed relevance, resurrected by new kinds of societal shifts and accompanying tensions that have once again put solidarity into the spotlight. Prominent among these transformations have been the growing prevalence of ethnonationalism, secessionist movements, civil wars, far right political parties and xenophobia, particularly since the conclusion of the Cold War. Also of relevance has been the political mobilisation of indigenous peoples, the widening rift between Muslim and non-Muslim populations in Western democracies especially since September 11, and the backlash directed at immigrant multiculturalism in recent times (Kymlicka 2007b).

Yet, beyond statements of necessity, there seems to be little else that unites analyses of solidarity. When one takes the bolder step of assessing how solidarity is ideally pursued, the phenomenon very quickly becomes the site of contestation and controversy, creating more divisions than it is supposed to overcome. At the level of policy making, all governments react with alarm at the sight of national disunity, but employ vastly different strategies to contain this threat. Some governments see it as necessary to further extend the reach of the state by centralising power away from troublesome minorities, ramping up nation-building programmes that reassert the culture of the dominant group, and in some extreme instances, restricting civil rights so that minorities are denied the freedom to practise and replicate their cultures in all facets of their lives. Others adopt a more relaxed approach, hoping the pacification of the unruly and disenchanted will come about through meeting the demands they are raising over self-government, constitutional amendments, affirmative action programmes, anti-discrimination legislation, language rights, representation quotas, among a host of other group-focused entitlements. Social scientists studying these actions cannot agree on their merits. Some regard a humane version of the former response as more effective, emphasising the monumental success of nation-building programmes in creating a common sense of community across vast territories (Miller 1995). Others endorse the latter response, stressing that many states are in fact multination- or multicultural-states, rather than nation- or monocultural states, held together through the institutional recognition of this demographic fact (Kymlicka 1995).

The result is those looking for a widely shared set of answers to problems of deep division and conflict have nowhere to go. Solidarity remains a core objective of governments and a central component of scholarship on justice and democracy. But there is no universally favoured route for its attainment and no universally accepted theory of its underlying conditions. Instead, studies of multicultural solidarity are characterised by mutually opposing assumptions on its preconditions, with each perspective claiming analytical superiority over the other, and each perspective able to point to historical evidence that casts doubt over the tenability of the other.

In this book, I identify the obstacles and possibilities for the realisation of solidarity in light of the confusion surrounding it. I offer a theoretical foundation from which to comprehend the normative demands of solidarity, and a corresponding set of institutional proposals that can function as guideposts for the reconstruction of societies divided across cultural and ethnic differences so that mutual answerability is patterned into the relations of historical antagonists.

While I provide widely applicable answers to the conceptual and institutional puzzles animating sociological and philosophical debates on solidarity, I do not claim to capture immutable laws of society, and nor do I believe such laws are out there waiting to be discovered. The empirical world is too disorderly for a tidy set of prescriptions to work equally effectively and smoothly everywhere and always, while as an ideal, solidarity is constituted by pluralist and unifying demands that stand in tension with one another and make its translation into practice a normatively delicate endeavour that dictates different policy interventions for different circumstances in order to avoid the creation of new injustices.

Nevertheless, I do believe certain generalisations can be made about what kind of institutional arrangements are more conducive to the attainment of cooperative and respectful relations. I also believe that certain universally valid suppositions can be made around what solidarity does and does not mean within a philosophical tradition that upholds democracy and respect for the integrity of individuals as foundational commitments to human life. It is with these assumptions in mind that the book proceeds, offering a progressive vision of solidarity in spite of the countervailing tendencies that stand in the way of complete control in social change and final answers on what solidarity ought to mean.

The challenges to theorising and grounding solidarity

It is tempting to conclude that the prevalence of contradictory assumptions around solidarity is a factor of insufficient evidence documenting the effects of different interventions designed to accommodate cultural diversity. From this perspective, disputes over the conditions of solidarity could be settled with further empirical research that compares policies within and across societies and establishes which ones have most successfully contributed to the deepening of bonds between diverse citizens. However, such research already exists, and does so in relative abundance.[1] It has nevertheless failed to provide widely sanctioned and generally agreed upon answers to the expansion of solidarity. The reasons for this are three-fold, each of which remains a challenge scholarship must meet.

First, solidarity is a contingent phenomenon. The causes of its decline are likely to be different from one society to the next. Correspondingly, its regeneration may not always presuppose the same course of action. This context dependence means there are limits to what lessons can be drawn from past experience to guide future attempts towards the realisation of solidarity. Consider consociational arrangements. They might have been pivotal in the management and eventual elimination of deep social cleavages in Western Europe last century. But they have not achieved anywhere near the level of success outside that context since, as attested by various failed and struggling consociations that have followed. Similarly, nationalism might have been a powerful unifying force in the eighteenth century, turning peasants into Frenchmen and Sardinians into Italians. Yet it has also functioned as a powerful dividing force in a number of notable contemporary cases, stimulating secessionist movements and political violence as minorities resist, rather than submit to, the national ideology cast over them (e.g., Kurds in Turkey, Albanians in Kosovo, Albanians in Macedonia, Tamils in Sri Lanka, Muslims in Thailand, Corsicans in France, and so on).

Clearly, there is a multiplicity of causally interlocked historical, cultural, socio-economic and geopolitical factors that influence how ethnic groups relate to one another. As these factors vary from one context to the next, so too will the success of any intervention chosen to render difficult circumstances more amenable to solidarity. The multifactor dimension to solidarity explains why comparative data remains so open to competing interpretations and why the advocacy of institutional reform remains such a vexed topic. Historical specificity between cases ensures a degree of uncertainty remains over what are associations between causes and effects. This leaves open an explanatory vacuum in which analysts squabble over the merits of assumptions and strategies for solidarity.

Second, solidarity is not only context dependent; the pathways for its generation are complex. Policies intended to defuse conflict and generate bonds of reciprocity do not always follow a linear pattern of causes and effects, but can sometimes produce impacts that are unforeseen and unwelcome. This non-linearity has been well documented through affirmative action programmes. While they were originally introduced to address inequalities stemming from prior or current discrimination by guaranteeing inclusion in the public service, education and the economic sector, affirmative action policies sometimes came with the unanticipated and unwanted baggage of stigmatisation, as quotas designed to equalise representation marked out targeted groups as undeserving recipients of state largesse in the eyes of the wider population (Fraser 1995). Moreover, such policies also worked to further disadvantage marginalised citizens excluded from their benefits. These non-beneficiaries of affirmative action had to compete for the finite social goods being pre-allocated to members of another group, further skewing opportunity structures against their identities.[2]

The extent to which stigmatisation, heighted social divisions or any other unwanted behavioural shift will follow a given application of affirmative action (or indeed other group-based entitlements) cannot be straightforwardly determined with reference to past events. Such policy interventions will always carry a measure of unpredictability. They embody complex cause and effect relations, rather than simply stable linear ones, making it impossible to model the future course of events with absolute precision (Geyer 2003; Little 2012).

The third, and perhaps the most critical, challenge facing the study of solidarity relates to the phenomenon's paradoxical nature. We have already witnessed that solidarity, at its most basic, involves an orientation of mutual answerability. It therefore contains joint demands of accountability and autonomy, which by their very nature, pull in opposite directions. The accountability dimension of solidarity is the requirement that people think and act with a sensitivity to the interests of others. The autonomy dimension is the requirement that respect is being shown for people's integrity and chosen ways of life as they are called upon to show deference to others. Thus, an overzealous desire to have people account for the interests of others can easily become an encroachment on people's freedom to pursue their chosen life-plans. The Jacobin state's uncompromising goal of creating a nation of equals is one such example. Individuals were forced to set aside their particular preferences to identify fully with what was deemed the common good on the assumption that this would establish genuine popular sovereignty (Weymans 2005: 271–2). Republican ideals of society focused on the expression of a 'thick' notion of the good are a philosophically more palatable expression of the Jacobin mission to enact a common will. But in continuing to long for a common vision of the political community, republicanism still remains at risk of descending into the same panoptic bureaucratic control of populations when actualised, particularly into contexts of deep disagreement and diversity (O'Flynn 2006: 69–72).

The same point can be made from the opposing perspective of an overzealous autonomy. Encouraging the unabridged realisation of life-plans can take away from the ability of others to realise their own life-plans, especially when access to scarce social goods is in question. Isaiah Berlin's famous defence of negative liberty is a prime example of how such a blinkered focus on autonomy can be self-refuting. In Berlin's (1969: 166) view, the appeal of a given society could be measured by the degree to which its members are left to do or be what they wish to do or be, without having such wishes frustrated by other human beings. However, the actualisation of Berlin's absolutist autonomy paves the way for the strong to dominate the weak. When interests, needs and values collide, encouraging their untempered realisation becomes a display of countervailing wills, where the claims of the powerful ultimately win out over those of the vulnerable.

As a result of this inherent normative tension, attempts to revive solidarity where it has broken down constantly walk a fine line, always at risk of demanding too much or too little of citizens expected to transcend group loyalties in their moral and political judgements. What I would describe as 'monist programmes' attempt to foster wider loyalties through the spread of a common national culture or national set of values that are intended to bring diverse citizens to treat each other justly.[3] According to this position, solidarity presupposes some form of normative or cultural integration at the national level, as this produces the collective loyalty necessary for strangers to cooperate and make sacrifices on each other's behalf. As a consequence, the state's role is not to sit back and remain agnostic on the identity of the nation, but to take an activist stance, nurturing a public discussion to determine what is a nationally shared notion of the good and then promoting this vision over the territory so that it comes to be shared by, if not all, then the greatest number of citizens possible.

However, built into such programmes is an unforgiving consequentialism, the means of which sit uncomfortably with the tenets of solidarity and the ends of which are, in any case, unattainable. There is no nation-state that can boast ever having approached, let alone achieved, universal popular support over the values that will underpin its institutions and public life. National constituencies are culturally too diverse and ideologically too intractable for this to ever be the case. The upshot is that when the state is put to the task of spreading a contested culture or set of values over its territory, it is engaged in the coercive activity of assimilation, since it is pressuring its citizens to adopt an identity they may have good reasons to reject. Insofar as solidarity requires ties of obligation to emerge through respect for people's chosen ways of life, and not their subordination, such programmes will always be in danger of denying autonomy for the grander purpose of an elusive national sameness.

What I would describe as 'pluralist programmes' do not offend against this normative demand, permitting, even encouraging, citizens to maintain their distinctive ways of life without the caveat that they internalise a set of nationally ascribed values, beliefs and preferences.[4] However, the satisfaction of this conceptual criterion comes at a potentially fatal cost – it is won at the expense of a unifying concept capable of orienting citizens towards one another. That is, if not a common evaluative platform, what is it that keeps a political community from fragmenting into its constituent cultural parts? And what compels its members to approach common problems in terms of 'what is good for my society' as opposed to 'what is good for my group'?

The commonplace response against this charge has been to assert that pluralist arrangements, such as devolved sovereign powers and group entitlements, eliminate barriers to participation, and therefore give minorities a motive to embrace political institutions and develop a sense of shared civic purpose. Yet this defence of pluralist arrangements offers cold comfort for those still waiting for reciprocal bonds to emerge in divided societies already ordered politically and bureaucratically along group lines. One does not have to search far to find examples where generous group entitlements involving power-sharing and federalism have failed to bring divided citizens closer, and in some instances, have actually coincided with a dramatic deterioration in relations. Bosnia, Belgium, Macedonia, Northern Ireland, Lebanon, Sri Lanka, Fiji, Nigeria, Yugoslavia, Czechoslovakia, the Soviet Union, the Ottoman Empire and the Austro-Hungarian Empire are just a few contemporary and historical examples demonstrating this.

In sum, those wishing to promote solidarity are caught in a bind. To seek it through national commonality is to offer a tangible source of unity but to risk coercive homogenisation and an almost certain hostile reaction from minorities. To seek it through the pluralisation of public institutions is to appease minorities and live up to standards of justice, but to risk cementing prevailing divisions by encouraging citizens to confront common problems as members of this or that group, rather than members of society. Whatever course of action one advocates, it seems bound to stray from the practical and conceptual demands of solidarity.

While solidarity's background properties – its contextual dependence, complexity and paradoxical nature – raise dilemmas that are very real and perplexing, this need not lead us down normative and institutional dead ends. Context dependence and complexity do not equate with complete randomness or an inability to make any generalisations from previous experience. They merely point to the reality that a measure of uncertainty will accompany all predictions on the effects of our interventions. This means we can still assume causal regularity (Wimmer 2013: 9) and plan for the future, as opposed to being prescriptively indeterminate to the point of inaction. It is just that we must be attuned to the ever-present possibility that the policies we put forward are fallible and therefore best left open to revision and readjustment as empirical circumstances alter and unforeseen shortcomings in our previous thinking reveal themselves.

Similarly, solidarity might contain constituent demands that sit in tension with one another. But it does not follow that it is a doomed project, one in which autonomy is destined to subsume accountability or vice versa. Solidarity can be coherently conceptualised and promoted. But, for this to be the case, we must move away from the stifling conformity of monist conceptions, and have as the starting point of our analysis a pluralist insight into the phenomenon. Only then can we have any hope of remaining true to the normative imperative of expressing care and answerability across difference and not merely towards people who are just like us.

Of course, in opting for this route, we must address the difficult question of how a pluralist conception of solidarity would maintain, rather than jettison, a unifying dimension in the midst of the often antagonistic ways of life it hopes to respect. A satisfactory answer to this question requires specifying what forces of unity exist outside the easy to grasp, but empirically unsustainable, notion of national sameness. It also requires making sense of how pluralist institutional arrangements can be a mechanism for group freedom without group dissociation, sectarianism and social fragmentation. There are three themes I cover in this book towards meeting these objectives, doing so with contexts of deep division and ethnic conflict in mind.

1. A definition of solidarity not dependent on national essences to unite people.

I show that solidarity exists when and to the extent that differently situated actors are responsive to each other's stated desires around three fundamental aspects of collective existence: the enjoyment of freedom (self-determination); the respect people believe their identity is due (recognition); and the material conditions that enable people to live dignified lives (redistribution). These three aspects of human relationships, as opposed to shared national essences, are defining elements of solidarity for two reasons. First, each is central to the maintenance of people's well-being and is therefore the basis of how people enter into relationships of moral mutuality with one another. Second, the fragmentation of societies is frequently traced back to a failed realisation of idealisations around these practices, which stimulates conflict and leads to the genesis of identities that would normally remain politically or socially irrelevant.

2. The conditions of solidarity.

I defend two mechanisms of behavioural change that can pattern responsiveness around claims for self-determination, recognition and redistribution between rival actors: strategic action; and group rights.

  i. While theorists tend to view strategic action as inimical to solidarity and communicative action as conducive to it, I argue that this distinction is too starkly drawn, as in practice strategic and other non-communicative forms of engagement must be enlisted to bring mutually hostile groups to interact in a manner reflective of solidarity. Appeals to reason and argumentative persuasion alone fail to motivate groups to place themselves in the positions of vulnerability associated with acting on each other's concerns, especially when relations are characterised by deep antipathy and mistrust. Therefore, inducing reciprocal behaviour under such circumstances requires incentivising it so that it is perceived as beneficial, or at the very least not harmful, to group interests.

  ii. Similarly, there is a tendency to one-sidedly view group entitlements as incompatible with solidarity on the assumption that they encourage group insularity and selfishness at the expense of civic-mindedness. However, this represents only part of the picture, as group entitlements can and have awakened goodwill between groups. I contend that what matters most from the perspective of solidarity is not the presence or absence of group entitlements, but the specific constellation of group entitlements introduced to accommodate diversity. This constellation is conducive to solidarity when it alters incentive structures in a manner that makes other-regarding behaviour politically more rewarding than purely self-regarding behaviour in the pursuit of goals. I explore the various institutional avenues available for the cultivation of such incentive structures in social environments defined by historical rivalry and hostility.

3. The promotion of solidarity.

If these are the conditions of solidarity, then how can societies get there? This is a crucial question to address, given that the powerful are likely to be deeply resistant to institutional change that threatens their position of privilege, and given that new and enlarged understandings between groups will be difficult to generate in the face of entrenched stereotypes and antipathies.

I offer a two-pronged response to this problem. The first documents change at the level of the state. I argue that where disparities in power allow privileged groups to ignore calls for reform geared towards the elimination of unjust institutional arrangements, the hand of such groups must be forced through a combination of unruly behaviour by the marginalised and intervention from external actors sufficient to make it politically costly for the privileged to continue resisting change. The second documents change at the level of attitudes and inter-group perceptions. I argue that where cultural, spatial or linguistic divisions impede deliberations across group lines, or where deep resentment makes this a potentially explosive practice, in-group deliberations offer the most plausible pathway for bringing groups to perceive each other as worthy of just treatment.

Key concepts and the outline of the book

This is a book on solidarity across *ethnic divides*, and a word is required on what this, and associated concepts, mean. I use the terms 'ethnic', 'ethnicity', and 'ethnic group' rather loosely to refer to 'agents who consider themselves as culturally distinctive from members of other groups with whom they have a minimum of regular interaction' (Eriksen 2003: 12). Some analysts believe it 'is vital to establish a clear-cut distinction between an ethnic group and a nation', whereby the existence of a claim to self-determination should serve as the defining marker of a nation as distinguishable from an ethnic group (Guibernau 2007: 60). I do not adopt this strict categorisation, as I do not believe it is always workable. All self-identifying ethnic groups wish to be self-determining in some way, and many actually aspire to have their own nation-state. As Stefan Wolff (2006: 54) puts it, 'nations are often nothing but state-seeking or state-controlling ethnic groups'. Thus, while I recognise there is some analytical benefit in referring to certain cultural groups as nations and others as ethnic groups (such as those not making claims to statehood, like immigrants), I use the terms interchangeably, unless I am engaging with the work of theorists who favour a stricter usage.

While deep division is a core theme of this book, its case selection is not restricted to societies commonly classified as 'divided' or 'deeply divided', even though such societies do feature prominently in the analysis. In the conflict studies and political theory literature, divided societies tend to be treated as a context apart, as they have properties that make the mediation of conflict and the institutionalisation of philosophical ideals onerous tasks. These properties include a lingering threat of political violence, legitimacy deficits around the state, and parallel social and public institutions with exclusively defined ethnic membership (Horowitz 1985: 17–21; Guelke 2012: 30–2). This would make divided societies the most logical starting point for a study on ethnically based conflict. Nevertheless, these are not the only sites of ethnic antagonism and associated injustices worth analysing. In fact, so-called integrated plural societies, like Greece, Bulgaria, France, the United States, among others, have been the location of ethnically targeted hostilities and maltreatment just as intense and egregious as any observed in archetypal divided societies, even though these integrated societies have remained unburdened by the severe institutional segmentation characteristic of divided societies. For this reason, I cast my net beyond quintessential divided societies like Northern Ireland, Macedonia, Bosnia and South Africa to also incorporate a number of integrated plural societies into the analysis, which provide equally relevant illustrations of the phenomena under investigation in the book.

The 'moral point of view' is another recurring theme of the book, and underpins the notion of solidarity I wish to defend. It is a term borrowed from Jürgen Habermas (1998: 6–7, 27–34) to refer to an attitude of seeking acceptance for a course of action from the perspective of each person concerned. In supporting such an ethic, my aim is not to advance a privileged moral truth (despite the moral vocabulary surrounding the ethic), but rather, to point to the unavoidability of role taking in the exercise of impartial judgement. What makes judgement impartial is the process of going beyond the first person singular perspective to adopt the perspective of the other. This can be distinguished from transcontextual understandings of impartiality, where independent judgement is supposed to arise through removal from, rather than embeddedness in, social context to adopt a kind of 'God's eye view' from nowhere. Not only is it impossible to exercise judgement in this socially detached way (Sandel 1984), to proceed as though it were serves to mask biases and dominant subject positions, given the unavoidability of context in human life and action (Kingwell 1995: 16). Thus, the centrality of role taking in the book is recognition of the fact that the achievement of mutual understanding presupposes taking in the self-understandings of partners to society. It is also recognition of the fact that sensitivity and openness to diverse claims presupposes permitting received customs, norms and ways of life to be voiced during reasoned discussion, rather than compelling discussants to set them aside as part of a (mistaken) formula for arriving at a common good (Ercan 2011: 82–4).

The book is organised as follows. Chapter 1 develops a pluralist account of solidarity against monist assertions tying the phenomenon to national essences. Solidarity, it proposes, is what differently situated actors experience when they are prepared to respect each other's concerns around self-determination, recognition and distribution.

The following two chapters consider the institutional implications of this definition of solidarity. Chapter 2 examines some prominent models of multicultural coexistence, and defends deliberative models as most consistent with the demands of solidarity. Through their emphasis on reason-giving and empathetic imagining, deliberative models offer a basis for the practical and democratic realisation of solidarity's core tenet of responsibility across difference. Nevertheless, it is also conceded that a deliberative approach brings with it its own set of problems that impede the expansion of solidarity. Specifically, where deliberation ensues from a starting point of marginalisation and disrespect, we can expect it to replicate, rather than overcome, these non-ideal conditions. The final section brings this problem to light in preparation for the subsequent chapters, which focus on how it can be overcome.

Chapter 3 analyses institutional designs that are supportive of solidarity. It challenges the view put forward by defenders of institutional homogeneity that group entitlements corrode solidarity by supposedly encouraging parochial behaviour over other-regarding behaviour. It is argued that this view is too one-sided, as it overlooks how group entitlements can compel majorities to orient themselves towards the concerns of marginalised minorities they otherwise have little incentive to respond to under majoritarian decision-making structures.

The following two chapters look at how social transformations reflective of solidarity can be initiated and carried through under conditions of inequality and antipathy. Chapter 4 takes up this question from the perspective of institutional reform, exploring the mechanisms through which political actors in positions of power can be influenced to dismantle unjust decision-making and legal structures from which they benefit. It is argued that when such actors are hostile towards principled reform and have the ability to withstand democratic challenges to their privileged position, a combination of civil disobedience and intervention by actors external to the society is required to compel them out of their intransigence. The chapter presents conditionality and transnational networking as practical expressions of this mode of structural change and considers how these practices can inform future efforts at principled reform.

Chapter 5 takes up the question of social transformation from the perspective of attitudes, social norms, and patterned behaviours at the everyday level. It examines how these can be altered to reflect a situation in which groups are encountering each other from the moral point of view when, previously, misconceptions, disparaging stereotypes or a history of violence left them harbouring dehumanising images of one another. The chapter presents in-group deliberation as a promising, yet underappreciated, vehicle for the achievement of such actor transformations. This claim is supported with reference to case studies showing that public sphere deliberations among like members are just as, if not more, consequential in fostering acceptance of outsiders than deliberations among unlike members, especially when antipathy defines group relations. What characterises such deliberations is the presence of 'integrative leaders', that is, individuals who take a leading role in persuading their group to develop a more enlarged and considered understanding of its relationship with another.

Chapter 6 reflects on and defends the book's central claim that the deliberative approach offers the most appealing framework for the democratic expression of solidarity. It does so against agonistic assertions that deliberative democracy's focus on the attainment of consensus takes away from the egalitarian expression of diversity. It is argued that a complete rejection of consensus is both unsustainable and undesirable from the very pluralist perspective agonists seek to uphold. In the place of agonists' wholesale rejection of consensus, the chapter puts forward a conceptualisation of consensus that conceives it as a matter of degree. This conceptualisation not only better captures the complexity of human relations. It also allows us to distinguish the potential accomplishments of aspiring towards consensus from the potential hazards.

Notes

1. A methodologically eclectic set of examples would include Lijphart (1977), Anderson (1983), Gellner (1983), Horowitz (1985), Kymlicka and Opalski (2001), Reynolds (2002) and Wimmer (2013).
2. This point is illustrated in the controversy over working-class Whites missing out on university placements in the United States in response to affirmative action programmes aimed at boosting the admission of Blacks.
3. Examples include Sandel (1996), Miller (2000), Pettit (2005), Walzer (2006), Putnam (2007) and Pevnick (2009).
4. Examples include Habermas (1998), Mouffe (2000), Bauböck (2001), Kymlicka (2001), Abizadeh (2002), O'Flynn (2006) and Schaap (2006).

1   Non-essentialist Solidarity

In this chapter, I take up the challenge of moving beyond a monist approach to solidarity. The notion that diverse citizens become obligated towards one another only through sharing national commonalities is a deeply influential one. It pervades everyday perceptions of the social world, witnessed through, on the one hand, the growing expectation in public discourses and naturalisation tests that immigrants internalise national values, and on the other hand, the public backlash in Western democracies towards multicultural policies deemed to encourage social fragmentation. It has, moreover, gained a respectable following in philosophical circles, where nationally defined principles of justice, values and cultures are extolled for their supposed indispensability in cultivating bonds between diverse strangers.

I argue such monist insights need to be rejected, as they are founded on mistaken assumptions about the nature of collective identity and imply a programme of national socialisation that is both normatively unsustainable and lacks practicality in contexts of deep diversity. What monists identify as *common* national culture, values, principles, traditions, and so on, are, on closer inspection, not so common at all, but artefacts of dominant actors whose position of privilege allow them to present these artefacts as normal and matter of fact aspects of social life. Moreover, monists complacently assume that the promotion of these artefacts is a benign process of simply putting aside supposedly 'selfish' or 'sectarian' interests in the name of converging around a common national good. In doing so, monists are blind to the structures of domination their programme sanctifies and naive about the potential of their programme's promise to bring about cooperation and fellow-feeling, rather than hostility and division.

In the place of the essentialism of monist theories, I develop a concept of solidarity that avoids dependence on shared cultural attributes. Solidarity, I propose, is what differently situated actors experience when they are prepared to respect each other's stated desires for self-determination, recognition and distribution. This non-essentialist account is both empirically and conceptually superior to the essentialist accounts of monists: *empirically* insofar as the decline in bonds of solidarity is frequently traceable back to a failure of actual experience to live up to people's idealisations around the enjoyment of freedom, the public evaluation of their identity, and the relative allocation of material resources; and *conceptually* insofar as being in a relation of solidarity presupposes a readiness to be attentive to another's stated desires on each of these core aspects of human well-being. This definition is non-essentialist as it is not reliant on shared social attributes to explain citizens' moral orientation towards one another. Rather, the emphasis is on three elements of social existence through which ties of responsibility manifest themselves.

Monist solidarity

In a plural society, solidarity denotes the disposition of taking an interest in those who are different, even unfamiliar, to oneself. This orientation of attentiveness across difference remains a cornerstone of normative thinking, as it is indispensable in the realisation of goals prized by democrats. On one level, solidarity has intrinsic relevance, as it is constitutively linked to justice and respect for the worth of all people. As Jürgen Habermas puts it, 'solidarity is simply the reverse side of justice', given that justice requires taking into account 'what is equally good for all' (1998: 29). Thus, a society which fails to extend moral attentiveness equally to all, but ranks it along the particularistic lines of ethnicity, religion, race or sexuality, is a society that has fallen short of meeting a key criterion of what it means to treat people as ends in themselves. Instead, the lives of those more familiar and similar to our own are being arbitrarily privileged ahead of those which are different and foreign, reflecting a hierarchy of humanity (Butler 2004: 34, 38).

On another level, solidarity serves functionally prized goals by permitting democratic practice to run smoothly and redistribution to occur voluntarily in the plural and anonymous spheres of mass societies. In the presence of bonds of responsibility, rule by consent becomes tenable, as citizens will be inclined to accept democratic outcomes that favour the interests of others ahead of their own (Tully 2004: 92). Similarly, the redistributive enterprise is freed up to get on with the task of reallocation, as citizens will see a rightful place for the apportioning of material goods beyond the scope of their narrowly defined social networks and communities of origin (Miller 2000: 32).

However, while agreeing on the normative and functional merits of solidarity, democrats are deeply at odds on how it is to be conceptualised. The main areas of contention lie with whether or not solidarity assumes an ethical or cultural unifying field that binds diverse citizens, and whether or not the promotion of such a unifying field can be endorsed in societies committed to pluralism, given that the attempt to institute cultural and ethical homogeneity is fraught with assimilatory and exclusionary influences.

The theorists I have loosely termed monists recognise the tension between the pluralist and unifying elements of solidarity, but believe it is unproblematically overcome through the presence of an overarching layer of social commonality provided by an inclusive national culture (Tamir 1993; Canovan 2000; Miller 2000; Walzer 2006). The defence of this understanding of solidarity begins with the frequently invoked historical observation that nationality is what has enabled fellow-feeling to take foot among strangers previously inclined to develop bonds through membership in face-to-face communities and regional ties. Through its 'mythical' and 'imaginary elements' nationality brought people who did not know one another and would never meet one another to imagine themselves as part of the same people collectively determining its own destiny. In doing so, nationality answered, as David Miller puts it, 'one of the most pressing needs of the modern world, namely how to maintain solidarity among the populations of states that are large and anonymous, such that their citizens cannot possibility enjoy the kind of community that relies on kinship or face-to-face interaction' (2000: 31–2).

Not surprisingly, adherents of this position have been quick to dismiss any attempt to locate sources of solidarity beyond common national traits. This, they hold, is as an exercise in futility, as a polity stripped of nationally shared elements would be a polity deprived of the very cohesive medium that enables wider social affinities and attachments to state institutions. According to Michael Walzer, this explains why the proletariat of the world could never unite. Unlike individuals sharing a nationality, they lacked common cultural artefacts in the form of language, religion, historical memory, the calendar and its holidays, a sense of place, and a specific experience of art and music, thus spelling the demise of Marxist internationalism (2006: 28). Similarly, Margaret Canovan concludes Habermas' notion of 'constitutional patriotism' can only ever be an academic exercise, as its attempt to garner loyalties through empty abstractions centred on legal norms offers no basis for a 'people' to emerge. A people, she contends, presupposes a shared history and traditions that go back in time – as she puts it, the polity is recognised as 'ours' because 'it was our parents' before us' (2000: 286).

However, a careful sociology of national polities would reveal that such constituencies are too vast and socially complex for any meaningful and inclusive commonality to be possible. Indeed, nation-states are sites of seemingly endless social conflict, as they are far-flung and unwieldy communities comprising a pluralism of identities sustained in opposition to one another. Feminists and Catholics, secularists and Islamists, homosexuals and traditionalists, unitary nationalists and autonomist minorities, libertarians and social democrats, indigenous groups and animal liberationists, to name but a few conflicting social groups, will all have irreconcilable visions of what set of laws, practices and values ought to prevail over a state territory. Here the idealisations of one social identity can only be won at the expense of the other, pointing to the futility of seeking an umbrella culture that is universally inclusive and capable of being equally appreciated by all.

In the presence of such social complexity, any assertion that common national traits have been discovered is indicative of at least one of two outcomes, each of which is unsatisfactory as a basis for establishing relations of solidarity. The first outcome is a commonality that is hollow, embodying a representation of the nation that is so detached from concrete circumstances that it can no longer be the site of dispute. In its uprootedness from empirical realities, this national commonality ends up specifying nothing, or at least nothing that provides critical direction for a community, remaining, instead, a fuzzy abstraction. The most commonplace instance of this is the cliché expressed in the media and by politicians that 'freedom and equality are defining values of our nation'. If such markers of commonality succeed in encompassing the identities of all members of the polity, they do so only because they are expressed at an abstract enough level to be open to a range of contradictory interpretations. More to the point, there is nothing in this mode of allegiance indicative of solidarity. Rival actors can all express their deepest commitments to freedom, and yet continue to reject each other's identity and place in the polity, as commonly occurs among ethnic groups in divided liberal democracies.

The second outcome would be reflective of the opposite scenario, whereby representative claim-making is reductionist. This is observed whenever a concrete, rather than abstract, articulation of the nation is put forward. Here, what it means to be a member is specified with reference to historical events and cultural practices that are empirically situated and embellished with tangible details supposedly familiar and homely to everyone. Such situatedness lends a level of meaningfulness to representations of the nation absent under abstractly defined ones. But it also takes away from the inclusiveness to which representations can lay claim, as in the face of social complexity and contested histories, one particularistic set of characterisations and idealisations is overshadowing another competing set in its claim to universality. Such representations are emblematic of what Ernesto Laclau and Chantal Mouffe (1985) term hegemonies, insofar as the symbolisation of social reality is assuming a false totality. Commonality is being postulated through an over-determination of what 'shared' values represent, and therefore through a masking of the particularity such values are supposed to have overcome.

Miller is complicit in this form of reductionism when he identifies convict ancestry as a generally shared national characteristic that defines Australians. In his view, 'there is nothing more illustrious for an Australian today than to have an ancestor who was carried over in chains by the First Fleet' (2000: 30). Yet to make this generalisation is to omit the experiences and sentiments of vast categories of citizens who neither relate, nor warm, to this romanticised colonial era narrative of Australia. For the majority of Australians, free immigration defines their family histories, given that it has been the country's dominant mode of migration. For others, British colonisation will be something they learn about at school, but feel little cultural connection with as a result of belonging to an ethnicity that is far removed from Anglo-Celtic ones predominating the events of that time. For others still, such as Indigenous people, convict era Australia represents the beginning of a dark period of dispossession, disease and cultural annihilation, as opposed to anything to be celebrated.

In opposing national commonalities as a basis for political community, my point is not to oppose any notion of searching for common ground. On the contrary, the very vibrancy of a diverse society is dependent on its members entering political interactions with a preparedness to be persuaded by each other and to eventually accept the legitimacy of each other's disputed positions (Chapter 6). Nevertheless, such deliberative openness is not brought about simply by making people bearers of national values. This course of action remains beside the point. A nationalist crusade to spread common attributes fails to acknowledge and address the concrete concerns that lead antagonists to view each other's commitments as mutually incompatible. Instead, it naively assumes antagonists will forget about them in readiness to be guided by a set of transcendent principles proclaimed as national. In sum, such analysis should be rejected as it is premised on a false diagnosis of a collective problem – the lack of cultural commonalities – which consequently leads one down a false path of prescription – the spread of cultural commonalities.

At this point, monists might object that the analysis misses the mark, for it overlooks how people of diverse backgrounds can and do come to embrace a common national standpoint so long as they avoid letting sectional and group affiliations obstruct their political dealings with one another. This is the view put forward by Miller in his vehement opposition to the group oriented politics favoured by difference theorists like Iris Marion Young. In Miller's view, group based politics is to be avoided, as it takes away from the 'emergence of a shared public culture' by encouraging people to confront one another not through generalisable principles of justice, but on the basis of sectional interests and demands connected to religion, ethnicity, race, gender and sexuality. Far from nurturing mutual obligation, this supposedly encourages self-interested behaviour, because the partial standpoints citizens bring to the political forum leave no grounds for appealing to a common good (2000: 62–80).

However, Miller's argument is tautological, as it presupposes the very conditions it hopes to bring about. If the discovery of common ground rests on sidelining those aspects of identity that divide people, it follows people have no reason to go into political deliberations in the first place. There would be no conflict between them, leaving nothing to contest or seek agreement over. In practice, Miller's appeal amounts to a circular assertion that: Nationalists and Unionists in Northern Ireland would resolve their differences were they to put aside their sectarian identities; Bosniaks, Serbs and Croats in Bosnia their ethnic identities; Turkey's secularists and Islamists Atatürk and the Koran; homosexuals and Christians sexuality and the Bible; Marxists and capitalists *Das Kapital* and *The Wealth of Nations*; and so on. Clearly, these 'sub-national' identities would no longer be the source of deep social division if their adherents voluntarily privatised them in the manner desired by Miller. Yet, that they are failing to do so is the very issue. In reality, fully constituted individuals are the empirical starting point from which all practical deliberations must begin, for were participants to check at the door those aspects of their identity that define and divide them, reconciliation would be achieved before politics had even begun (Benhabib 1996: 125–6; O'Flynn 2006: 70–1).

There is also a serious normative concern with programmes seeking to foster solidarity through the relegation of 'nonnational' identities to a private realm. To introduce a condition of citizenship demanding conformity to a national culture steers public policy towards assimilation, self-censorship and arbitrary control, as what is extolled as national, impartial and open to all will in fact be embedded in the norms, habits and symbols of specific groups, given, as we have seen, the empirical reality of value pluralism (Young 1990: 181–7; Bauböck 2001: 4). Where such cultural and ethical hierarchies go unrecognised and unacknowledged, the interests and values of dominant actors will be normalised in public life, rendering alternative perspectives invisible, inferior or troublesome when they are asserted as worthy of consideration.

This pattern of domination is witnessed in societies ordered around a strong expectation that minorities will bring their identities in line with an idealised national one. The preservation of ideal national images in such instances plays out as symbolic, and sometimes physical, violence towards minorities deemed to stand in the way. In contexts of immigration, this ensues as the control and domestication of immigrant populations so that their otherness no longer poses a threat to the nation or the privileged mode of being enjoyed by some within it (Gozdecka et al. 2014: 54–7). In these situations, immigrant members are routinely summoned to prove they actively support liberal values (Bauböck 2002: 7) or that they have adopted the cultural features of the majority in order to be naturalised (Humphrey 2009). What compounds the arbitrariness of this practice is that those doing the summoning are neither put on public trial in the same manner nor do they hold beliefs that come close to measuring up against the liberal standards they demand of others (Bauböck 2002: 7).

In the context of interethnic politics, such domination takes the form of ethnic minorities being obstructed from pursuing objectives that clash with the interests of the 'nation', which by extension, are the interests of the majority ethnicity. Here, the sanctity of a hegemonic national image functions to disarm minority dissent, as the claims made by minorities, even when they are couched in the universal language of inclusion, equality and anti-discrimination, are represented in public discourse as a threat to the identity of the 'people' and its state. Consequently, political mobilisation by the minorities becomes a matter of state security, anxiety and ultimately control when it would normally be interpreted as a more banal aspect of everyday politics. The ultimate effect is to deprive minorities of a democratic route for the realisation of their goals (Kymlicka 2007a: 190–6).

All these examples demonstrate how the monist pathway to solidarity is bound up with dubious practices of policing and cultural vigilance, as opposed to relations of care and responsibility. Someone has to ensure citizens are defining themselves against a common background. Ultimately, this duty will be assumed by those embodying the greatest share of cultural capital associated with the nation, as the rich possession of such capital legitimates one's managerial role over society and one's power to symbolically and spatially position within it people defined as different (Hage 1998: 65, 66). In short, actors embodying otherness become what Ghassan Hage has termed, 'manageable objects' (1998: 42). They inhabit social spaces not as autonomous subjects, but as objects to be positioned or removed by those occupying the privileged mode of being within that space. Such arrangements cannot be endorsed under a definition of solidarity. They not only amount to a coercive mode of socialisation, but reproduce a social order in which some citizens enjoy a relation of domination over others in virtue of arbitrary distinctions pertaining to cultural characteristics.

Non-essentialist solidarity

If solidarity must be understood as a phenomenon that emerges precisely where people do not share cultural traits or a common ethical background, in what sense can we speak of it as being in existence? To answer this question, it is instructive to begin with James Tully's remarks on the sources of mutual ties.

For Tully, it cannot be anything citizens agree on that holds them together, as public life will be marked by competition and disagreement. In his view, what orients people towards one another is 'nothing more or less than participation in the activities of public dialogue and negotiation themselves' (2000: 215). Under this post-teleological notion of democracy, it is not a society's arrival at a final end state of reconciliation that functions as a source of bonds, but the open-ended engagement in 'agonic and interminable public discussions and negotiations, both within and over the conditions of citizenship' (2000: 216). This continuously conciliated order nurtures wider identifications among people, as the state of freedom it leaves them in leads to the development of respect towards others playing the same game – in Tully's words, it 'constitutes and sustains identities as "free citizens" and generates a sense of belonging to a "free people"' (2000: 216). Similarly, the '"agonic" to-and-fro activity of mutual disclosure and mutual acknowledgement' embodying this mode of being has a cathartic effect that limits the accumulation of bad feelings. Rather than keeping ill-feelings pent up, those taking part will 'discharge resentment at a present structure of recognition' by disclosing the identities they wish to see recognised (2000: 216, 231).

Tully's agonistic version of solidarity directs us towards sources of attachment not premised on cultural conformity. Yet in order to be empirically precise, it requires further refinement into strong and weak claims. As a strong claim, the relationship between contestation and solidarity would be couched as a direct one, whereby the very act struggling both within and over the rules of a political community is what generates sentiments of fellow feeling. However, pitched in this way, the relationship risks overstatement, as empirical evidence strongly speaks against the solidarity producing effects of political contestation *per se*, especially where it ensues against a backdrop of mutual hostilities. Indeed, it is precisely when the rules of the game are up for grabs that the worst behaviour emerges among competitors already unfriendly towards one another, as the redistribution in sovereign power this implies significantly raises the stakes of failure and compels actors to interpret their situation in zero-sum terms (Dryzek 2005).

As a weak, more persuasive claim, the relationship between contestation and solidarity is understood as an indirect and more contingent one. Here, it is not the cathartic act of dispelling suppressed grievances that stimulates solidarity, but, more specifically, the favourable shifts in attitudes, patterned behaviours, decision-making structures and legal norms which dialogic encounters can facilitate. Such shifts, I will now argue, are conducive to solidarity when they are emblematic of a move away from arrangements that leave groups exposed to domination, disparagement and material deprivation and a move towards arrangements that respect the aspirations of groups for self-determination, recognition and distribution. Through these alterations, the social conditions stimulating ill-feeling and hostility are attenuated. However, as I shall also point out, the relationship between these three dimensions of interaction and solidarity is not merely causal; it is also conceptual, as being in a relation of solidarity with someone assumes his/her requirements for self-determination, recognition and distribution are being sufficiently met. Let us consider each of these points in detail.

Self-determination

Self-determination refers to the freedom of people to exercise choice over their lives. At the level of the individual, it entails being an autonomous chooser of ends, unconstrained in the activity of choosing a conception of the good life, revising this conception, and pursuing an alternative one if that is what is desired (Kymlicka 1995: 80). At the collective level, it denotes the authority of a group to decide how to maintain and promote its existence as distinct from wider society.

The constitutive relationship of self-determination with solidarity is made evident by considering the implications arising from its arbitrary suppression. Where people are denied the ability to be self-determining, they will be unable to participate in social and political life as equals. They will instead be subject to another's mastery, being, as Philip Pettit has described, in a 'position where fear and deference will be the normal order of the day, not the frankness that goes with intersubjective equality' (1997: 64). Such mastery by others plays out as the capacity to carry out any number of interfering behaviours calculated to worsen the choice options of another for one's own aggrandisement (1997: 53). At the aggregate level, it can manifest itself as a capacity to summarily assimilate or exclude people from structures of governance. Here, members of a specific identity are either coerced into determining their actions according to the terms set by others (assimilation), or are simply denied any role in determining decisions that have a significant bearing on their lives and development (exclusion) (Tully 2002: 221). Both instances represent a denial of self-determination and therefore solidarity insofar as groups are being forced down a path that conflicts with what they desire and take to be important for their own existence.

Yet the curtailment of self-determination is not merely a conceptual issue. Importantly, it also has a causal dimension, functioning to stimulate conflict and division between those retracting freedom and those at the whim of such behaviour. Where a group feels it is being denied the ability to meaningfully determine its own fate, its members will be prone to feeling it no longer pays to be a citizen (Habermas 2001: 77). The democratic process will consistently fail to take up their perspectives, leaving them with few incentives to participate in it or play by its rules. Furthermore, they are likely to lack identification with the political order as a whole, associating it with those sections of society benefiting from it most. Entwined with these strategic calculations are often visceral ones in which subjugated citizens develop a deep-seated resentment towards those held responsible for their undignified treatment. The result of these legitimacy deficits and social antipathies is instability and disintegration, as excluded actors will be contemplating how to 'get in' or secede from the larger political association to create their own where they can regain the capacity to be publicly autonomous (Tully 2000: 216).

These reactions are witnessed among a range of social groups. Violent campaigns for political empowerment by ethnic minorities typically arise in response to the sense of indignation they feel at being kept in a relation of subordination by a domineering majority. For example, the turmoil of the Troubles in Northern Ireland was the result of Catholics seeking to overcome systematic discrimination by a Protestant controlled government in housing allocation, employment and electoral procedures. In Macedonia, the Albanian minority took to arms in 2001 to bring about institutional change that would grant them a meaningful presence in influential sites of decision making in response to their historical exclusion from them by the Macedonian majority seeking to keep them politically subordinate. In Milosevic era Kosovo, it was the Albanian minority's exposure to severe forms of state-sanctioned repression and violence that added fuel to their secessionist aspirations. Other examples would include the conflict between Sinhalese and Tamils in Sri Lanka, Turks and Kurds in Turkey, Bosniaks and Serbs in Bosnia, and Buddhists and Muslims in Southern Thailand. In all these examples, separatism is fuelled by one group's perceptions that another group is using its privileged position in policy-making arenas and its control of state apparatuses of coercion to assert its will or identity over others.

Political and social stratification also follows the subordination of groups distinguishable along markers of race, religion, class, sexuality and gender. Where such groups lack the ability to participate effectively in a democratic system rigged in favour of other identities or where they feel their capacity for choice is being constrained by an unduly paternalistic state, they typically retreat into their own 'sub-altern counterpublics' from which they 'can invent and circulate counter discourse so as to formulate oppositional interpretations of their identities, interests and needs' (Fraser 1993: 14).

One witnesses this pattern of retreat and resistance in the subversive reaction of immigrants towards the French state's suppression of veiling in the 1990s. While public officials justified the measure as necessary for the 'emancipation' of women from religious and sexual subordination, some women experienced it as an illegitimate intrusion on their autonomy to determine how they, and not others, could pursue their lives. In response, they defiantly chose to take up the practice in the very public spaces from which it was banned, doing so with the express purpose of carving out an identity for themselves that was distinctive from the vigilantly secularist one being imposed by the state. The outcome was to reify group distinctions, rather than nurture the homogeneity desired by officials, as the assimilatory effects of maintaining a public sphere purged of religious symbolism served to orient Islamic women increasingly towards their communities of birth and away from the republican identity espoused by the French state (Benhabib 2002: 94–100).

This point can be made more broadly with reference to a number of defining struggles against domination, including those over apartheid, civil rights, women's suffrage, gay rights, and indigenous rights. In all these instances, the experience of being unduly denied the ability to be self-determining through restrictions on voting rights, curtailments on freedoms of association and organisation, exclusion through majoritarian decision making, social segregation, external control over one's body and sexuality, cultural annihilation and police brutality functioned as a driver of social division by spawning movements, ideologies and practices oppositional to the identity espoused by the agents of domination.

It follows then, that at least one enabling factor of solidarity is the parity of social and political participation that comes from being self-determining. It is both at the heart of what it means to respect another's integrity and is a vital ingredient for inducing citizens to willingly orient themselves towards one another when they would otherwise have reasons not to. Note that this source of solidarity is non-monist, as what is binding diverse citizens together is not a shared essence, but the experience of relating to one another on equitable terms and of being treated as voices worth listening to. That is, people are expressing a sense of obligation towards differently situated others because these others are permitting them to pursue their plans in accordance with their desires. Likewise, they maintain a sense of attachment to a political order because it enables them to exercise influence over decisions they consider central to their identity. No doubt, attempts to bring about this complementarity in group freedoms will not always prove successful. It is nevertheless a factor of solidarity.

Recognition

Whereas self-determination refers to practices of freedom, recognition refers to social judgements of worth. It designates the experiences of intersubjective interpretation and acknowledgement of identity which secure human dignity (Honneth 1992). In a society where an ideal of recognition is upheld, its members would be receiving the public acknowledgement they believe they rightfully deserve, while their mode of being would be upheld as legitimate next to that of others present in society (Thompson 2006: 3).

There are several levels along which a failure of recognition can be considered a violation of solidarity. When people are misrecog-nised, and when they are subjected to contemptible images of themselves, they are – as with arbitrary curtailments of freedom – denied the potential to participate on equitable terms with the rest of society. If one's identity is devalued and despised, one's viewpoints and concerns will count for less, because they will not be appreciated on terms equal with others. From this perspective, misrecognition is 'an institutionalized relation of social subor-dination' (Fraser 2000: 113). The core violation concerns the constitution of some social actors as less than full members under prevailing patterns of cultural evaluation, preventing them from participating on a par with their peers (Fraser 2000: 114).

Yet, failures of recognition are equivalent to collapsed solidar-ity not merely through their association with stunted political agency, but for the more prior reason that they can be tied to psychological harm. Such harm is experienced as crippling self-hatred and deflated self-esteem, whereby the ongoing exposure to insult and degradation impairs people in their positive under-standing of self (Honneth 1992: 188–9).

As with self-determination, recognition is also causally related to solidarity, as exposure to identity-based degradation can lead to a process of antagonistic group formation. Such transforma-tions frequently play out as a regressive struggle for recognition, whereby groups lock themselves into a self-subverting pattern of proving themselves equal to one another according to the terms set by a disparaging other (Schaap 2004: 530–4). In such modes of social interaction, the over-determination of groups becomes commonplace, as they become fixated on asserting an 'authentic' and 'original' identity as a means to overcoming the undesirable image cast over them. This serves to constrain, rather than enable possibilities for self-creation, as groups are obsessively defining their world in relation to the negative images asserted by their misrecogniser.

A case in point is offered by the conflict in Northern Ireland. During and after the Troubles, the attempt at self-realisation by Unionists and Nationalists has led to an emphasis on particularis-tic symbols and rituals that are mutually exclusive and expressly negate, rather than incorporate, the other's stated desires for recognition. At the everyday level, this has played out as a totalising display of what each community takes as its authentic identity, involving ostentatious assertions of Britishness in Unionist neighbourhoods and Irishness in Nationalist ones through the adornment of thoroughfares with Union Jacks in the former and Irish tricolours and Gaelic script in the latter. Such symbolism, though banal on the face of it, can be interpreted as a bold exhibition by each community of its round rejection of the aspirations associated with the other's identity (the rejection by Unionists of a united Ireland and the rejection by Nationalists of strengthened union with the United Kingdom). It is also a display of each group's attempt to establish a hierarchical rather than coequal ordering of identities, as these are presented as a zero-sum game in which one must take precedence over the other (Little 2003: 380).

This regressive struggle for recognition has also played out as a totalising exercise of spatial sovereignty, captured most vividly through the sectarian hatred and violence that has come to surround Orange Order marches routed through Nationalist neighbourhoods. For Nationalists, such marches represent a provocative display of disrespect, as they perceive them as assertions of British and Protestant supremacy in a space considered their own. For Orangemen, any attempt to restrict their parades is an affront to their dignity, as they regard the freedom to parade along the 'traditional' routes situated in Nationalist neighbourhoods as their religious and political right (O'Neill 2002: 182). Thus, the experience of misrecognition here has consolidated identifications and cultural practices which each group takes as true to its original self, but which is experienced by the other as a profound violation of its being. To paraphrase Andrew Schaap (2004: 531), each group is attempting to 'turn the tables on the other', and to make the other the object of its own annihilating image, taking this as a route to the realisation of a more desirable projection of itself.

Other examples of antagonistic group formations arising from the experience of misrecognition would include: the widening rift between Muslims and majority groups in Western democracies through the intensification of contemptible depictions of Muslims in mainstream discourses; the Black is Beautiful Movement positively affirming Black physical features to overcome a racialised aesthetic that constructs them as ugly; the Gay Pride Movement's promotion and celebration of gender plurality and sexual variance to displace social stigmas depicting gay, lesbian, bisexual and transgender people as deviant beings; and feminist consciousness-raising revaluing feminine activity by disrupting masculine coded norms and styles that leave women inferior and objectified (Young 1990: 176–7). In all these examples, group differentiation is embedded in some failure of recognition. The experience of being subject to, but also staving off, evaluative hierarchies and imagery that generates feelings of humiliation, abjection and inferiority is leading to the genesis of mutually opposed groups that would normally remain politically and socially irrelevant.

Recognition is therefore constitutive of solidarity, but also an ingredient for its further empirical expansion by promoting the very conditions that orient groups towards one another. Where people feel their identity is being accorded the respect it is due, they are more likely to reciprocate that respect by acknowledging the worth of those outside their group. Where they feel it is being disparaged, they are more likely to seek to distance themselves from those responsible, to harbour a desire to harm and dominate them, or to cluster in social formations that provide relief from, and a platform for challenging, the demeaning images cast over them. Note, again, that recognition is a pluralist, and not a monist, element of solidarity. It takes the form of the expansion and deepening of group relations through an upward revaluation of 'disrespected identities and the cultural products of maligned groups' (Fraser 1997a: 15), and not a call for their displacement by a master (national) identity.

Distribution

Distribution refers to the economic and material dimension of social existence. It encompasses the allocation of wealth, income, resources, property, education, healthcare and leisure time across a society. It also refers to the allocation of occupations among individuals and groups, along with the nature of the meanings and values behind these occupations and their specific tasks (Young 1990: 23; Fraser 1997a: 11).

Distribution is constitutive of solidarity, as some patterns of distribution have the effect of limiting reasoned human agency and equality of participation. As Isaiah Berlin put it, 'to offer political rights . . . to men who are half-naked, illiterate, underfed and diseased is to mock their condition; they need medical help or education before they can understand or make use of, an increase in their freedom' (1969: 124). Yet violations of solidarity do not cease with more obvious manifestations of deprivation rooted in access to food, shelter and material resources. More invidiously, they arise through divisions of labour that exploit categories of people through their confinement to menial professions with low status, income and decision-making power. Such relations are inconsistent with solidarity's requirement of attentiveness across difference, as they are reflective of a situation where, in the words of Iris Marion Young, 'the energies of the have-nots are continuously expended to maintain and augment the power, status and wealth of the haves' (1990: 50). In a labour market comprised of exploitative social segmentations, women, racialised groups and cultural groups are performing servile work that goes unnoticed and undercompensated, leaving them lacking autonomy next to individuals this work is geared to please and benefit.

Distribution becomes the site of diminishing solidarity when judgements about 'what individual persons have, how much they have, and how that amount compares with what other persons have' (Young 1990: 25) yield answers falling short of people's standards of what is fair and what they believe they are rightfully owed. There are several levels along which such distributive assessments lead to a breakdown in solidarity.

First, it occurs against the backdrop of downward social mobility, or its very threat, as this has the tendency to move segments of the population towards extremist views and entice them to follow extremist leaders. Indeed, the relationship between economic insecurity and support for political extremism is well documented through the rise of Nazi racial ideology in Weimar Germany, membership to the Nation of Islam in the United States, the rise of right-wing skin-heads in Eastern Europe and the electoral success of far right political parties (Chambers and Kopstein 2001: 847, 858). In the face of anxiety and powerlessness caused by poverty and diminished economic expectations, such groups were able to offer much sought-after solace by venting anger and hate at clearly identified villains.

Second, disaffection can flow in the opposite direction, channelled from the economically privileged towards the underprivileged. This is witnessed in the stigmatisation of people dependent on welfare programmes as lazy and parasitic on society. It is also witnessed in the resentment stimulated by redistributions between developed and underdeveloped regions. Whenever an economically prosperous and resource-rich region is relied on to subsidise other parts of a territory, friction with the centre is never too far away, as the wealthy region's disproportionate contribution to the overall economy can produce the perception that its own development is being encumbered by an alien authority siphoning away its earnings and resources. Such sentiments played a notable part in fuelling Slovenia's secession from Yugoslavia, Aceh's push for autonomy in Indonesia and the Northern League's desire to detach northern Italy from the rest of the state.

Finally, the loss of solidarity tied to distributive matters can ensue in the context of a segmented labour market. Where a society's division of labour closely coincides with a set of cultural or physical markers, social segregation can be reproduced and intensified, especially when the occupations in question are low-paid, menial and dirty. The confinement of particular individuals to such work can have the effect of endowing them with class-like characteristics that become the object of conscious and unconscious aversions (Fraser 1997a: 20–1). This process of group differentiation sustains the social relevance of India's caste system, despite its de jure abolition over half a century ago. While affirmative action programmes have improved the quality of life for Dalits, their continued association with ritually impure occupations, such as the cleaning of streets, latrines and sewers, serves to sustain caste norms and reveal people's caste origins, thereby marking them out for ongoing discrimination and social segregation. Other relevant examples include Mexican labourers in the United States, Southeast Asian and South Asian labourers in the

Gulf States, and until more recently, guest workers in Germany. The disproportionate location of these workers in low-status or domesticated work has constituted them as inside aliens and an underclass that is separate from the rest of society.

Yet, for a segmented labour market to undermine solidarity, it need not be rooted in base economic exploitation. It may be the case that solidarity is obstructed by occupational monopolisation around a limited set of influential and high-earning professions, the very presence of which stirs intense rivalry through a heightening of anxiety over economic expectations. Indeed, when prized occupations, offices and trades are well known as the preserve of one group to the exclusion of another, they can serve as a source of perennial friction, as some are led to believe their rival's monopoly over these occupations skews the structure of economic opportunities away from them (Horowitz 1985: 108–13). This can generate intense prejudices, distrust, conspiracy theories and ultimately a desire to control the other.

A case in point is the troubled relations between Malaysia's Chinese minority and its Malay majority. Fearing future domination under a powerful Chinese minority, Malays have sought to curb their economic might, introducing policies that give preference to Malays in job allocation, education and ownership stakes in Malaysian companies. The introduction of such measures has been driven by a desire to ensure Chinese economic influence does not translate into political and cultural forms of power that would threaten Malay pre-eminence over the territory (Freedman 2000: 50; Brown 1994: 321).

Similar remarks can be made about the economic rivalries between minority Chinese and the majority ethnic groups throughout Southeast Asia, along with Jews and the majority ethnic groups of some of the former Soviet nation-states, and South Asians and the societies of many East African nation-states (Horowitz 1985; Chua 2003). In all of these instances, a segmented labour market functions as a hindrance to solidarity by imbuing a cultural group with a threatening quality and ultimately compelling an insecure majority to react oppressively, even violently.

Distribution is therefore an additional chief medium of solidarity, as particular allocations of materially derived burdens and benefits play a vital role in supporting people's agency and integrity, but also influentially shaping their sense of self and how they choose to relate to others. Note that distribution too is a pluralist, rather than monist, aspect of solidarity, as relations of obligation arise not from the levelling of cultural and ethical variance, but from the modes of production and economic institutions that meet people's basic material needs and what they consider integral to taking advantage of opportunities relative to others. If any aspects of identity are sacrificed under solidarity promoting distributive arrangements, it is the agency inhibiting stigmatisations and class-like differentiations produced by exacerbated material inequalities and exploitative relations of production. Insofar as these are markers of social differentiation tied to oppression, their sacrifice is a very requirement of solidarity, and not its obstacle.

Relationality

I hope I have said enough to establish that solidarity is not dependent on cultural commonality. The key consideration, as we have witnessed, is the satisfaction of people's criteria for the enjoyment of freedom, the respect their identity is due, and the material conditions that enable them to lead dignified lives. Where a failure of one or more of these practices is occurring, we cannot equate the situation at hand with solidarity, and nor can we expect a society to be in a cohesive state.

However, in its current shape, this definition encounters a significant problem. Not all claims made in the name of self-determination, recognition and distribution can be considered consistent with solidarity. Indeed, it is often the case that solidarity is absent because groups are striving to achieve their autonomy, dignity and material well-being at the expense of each other. In reality, these aspects of social life will also be sites of incompatibility and tension, rather than harmony and reconciliation. Given this, on what basis can it be said that they are constitutive of solidarity?

The response to this question is that solidarity's core requirement of attentiveness across difference does not assume the attainment of a perfectly aligned constellation of self-determination, recognition and distribution satisfying to an ultimate degree the wishes of all concerned. This, it should be evident by now, remains an empty hope in the face of social complexity and finite resources. Rather, what matters is that people are prepared to compromise and accept as legitimate imperfectly realised aspirations around these defining practices in view of how their realisation poses harm to others. This relational insight implies that self-determination, recognition and distribution do not take on an absolutist and insular quality, but are outward looking and amenable to renegotiation so that they are supportive of the agency of people with whom one comes into contact. The stated goals tied to these practices are being held as provisional and contingent, subject to constant consideration of the effects they have on partners to society. Where the pursuit of objectives ensues in this self-reflexive fashion and where people are prepared to revise their intended plans when it comes to light that they adversely impact on those with whom they are socially interconnected, we can conclude a state of affairs is reflective of solidarity. From the perspective of self-determination, this implies a move away from unbridled choice towards the acceptance of certain kinds of constraint; from the perspective of recognition, it implies a move away from an uncritical acceptance of what accords respect to one's own identity and openness towards renegotiating the terms by which one's desire for respect can be satisfied; and from the perspective of distribution, it implies a move away from the patterning of distributions according to one's own distributive criterion towards a plurality of criteria sensitive to the value others attach to the goods being distributed.

This relational notion of solidarity is sensitive to the interconnections existing between humans that make compromise both a functional necessity of democracy and an unavoidable component of justice. Indeed, people are bound to each other in many ways they have not chosen – be it through economic interaction, history, proximity, or the unintended consequences of action – and in virtue of such interdependencies are able to thwart, and not only support, one another (Young 2000: 258). In the face of this mutual vulnerability, a relation of solidarity assumes a readiness to exercise curbs on desires for freedom when it comes to light that such desires limit the agency of others. Insofar as we do not exercise choice in isolation, and insofar as others can be adversely impacted by our actions, attentiveness to their well-being implies they are having some kind of input over our actions when such actions cause them harm, rather than enduring them for the sake of our own freedom.

The same point can be made in relation to recognition and distribution. Under an absolutist notion of recognition, those feeling disrespected would be receiving the recognition they believed they were due without any need to justify their demands beyond some subjective experience of wounded dignity, and without any need to consider the repercussions their desired mode of recognition would have on others. Yet we cannot take a claim of disrespect or insult to, in its own right, be conclusive evidence of mistreatment, as sometimes groups feel mistreated or hurt on the basis of being denied the opportunity to live out desires predicated on the mistreatment of others. The offence a nationalist feels at the arrival of immigrants altering the cultural characteristics of his/her society or acquiring jobs that he/she believes should be reserved for co-nationals is one such example, as it is an offence arising from false perceptions of unfair discrimination on the one hand and a notion of society that treats immigrants as subservient to 'natives' on the other (Thompson 2006: 168). Accordingly, to accept as valid the recognition such actors believe they are due would be to hinder, rather than promote, solidarity, as the inflation of one identity is reliant on the degradation of another.

To the extent that a desire for recognition risks being a desire for domination, a purely self-regarding understanding of recognition will be unsupportive of solidarity. Instead, people must be ready to renegotiate their claims when they stand to produce gains in their own self-esteem at the expense of the self-esteem of others. Otherwise, far from living up to its emancipatory potential, recognition will be an imposition on those who are called upon to do the recognising. One would be reduced to accepting another's characterisation of his/her identity for the sake of this person's achievement of a sense of sovereignty and invulnerability

(Markell 2003: 5, 7). In short, there would be no reciprocity in the relationship, and therefore no solidarity.

In the case of distribution, an absolutist and insular manifestation of the practice would involve an actor or set of actors pursuing goals around the allocation of finite goods as atomised egoists. They would be seeking to maximise their own share of the goods unperturbed by how this takes away from their possession by others, even though these others might have an equal stake in their acquisition.

The relational alternative emblematic of solidarity would entail distributive claim-making through self-limitation, whereby actors display sensitivity to how their own acquisition of a finite good takes away from its acquisition by others. Actors vying for access to goods are aware of and accountable for the various effects their intentions for distribution will carry, and are adjusting their intentions as they listen to those who will feel their negative repercussions. This does not imply everyone's needs have been met to the same or to the ultimate degree. Such an outcome will be unlikely in a context of scarcity of resources (Walzer 1983: 66–7). However, even though needs must be met imperfectly, they are being met imperfectly through a responsiveness to what people have to say about their own material situation, and not by satisfying the wishes of a narrowly defined section of society.

Conclusion

The aim of this chapter has been to identify the characteristics and background conditions of solidarity against accounts which equate it with national commonality. It was argued that solidarity denotes the associations people share when, and to the degree that, they are taking into account one another's concerns for self-determination, recognition and distribution. This definition avoids dependence on commonality, as it does not rely on a single social attribute to explain relations of mutual attentiveness. Rather, mutual attentiveness exists through people's tempering and revision of objectives around these three aspects of social coexistence. This assumes the preservation, and not elimination, of distinctiveness, even though the nature of such distinctiveness can be expected to alter in the course of social interaction. In the proceeding chapter, I turn to existing models of multicultural coexistence and assess their suitability as blueprints for solidarity.

2 Three Models of Coexistence

This chapter continues with the task of laying down the conceptual foundations of the book. While the previous chapter concerned itself with the nature of solidarity, the current one focuses on models of coexistence that best embody it.

I consider three commonly advanced ideals of social and political organisation for diverse societies – liberal multiculturalism, consociationalism and deliberative democracy – and assess the extent to which they can serve as a basis for mutual attentiveness across difference. While I analyse these models separately, they are not mutually exclusive. Indeed, a deliberative framework can inform the overall design of consociations by showing how group elites can engage in a manner that increases the likelihood of favourable conflict transformation, if not resolution (O'Flynn 2009), while the elite centrism of consociations can function as a backdrop for deliberations whenever open and unconstrained dialogue at the grass roots risks inflaming hostilities. Similarly, liberal multiculturalism provides philosophical grist to the empty proceduralism of deliberative practice by specifying which cultural rights are consistent with individual autonomy and which are not, while the inclusive and uncoerced dialogue of deliberative practice is how disagreements over the institutionalisation of cultural rights claims come to be managed fairly (Ercan 2011).

Nevertheless, each of these models contains its own overriding logic for the accommodation of difference, and this logic will approach standards of solidarity to lesser or greater degrees. As such, it matters a great deal which model is favoured as a guide for structuring group interactions. I contend that a society reflecting a norm of solidarity is one that is fashioned along deliberative tenets. Through its emphasis on public reason-giving and critical reflection in the pursuit of preferences, a deliberative approach tends towards a notion of collective organisation that best reflects the spirit of mutual obligation and reciprocity inherent to a relation of solidarity.

However, this is an idealised picture of deliberation. It says nothing of what we can expect from the practice when it is put to the task of guiding behaviour in the gritty and uncompromising settings of the empirical world. In the final part of the chapter, I address some of the issues deliberation encounters in contexts of deep inequality and ethnic antagonism. These issues include: the reluctance of participants to expose their viewpoints to critical examination; their unwillingness to consider as reasonable those of their opponents; and the potential for the powerful to manipulate the forum for their own gain. This analysis will provide a sociological backdrop for the subsequent chapters, which offer prescriptions for making people take reciprocal thinking seriously.

Liberal multiculturalism

Will Kymlicka (1995) offers a compelling defence of group entitlements from a liberal perspective, the complexity and nuance of which I cannot do justice to in the rather truncated analysis of his work that will follow. I can, nevertheless, identify where his argument comes into tension with the requirements of solidarity, and thereby provide clues as to how his rationale for group entitlements can be modified to have a more central place for mutual answerability.

The basic premise of Kymlicka's argument is as follows: how a state decides to accommodate the demands of its cultural groups ought to be informed by how the cultural groups were historically incorporated into the state. Those that were incorporated involuntarily, through non-consensual state expansion, have a claim to maintain a distinctive identity alongside the identity of the majority cultural group, while those that reside in the state as a result of making a voluntary choice to migrate there have a duty to integrate into its mainstream institutions constructed in the identity of the majority ethnicity.

This touchstone for assessing group claims is given practical currency through two corresponding normative categories of diversity, each of which is constructed according to the assumed desires and intentions of the cultural groups they signify. These categories are 'national minorities' on the one hand and 'immigrant groups' on the other.[1] National minorities correspond to those ethnic groups incorporated into the state involuntarily. As a result of this historical contingency, they typically wish to maintain themselves as distinct groups alongside the majority nation, demanding various forms of autonomy or self-government to ensure their survival (1995: 10). Immigrant groups, by contrast are those which voluntarily arrived in the country. As a consequence of having made a voluntary choice to leave their society of origin, they typically do not wish to become a separate and self-governing nation, but, rather, to integrate into the society of their new country and to be accepted as full members (1995: 11).

It is on the basis of these distinctive desires and historical backgrounds that Kymlicka argues national minorities have a right to maintain and develop a nation that is distinct and protected from the dominant nation, while immigrant groups do not, and should instead be offered assistance to integrate into the societal culture in which they find themselves (1995: 27–31).

In what sense does liberal multiculturalism provide a basis for solidarity? If we recall that solidarity assumes differently situated actors are taking into account each other's concerns for self-determination, recognition and distribution, we find that liberal multiculturalism offers robust directives for the promotion of each of these core elements of human interaction. Self-determination is promoted by permitting national minorities to preserve their distinctive ways of life next to the majority nation. They will 'have the same tools of nation-building available to them as the majority nation, subject to the same liberal limitations' (2001: 29). This includes such measures as 'control over the language and curriculum of schooling, the language of government employment, the requirements of immigration and naturalisation, and the drawing of internal boundaries' (2001: 28). While liberal multiculturalism seeks to integrate, rather than promote the separate existence of immigrants, this too is consistent with self-determination, as immigrants do not normally pursue separatist objectives, but seek incorporation into existing institutions. Insofar as liberal multiculturalism attempts to make the terms of such incorporation fair, through, for example, curriculum reform in schools to give greater recognition to the historical and cultural contributions of immigrants, the accommodation of religious practices and holidays of immigrants in public institutions, cultural development programmes involving the funding of ethnic festivals and mother tongue literary courses for adult immigrants, and affirmative action to increase immigrants' access to education, training and employment (2001: 159–61), it can be seen to support the autonomy of immigrants, rather than to arbitrarily restrict it.

Similarly, there are important ways that liberal multiculturalism functions as a vehicle for the promotion of recognition. Group entitlements, be they of the group preserving or group integrating kind, have a commanding role in determining group status by according prestige to a recipient group. They signal to society that the group in question is important enough to warrant attention and treatment by the state not afforded to others. Thus, where a minority identity is devalued, the acquisition of group entitlements can raise its status, not only in the eyes of its own members, but also in the eyes of those outside the group.

Finally, liberal multiculturalism also functions as a framework for redistribution. Group entitlements not only enhance freedom and status, they have a direct bearing on the allocation of resources and opportunities between groups (Phillips 1999: 30–1). To grant powers of self-government to a national minority is to increase its control over patterns of provision. This, in turn, can assist in narrowing material inequalities where these are the result of a more populous group using majoritarian policy making to distort distributions for its own gain. Similarly, integration programmes enhance equality of opportunity for immigrants by, on the one hand, increasing their literacy, education and economic mobility, and on the other hand, altering the character of academic, economic and political institutions so that immigrants are more welcome, and more likely to succeed, in them.

While liberal multiculturalism offers provisions that can bring human relations closer to standards of solidarity, there are aspects of it that lead it astray from such standards. Perhaps the most relevant of these is its support of a 'simple' notion of equality in the distribution of group entitlements. Simple equality is a term famously coined by Michael Walzer to criticise a literal interpretation of equality in which the division of a society's social goods occurs according to identical allotments among citizens (1983: 47–8). Under such a notion, justice obtains when everyone has the same amount of wealth, the same amount of income, the same amount of land, the same amount of leisure time, and in the context of the current discussion, the same powers of nation building.

Simple equality is an intuitively appealing principle of justice. However, there are important reasons why we should eschew such a literal understanding of ethnic egalitarianism, not least, when it concerns shifting the balance of nation-building powers within a society. It is rather blunt to assert that justice is achieved only when, and to the extent that, an ethnic minority has powers of government equal in quantity and quality to a majority, as ethnic groups do not come with a ready-made desire or interest to have such powers, and nor can we conclude that in the absence of such powers ethnic minorities must be subject to oppression. Minorities have specific histories that lead them to understand themselves and their interests relative to majorities in different ways. Whether or not such understandings are tied to the possession of sovereign powers equal to a majority's will be a matter of contingency.

Indeed, significant variation exists across ethnic groups, but also within them among the many factions, on aspirations for collective selfhood. Some of these aspirations will be based on increased independence from the majority, and some of them will not. A principle of simple equality in nation-building is incapable of capturing this variability. Anything short of an interest in possessing nation-building powers cannot count as a legitimate self-understanding, since simple equality preassigns ethnic groups an inherent interest to be distinct and self-governing.

The untenability of simple equality can be further illustrated by turning to Kymlicka's core moral assertion that the right to equal nation-building powers derives from an ethnic group's forcible incorporation into the state. It is true that the expansion and consolidation of nation-states are historically unjust acts involving violence and assimilation, the redress of which may require some kind of restitution or public apology. However, this historical legacy does not in itself validate the extension of nation-building powers to minorities in the present. How a minority was dealt with at the time of a state's genesis or its territorial expansion does not tell us how the minority is faring in the present, the kinds of opportunities it enjoys, and what kind of self-conception it maintains relative to the majority. Once again, there is significant empirical variation on such matters across time and in different places.

Thus, in the case of some minorities, there is indeed a strong correlation between present day disadvantage and events in the distant historical past. The marginalisation of Indigenous people in former colonies and African Americans in the United States are two such examples, as the relative gains made by wider society can in part be attributed to the historical oppression of these groups from the moment of their incorporation – in the case of Indigenous people, through dispossession and cultural genocide, and African Americans, through slavery. Where state genesis or forced incorporation leave their mark on a society in this way, they certainly carry normative weight in the distribution of group rights in the present.

However, beyond such exceptional cases, the correlation between involuntary inclusion into a polity and the kinds of opportunities, status and mobility enjoyed by a minority in the present day remains weak or absent. Access to such social goods varies considerably among ethnic minorities, but also among immigrant groups, whose treatment at the hands of wider society is deeply divergent.

In fact, in many societies, ethnic minorities have become proficient in the official language of the state and have been incorporated into its institutions through intergenerational socialisation. Under such circumstances, 'the equality of opportunity' line of justification for nation-building powers becomes redundant, as nationally socialised ethnic minorities participate as full, rather than disadvantaged, members of a mainstream 'societal culture'. They have access to opportunities comparable to those of a majority, even though the majority's language governs the character of the society's institutions.[2] This is true for Bretons and Alsatians who are no more disadvantaged economically, educationally and politically than the rest of French society as a result of working and living in a Parisian French societal culture (even though matters were otherwise prior to their linguistic assimilation), or Welsh and Scots as a result of working and living in an Anglophone societal culture, Venetians and Friulians in an Italian societal culture, Volga Germans in the societal culture of former Soviet states, Sorbs in a German societal culture, Carinthian Slovenes and Burgenland Croats in an Austrian societal culture, Vlachs in the societal cultures of numerous Balkan States, and so on. The identities of such groups are entwined with the cultural forms of the majority. The bulk of their members use the official language of the state as their primary medium of exchange and typically lack the same level of proficiency in the language associated with their minority identity, owing to decades or centuries of participation in institutions centred on an official idiom. Under such circumstances, equal nation-building powers remain an irrelevant justice-promoting measure, even though such groups were forcibly incorporated into the state and were subject to its unjust policies of assimilation. The majority societal culture now functions as the chief medium through which diverse ethno-linguistic minorities express and pursue their objectives, meaning that, all other things held constant, opportunities for self-realisation will be the same.

Any attempt to reinfuse minority societal cultures in contexts where they have been displaced by majority ones risks limiting, rather than creating, opportunities, as those who lack proficiency in the minority language (which will be the bulk of minority members in the above examples) face barriers to participation in institutions reformed to operate in a new obligatory language. As Matthew Festenstein (2005: 78–9) notes in the context of Wales, compulsory education in the Welsh language in state schools and its promotion as a prerequisite for some public sector jobs enhances 'contexts of choice' for the relatively few monoglot Welsh speakers while narrowing the contexts of choice for the rest of society. By shifting the linguistic moorings of society, the official promotion of Welsh has caused disorientation and unfamiliarity for those lacking competency in the language, and therefore limited their capacity to pursue their conceptions of the good on equal terms with fluent Welsh speakers.

The cruel irony of assimilation is that the closer it comes to being accomplished, the less it functions as an agency depriving imposition, and the more it opens up opportunities for effective participation. Minority members who have acquired proficiency in the obligatory idiom take advantage of opportunities through structures of communication and action that are no more enabling or constraining for them than for the majority. In highlighting these matters, my point is not to endorse assimilation as a solution to the accommodation of ethnic minorities, but rather, to draw attention to the way nation-building powers can stray from their intended purpose of promoting justice when they are distributed simply with reference to the historical criterion of forced incorporation into the state. On the one hand, the extension of nation-building powers *teaches* minorities to be distinct as much as it permits them to be distinct. On the other hand, the lack of such powers and mere embeddedness in mainstream societal culture is insufficient proof that minorities are enduring injustices. For these reasons, a more careful and precise rationale for the distribution of nation-building powers is required than Kymlicka's liberal multiculturalism offers, which in principle, makes those powers available to all ethnonational groups.

In Chapter 3, I provide a defence of such a rationale, contending that the legitimacy of claims for group rights should be assessed according to a minority's exposure to oppression and disadvantage. This logic, I argue, brings group rights into closer alignment with justice-based concerns than apportioning them simply on the basis of a group's historical background. However, for the purposes of the current discussion, it has been adequate merely to highlight that simple equality in nation-building powers is not a necessary condition of justice, only a contingent one.

Consociationalism

Whereas liberal multiculturalism provides a defence of group entitlements from a moral perspective, consociationalism – or power-sharing as it is alternatively known – does so from the standpoint of political functionality. It offers, with workmanlike rigour, a set of practical insights for the generation of democracy-enabling stability where the potential for destructive conflict between mutually hostile ethnic groups remains an ever-present threat.

The political designs on which consociationalism lays its claim to practical superiority include a combination of all or most of the following features: 'Executive power-sharing', practised as grand coalition cabinets in parliamentary systems or as the distribution of the presidency and other higher offices among ethnic groups in presidential systems; 'segmental autonomy', which involves the delegation of decision-making freedoms to each ethnic group; 'proportionality', practised as the proportional representation of each ethnic group in key public institutions and the proportional allocation of public resources and expenditures to each group; and 'veto rights', involving the power to prevent change that affects vital group interests (Lijphart 1997: 277–8; McGarry and O'Leary 2006: 44). Taken together, these institutional mechanisms are seen to induce stabilising effects on divided societies by encouraging elite cooperation and blunting the force of appeals to extremism.

To what extent are these designs consistent with solidarity? Consociationalism has all the trappings that enable groups to relate to one another equitably and, over time, to renounce the mutual resentment that necessitated consociational designs in the first place. In a consociation, minority ethnic groups that gain representation are guaranteed a political voice when they would otherwise be outvoted and disregarded under majoritarian systems. In contrast to first-past-the-post electoral systems, proportional representation ensures a broader sweep of society's voices and perspectives are present in legislative assemblies by making it easier for smaller parties to gain seats. Likewise, the practice of segmental autonomy allows an enhancement of decision-making capacities among minorities through greater freedoms for self-organisation, territorial autonomy and/or reserved seats, while veto rights protect against a majority acting with impunity and thereby dominating the interests of minorities through the unchecked pursuit of its own. The presence of such measures enables minority freedom in a manner not possible under a homogenous public by levelling the playing field between the more powerful, who have the material, personal and organisational resources to speak and be heard, and the underprivileged who do not (Young 1990: 185).

A similar point can be made from the vantage points of group respect and distributions of material goods. Inclusion within a consociation can have powerful recognition-conferring effects. These emerge through the public and tangible ways that sovereign power is shared and ethnic identities are officialised – to have an identity gain constituent status in a consociation is to give its bearers a sense that they are socially included and publicly appreciated. Likewise, consociations can attenuate ethnically based socio-economic stratifications. Not only do they disrupt group monopolies of control over the allocation of finite resources, they level opportunities for the realisation of mobility aspirations between groups. For example, by gaining access to the levers of decision-making power, an economically underprivileged ethnic group can direct the attention of the welfare state to its own neglected members and encourage investment in infrastructure in regions where it is territorially concentrated. Similarly, opportunities for education and skills can be shifted towards the group, enhancing its access to influential occupations and boosting its representation among a broader sweep of social classes.

Where consociationalism does come into tension with solidarity is around the primacy it places on the achievement of social stability. The first and primary task of consociations is to nurture stable democratic institutions. This is evident in three normative priorities that distinguish consociations from other democracies: an emphasis on prescriptions that are feasible; the institutional inclusion of warring or numerically superior ethnic groups; and the restriction of politics to elite circles. As I will now argue, each of these features achieves stability through power politics and acts of exclusion, and given this, remains incompatible with the relation of mutual answerability demanded in an ideal of solidarity.

Feasibility

We have noted that consociationalism's claim to superiority is built on a promise to offer prescriptions that work where deep inter-group division and hostility purportedly leave philosophically derived ideals standing no chance. These realist credentials are best appreciated by considering consociationalism's origins as a descriptive theory in the field of comparative social science. Developed by the Dutch political scientist Arend Lijphart in the 1960s through his famous comparative analysis of pre- and post-Second World War societies in Western Europe, consociationalism explained why some divided countries did not exhibit the political immobilism and instability typical of other divided countries (Lijphart 1969: 208). Lijphart concluded that what accounted for this counterintuitive observation was the behaviour of political elites. In unstable, divided societies, the leaders of rival subcultures engaged in competitive behaviour and therefore aggravated mutual discord, while in stable divided societies they made deliberate efforts to counteract the volatility stimulated by social fragmentation, thus achieving a degree of political harmony quite out of proportion to the degree of social division present (1969: 211–12). Lijphart came to call these fragmented, but stable, political systems 'consociational democracies'.

These roots as a descriptive theory have added to consociationalism's reputation as a model of society that is actually attainable and not simply normatively desirable. Unlike many philosophically inspired models, consociationalism does not owe its origins to a process of abstract reasoning detached from empirical exigencies. It is in fact the product of empirical observation, formulated through what *has* happened in an actual world of power disparities and hostility, rather than what *would* happen in an imagined world of perfect and respected equals. Consociationalism thus boasts a proven formula. It offers theoretical constructions that have their origins in actual problems and avoid what Ian Shapiro calls the 'whiff of irrelevance' associated with the hypothetical thinking and counterfactuals of armchair speculation (Shapiro 1996: 5).

However, consociationalism's intimate association with the empirical world may be a virtue in one sense, but it is a liability in another, as it brings into question the theory's prescriptive status. As Ian O'Flynn has pointed out, democratic proposals that permit us to make informed decisions about public policy are not merely those that offer a clear understanding of what is institutionally feasible, but, also, what is justifiable independently of the empirical world as we currently find it (2006: 22–3). Where there is insufficient distance between a set of prescriptions and the empirical realities to which they apply, they are prescriptions in name only, as they are deprived of critical content. They reflect matters as they already are, rather than as they ought to be, and as a consequence, fail to confront the relations of power causing disadvantage.

Consociationalism is vulnerable to this charge, providing an approach that is 'almost entirely empirical' (O'Flynn 2006: 20). In its attempt to signal what works, it surrenders too much to existing practice and, with this, any hope for social transformation beyond entrenched hegemonies. It shows us how democracy can take place, but this gain in democratic functionality is pursued by harnessing status quo relations of power, rather than redefining them with a view to making societies more just. It is therefore of little surprise that consociationalism can boast so much expediency. The distance between 'what is' and what the theory believes 'should be' is so narrow that its objectives can only ever be widely attainable.

Institutional inclusion

Who and how one gains inclusion in a consociation is an additional aspect of the theory that puts it at odds with solidarity. Due to its prioritisation of stability ahead of other objectives, consociationalism supports schemes of representation that overlook groups subject to the gravest forms of oppression. This is particularly so when the groups in question do not pose an immediate threat to social stability. In a consociation, actors favoured for representation are typically those engaged in political violence or those that are numerically superior and well resourced, as it is their cooperation on which the viability of power-sharing depends (Jarstad 2008a: 22). They have the capacity to bring the legitimacy of a state into jeopardy by disrupting or withdrawing from mainstream institutions, by threatening secession or by turning to military and terrorist measures when they are excluded from government. As a result, consociational design will naturally gravitate towards the wishes of such actors ahead of the wishes of others. This is a route to the pacification of potential spoilers, and therefore the stability the theory promises.

To highlight this issue with consociations is not to say that attending to the demands of the unruly is always illegitimate. Minority activism and agitation is, after all, fuelled by perceived injustices at the hands of a majority. As such, representation in a power-sharing arrangement is how a minority can gain protection from further exposure to abuse of this kind.

Nevertheless, justice in a consociation attains not by design but as a by-product of bargains struck. Given that bargaining leverage diminishes with disadvantage, justice frequently falls by the wayside in consociational arrangements. Indeed, success in a bargaining environment depends on one's capacity to coerce, bribe and threaten interlocutors into compliance. To the extent that this is so, the groups prioritised for consociational representation are unlikely to be the ones which are subject to the gravest forms of deprivation at the hands of others, but those which already possess enough retaliatory powers to be taken seriously.

Perhaps the most striking illustration of this is the repeated sidelining of Roma in consociational settlements. No consociation has ever included the Roma as a segmental group, despite the gravity of their socio-economic and political dislocation, which far exceeds that experienced by any group admitted into a consociation. A consociational framework offers few normative avenues to condemn the continued exclusion of Roma, for even though consociationalism is about inclusive decision making, its objective is nevertheless to prioritise the inclusion of those 'groups that can threaten political stability if kept outside the arrangements' (Rothchild and Roeder 2005b: 31). The Roma have never sought reform through armed insurgency or threats of secession, and insofar as they do not put the integrity of a state into jeopardy, their absence from power-sharing arrangements is not a matter that consociational theory is equipped to address (Kymlicka 2007a: 220–1). The experience of the Roma tells us, as Anne Phillips has put it, that 'the most marginalised can be as marginal in a consociation as they are anywhere else. Neither the theory nor the practice is about levelling democratic weight' (1995: 15). It is instead about averting conflict.

An analogous point can be made in relation to the divisions existing within groups. Inclusion in government for the sake of peace directs attention towards ethnic factions most likely to engage in political violence, and not moderates committed to tolerance and compromise. Again, this tendency is not entirely problematic, and nor is it always avoidable. Currying favour with extremists and winning the loyalty of combatants towards a political order is often the only way to end a war and its associated human suffering. Furthermore, as difficult as this strategy is to stomach, it also has the added benefit of potentially transforming extremists into moderates, given that political institutions are as much schools of democracy as they are its arenas. Once extremists are in government they are under pressure to strive for broad-based democratic support in order to succeed. This implies a preparedness to compromise and the abandonment of a dogmatic adherence to ethnonationalist ideologies (Jarstad 2008a: 22). The IRA in Northern Ireland, the KLA in Kosovo and the NLA in Macedonia are all examples of violent insurgent groups that have undergone such transformations.

By the same token, peace through such means is won at a high price to justice. The ascendency of such actors occurs through their readiness to use brutal force, directed not just at members of opposing ethnic groups but at members within their own ethnic community who may be considered impediments to their cause. As such, to offer them concessions for peace will always be a bitter pill to swallow, especially if it is tied to amnesty for crimes committed, as was the case with the peace process in Northern Ireland and Macedonia. Such measures might offer a more immediate pathway to peace. But they permit human rights violations to go unaddressed (Jarstad 2008a: 22), and send the message that violence can be rewarding in the pursuit of power. This can be counterproductive for peace building efforts in the long run by inspiring others to turn to arms to achieve political objectives (Jarstad 2008b: 117, 124).

Elite centrism

In a consociation, democratic interaction occurs primarily between the elites of each ethnic group, rather than through the direct involvement of ordinary citizens, a process Lijphart aptly dubbed 'government by elite cartel' (1969: 222). The common justification offered for locating politics out of popular reach is that it remains the only way democratic decision making can be made possible where very little interaction occurs between mutually hostile groups. In addition, it is seen to guard against the spectre of interethnic violence, which it is feared would follow were democratic contestation to be broadly extended throughout society (Dryzek 2005: 222).

However, the pursuit of stability through elite politics works against the establishment of accountability from representatives to their constituencies, for in such a system of government representatives are absolved of considerable responsibility to justify their decisions beyond themselves. Secrecy is favoured over publicity, as politicians stand little chance of gaining public approval for the unpopular compromises they make across ethnic lines. Moreover, politicians risk inflaming an already volatile public when they make known the details of such compromises. As such, it is commonplace in a consociation for interethnic negotiations to take place behind closed doors, shielded from popular scrutiny and input. Under these circumstances, representatives operate unburdened by the gaze of stakeholders, passing decisions without the approval or authorship of actors those decisions affect.

In one sense, the promotion of secrecy in decision making need not lead to behaviour completely at odds with democracy. After all, secrecy liberates parties to exercise independent judgement, rather than to be tied down by the expectation to remain faithful to vested and narrow interests. It also protects politicians from extremists who portray them as soft or sell-outs whenever they change their position on a controversial issue following the consideration of an opponent's views (O'Flynn 2006: 118). Such freedom of judgement is an integral part of well-functioning democratic representation, as it is how representatives arrive at wise and just decisions after having listened to each other's viewpoints (Young 2000: 131).

Moreover, there are moments in political life when secrecy can be justified in public interest terms. It is wishful thinking, for example, to think that agreements ending wars could be forged through open and inclusive negotiations involving the general public's oversight of the proceedings of mediations. Peace agreements depend on secrecy, as the location of representatives behind closed doors frees them to make compromises that are unpalatable with polarised constituencies, but necessary for the establishment of peace.

By the same token, we cannot trust that such independent thinking will be oriented towards what is in everyone's best interests when an expectation of public accountability and justification remains weak. Politicians making decisions in a shroud of secrecy have little to discourage them from abusing their position (O'Flynn 2006: 103). Furthermore, in remaining detached from those they represent, politicians risk misconstruing or overlooking their perspectives when passing judgement, even when they are acting with honourable intentions (Chapter 3). By contrast, when decision making is made public, the scope for self-interested behaviour and misrepresentation is narrowed. Representatives are compelled to adopt what Hannah Arendt termed an 'enlarged mentality', as their actions undergo the scrutiny of a broad audience, which can hold them to account. In addition, the preservation of their reputation and career will depend on the extent to which they couch arguments through an appeal to generalisable interests, as this is the kind of behaviour the wider public would expect from elected representatives where a norm of public justification is strong (O'Flynn 2006: 112).

In sum, consociationalism is best thought of as a theory of necessity rather than justice. It signals how democratic politics can be established under conditions of state dysfunction and severe social fragmentation, but not how such politics can approach standards of fairness or function as a source of emancipation for those who are in need of it most. In this sense, consociationalism should not be supported for its own sake. Rather, it is best seen as an interim instrument for the eventual institutionalisation of more inclusive and accountable forms of coexistence.

The deliberative ideal

Deliberation can be defined as a critical and public exchange of arguments oriented towards producing reasonable and well-informed opinions. Through this reasoned exchange, participants are conceived as willing to revise their preferences in light of new information and claims made by fellow participants in the course of discussion (Chambers 2003: 309). In this manner, a democracy informed by deliberative tenets represents a turn away from aggregative and realist models, which see democracy as an arena where fixed preferences and interests compete via fair mechanisms of aggregation, most notably, via voting (Chambers 2003: 308). In a deliberative democracy, voting still takes place. But the focus is on the communicative processes of opinion and will formation that precede it. The legitimacy of a decision is based not merely on the fairness of voting rules, but, more importantly, on the quality of the conversations that culminate in a vote.

There are several core elements to this norm-guided notion of dialogue (Benhabib 1996: 72). First, participation in a deliberation must adhere to conditions of equality and symmetry in the sense that 'all have the same chances to initiate speech acts, to question, to interrogate, and to open debate'. Second, all taking part will have a right to question the assigned topics of conversation. Third, all participants will be free to challenge the actual rules of discourse procedure, including the way in which they are applied and carried out. There are to be no *prima facie* limitations on the agenda of a conversation or on the content of speech. What is important is that actors making a claim for inclusion in dialogue are able to prove they are relevantly affected by the proposed issue under debate. It is only when all of these features are satisfied that a democratically attained agreement can be considered valid from a deliberative standpoint.

I wish to argue that of the three models of coexistence under examination, deliberative democracy offers a rationale for the accommodation of diversity that sits closest to the demands of solidarity. Deliberative democracy calls for a certain reflexivity in the pursuit of preferences not available in liberal multiculturalism or consociationalism, as participants must advance their positions by articulating reasons that would count as valid for all others involved, and not simply for themselves. Under such a proposal, one is forced to think from the standpoint of all dialogically present, as nobody 'can convince others in public of her point of view without being able to state why what appears good, plausible, just, and expedient to her can also be considered so from the standpoint of all involved' (Benhabib 1996: 72).

We can consider these points specifically with reference to solidarity's core elements. Self-determination under a deliberative framework is promoted through reason-giving in the pursuit of preferences. Insofar as the acceptability of positions hinges on their justification to all potentially affected, participants are automatically placed in a tracking relationship to one another. Success is dependent on drawing on supporting reasons which go beyond narrowly defined, self-interested arguments, as this is a minimal requirement for the establishment of validity behind the preferences asserted. This distinctive emphasis on reason giving opens opportunities for citizens to learn, think and talk more about the issues connecting them. They do not simply receive and digest information and opinions in private. Rather, they talk with a wide variety of citizens, hearing and weighing opposing points of view on the process of coming to their own considered judgements (Fishkin and Luskin 2000: 18, 21).

A similar point can be made on matters of recognition. Through public discussions, the full nature and extent of experiences of insult and disrespect in a society are made known, and groups come to express how they would like to be understood and treated by the broader public in response (Festenstein 2000: 86). This permits a misrecognising group to better appreciate the rationale behind another's feeling of insult and indignity, but also, a misrecognised group to comprehend why its misrecogniser arrives at mistaken beliefs about it (Valadez 2001: 38).

From the perspective of distribution, demands for the reallocation of wealth and the control of a society's capital and resources cannot simply be handed down from officials deemed to possess, in Young's words 'transcendent normative verities' (1990: 92), but must run the gauntlet of public scrutiny before they can be put into practice under a deliberative framework. A procedure that submits distributive proposals to the judgement and input of all perspectives in this way fosters thinking about one's own needs in relation to the needs of others, for people will be called to account when their desired distributive outcome endangers others (1990: 91–5).

Practical deliberation

The foregoing account of deliberative democracy is a highly idealised one. In reality, democracies fall considerably short of living up to this ideal state, to say nothing of democracies marked by ethnic divisions and intolerance. A major issue with deliberative theory, as many of its more level-headed supporters would concede, is that it takes for granted the very empirical conditions it hopes to bring about. That is, for deliberation to reliably lead to just outcomes and mutual understanding, it must begin from a starting point of justice and mutual understanding. However, actual-world democracies contain structural inequalities that distort deliberative proceedings and disadvantage already marginalised participants. Such inequalities relate to matters of 'wealth, social and economic power, access to knowledge, status [and] work expectations' all of which contribute towards making some actors more effective deliberators than others (Young 2000: 34).

Likewise, a shared commitment towards mutual understanding and the achievement of free public reasoning in which citizens go beyond their self-interests and orient themselves to a common good is the exception rather than the rule. As Robyn Eckersley (2000: 126) observes, the forums in which anything approximating genuine deliberation occurs – Quaker meetings, university tutorials, reading groups, deliberative microcosms and town hall meetings – either contain participants who already share a steadfast commitment towards the practice of deliberation (Quakers have a pre-existing and deep-seated mutual understanding of and respect for one another; participants in university tutorials and reading groups share a culture of critical discourse), or in cases where they do not, discussions are well facilitated so as to harness the core ideals of the deliberative model (public meetings in the town hall; deliberative microcosms). Outside of such protected and semi-formal deliberative forums, and in everyday political contexts characterised by deep pluralism and inequalities in power and resources, forces other than communicative argumentation will inevitably influence decisions.

In the face of these realities, appeals to deliberation can appear circular at best and dangerous at worst, as recourse to deliberative practice risks reinforcing the injustices it is supposed to remove, despite the best intentions of its advocates. Where inequalities in social, economic and political power prevail, the powerful will be able to rely on deliberation to exclude or marginalise the voice and influence of some groups while magnifying the influence of others (Young 2000: 34).

These attributes of actual-world politics are pervasive and have provided ample ammunition for democratic realists to cast doubts over the feasibility of deliberative democracy.[3] While I share the view of realists that certain, unavoidable social, political, economic and historical conditions are hostile to the emergence of communicative openness, I do not share their conclusion that deliberation is ultimately a doomed and irrelevant procedural ethic as a result. That political practice does not properly correspond to ideal deliberation is not adequate grounds to dismiss its relevance out of hand, for this ignores the many public arenas in which it is already present, albeit in approximated forms. As Seyla Benhabib points out, the rationale of parliamentary opposition and the need for a free and independent media and sphere of public opinion are all practices that a theory of deliberative democracy elucidates (1996: 84). Furthermore, the intimations of ideal deliberation, as noted by John Dryzek, can be found in a number of contemporary practices aimed at resolving conflictual social problems, be it in the mediation of disputes (civil, labour, international and environmental), policy dialogue, principled negotiations, or 'problem-solving' workshops in international conflict resolution. What these practices share in common with ideal deliberation is that discussion among actors is governed by formal and informal canons of reasoned discourse that rule out threat, concealment of information, delaying tactics, statement of a bargaining position, and so on (Dryzek 1990: 44, cited in Benhabib 1996: 86). Given this, deliberative democracy is not merely a counterfactual thought experiment, but throws light on 'the already implicit principles and logic of existing democratic practices' (Benhabib 1996: 84).

Therefore, a more accurate assessment of deliberation would conclude it is a process that is seldom self-inducing and fully achievable in contexts of conflict, but one that can be nurtured and approximated closely enough to make it a viable promoter of just relations. How this can be achieved is a task of the proceeding chapters. For now, a more precise picture is required of how it flounders in contexts of group conflict and rivalry, as this will frame the discussion on institutional choices in the following chapters.

Deliberative exclusion and assimilation

Where disparities in political influence between ethnic groups are significant and where an orientation towards reasonableness is lacking, a deliberative process will be vulnerable to both exclusionary and assimilatory tendencies. Exclusion, in the context of deliberation, refers to the inability to initiate or participate in democratic procedures that lead to publicly relevant decisions. By contrast, assimilation refers to the incapacity to participate and influence such decisions on one's own terms.[4] Both phenomena are reflective of domination insofar as they involve the arbitrary denial of freedom to influence democratic outcomes and potentially alter the rules by which governing power is exercised.

Exclusion

The most obvious manifestation of exclusion is formal in nature, involving the denial of legal rights of association and organisation. A notorious example of this is South Africa under apartheid. The formal exclusion of Blacks occurred through the tightening or banning of the political activities of associations representing them. It also occurred through the disenfranchisement of Blacks under the 'homeland system', where their voting rights were restricted to the territory of so-called tribal homelands, and denied in what was deemed 'White South Africa'. Other, more general, examples of formally excluded groups that can be added to the list are asylum seekers, denizens, guest workers and their descendants, and women in fundamentalist Islamic states, all of whom have limited or no political rights as a result of being denied the full status of citizenship.

However, the majority of exclusion that occurs in liberal democracies is not typically of the formal kind, but can be traced to informal exclusions. In such instances, citizens have democratic rights constitutionally guaranteed. But the presence of hierarchical relations among them, due to inequalities in political power, continues to undermine the ability of the disadvantaged to be taken seriously in public deliberations that lead to democratic decisions (Bohman 1996: 110–12). Such exclusion, while not as obvious as formal exclusion, can be just as invidious because its very inconspicuousness contributes to the difficulties in its being overcome. Disadvantaged groups will have equal rights of citizenship, but will be denied the ability to initiate, or influence outcomes of public deliberations about themes and topics which affect their lives, leaving them in a state of perpetual, but invisible, marginalisation in policy making.

A clearer picture of informal exclusion is gained by encapsulating it within the institutional elements of what Dryzek calls a 'deliberative system' (2009: 1385–6). A deliberative system contains a 'public space', where people engage in critical discussions on an issue (for example, spaces associated with the media, social movements, activist associations, among others), and an 'empowered space', where collective decisions are made (most notably, the legislature, but also constitutional courts, councils committees, cabinets or any other institution mandated to make public decisions). Ideally, the viewpoints expressed in the public space are to be consequential in influencing the content of collective outcomes made in the empowered space (Ercan and Hendriks 2013: 427). But during instances of informal exclusion, public sphere deliberations fail to influence empowered spaces, even though the former does not contain legal restrictions on who can participate and what participants can say. All participants continue to have formal opportunities for input in public dialogue. What makes them informally exclusive is that dialogue on an issue either does not take ground (often as a result of affected actors lacking the necessary organisational capacities to achieve this), or when it does take ground, the viewpoints expressed simply fail to carry across to the empowered deliberative spaces. Viewpoints fail to carry across either because of a lack of discursive links between the two spaces, or more relevantly for contexts marked by group antipathies, as a result of group actors in the empowered space being unaccountable to actors of a rival identity in the public space.

Under such circumstances, a group's inability to be consequential in collective decisions is not a factor of some internal shortcoming that leaves it incapable of publicly articulating its desires (as would occur under capability-depriving conditions of material poverty, for example). Rather, it is a factor of external interference to deny it the opportunity to have its reasons count in democratic decision making. Under such circumstances, a group can possess the cultural resources (as in knowledge and access to information) necessary to lend validity behind its reasons and to make it a persuasive deliberator. It can, moreover, possess the economic wherewithal to participate as an equal in public sphere deliberations, having the material security and economic independence to direct its energies towards activism and engagement in the public space of a deliberative system. Ultimately, though, it stands little chance of converting its claims into policy outcomes because the dominant group uses the instruments of centralised government and majoritarian decision making to persistently shut them out of the empowered space.

It is precisely this form of purposive and calculated exclusion that characterises the situation of oppressed groups in contexts of deep ethnic division. In Northern Ireland, Unionists were in a position of vast political privilege in a democratic system that was strongly majoritarian before the introduction of power-sharing. They were able to use the force of numbers to manipulate democratic procedures in a way that ensured their continued dominance over the territory and left Nationalists impotent to act on their core concerns. This took the form of denying Nationalists any group rights beyond education and limiting their presence in the Cabinet, the Parliament, the courts, the security forces and the top echelons of the civil administration (Smooha 2001: 322–3). Unionists were able to do this within the parameters set by the law, using constitutionally enshrined majoritarian procedures to cement their hegemony and brush aside Nationalist calls for reform.

In Malaysia, ethnic Chinese have remained economically superior, but deliberatively inconsequential as a result of concerted efforts of Malays to ensure Chinese stay mute within the country's public spheres. Malays have impeded Chinese activism via a two-pronged process involving, on the one hand, the threat of hostile reprisals from radical Malay organisations and, on the other hand, curbs on associational activity by the Malay-controlled state (Freedman 2000: 53, 58, 83–4). Fearing a repeat of the murderous anti-Chinese rioting that took place in 1969, and seeking to avoid detainment by state authorities for 'disturbing public order', Chinese Malaysians have been driven to pursue collective goals through indirect and non-confrontational methods. Among these have been the backdoor channels of clientalistic relationships Chinese business elites have forged with influential Malay politicians (Chee-Beng 2002: 135). Though offering a means for Chinese concerns to reach empowered deliberative spaces, this rent-seeking arrangement has, for obvious reasons, been of greater benefit to Chinese entrepreneurs than it has to the Chinese community as a whole.

Similarly, the limited ability of Albanians to influence political decisions in Macedonia during the 1990s was attributable not to any shortcoming internal to the group itself. Rather, it was the result of the intentional actions of Macedonians to deny them a voice. In occupying the country's empowered spaces, Macedonians were able to ignore calls for reform being made by Albanians within the public sphere. Though Albanians were successful at drawing public attention to issues concerning their community, they were unsuccessful at converting this into tangible political outcomes, as Macedonians used their superiority in the decision-making organs of the state to exclude Albanian perspectives and to arrest any effort towards the empowerment of Albanians, seeing this as a means to protecting their own hegemony against a perceived challenge posed by an Albanian one (Vasilev 2013: 694–5).

Assimilation

Exclusion is a commonplace expression of domination where an ethnic group lacks accessibility to or accountability from an empowered deliberative space. Paradoxically, however, practices of exclusion are almost always accompanied by some form of assimilation. This too serves as a potent tool for the arbitrary restriction of a group's ability to influence political decisions during public sphere deliberations.

Relations of assimilation, as Tully notes, involve a social arrangement in which individuals and groups are permitted, even encouraged, to participate in deliberative practices, but are 'constrained to deliberate in a particular way, in a particular type of institution and over a particular range of issues so their agreements and disagreements serve to reinforce rather than challenge the status-quo' (2002: 223). Thus, the primary process by which citizens are dominated in an assimilative arrangement is the denial of freedom to phrase demands *qua* members of a specific identity. They are forced to conform to the practices and identity of the dominant, usually majority, group if they wish to take part in deliberations in which they have a stake. The pressure to conform in deliberations serves to undermine the ability of citizens to be both equal and different, as they must shape their participation according to standards that are not theirs and represent their demands in a fashion not reflective of their core concerns (Laden 2000: 159, 160).

By its very logic, the goal of assimilation is achieved when a group comes to relinquish its dissonant customs and ways, and acquires the consonant forms of identity characteristic of another group (Tully 2002: 223). But for assimilation to amount to domination, it does not need to rest on the pursuit of complete conformity. Assimilative action is also an expression of domination even when it seeks partial conformity if the party enacting and benefiting from such conformity cannot justify it in a manner others are likely to find credible (Pettit 1997). After all, what matters normatively is the degree to which one has a say and control over subjection to assimilatory pressures, rather than simply the presence or absence of such pressures. Relations of assimilation will be a fact of social life so long as diversity in culture and ways of being remain a fact of social life. Therefore, it is only when one is powerless to respond to acts of assimilation that we can conceive of them as inconsistent with what is right.

The most crude and oppressive form of assimilative domination involves the intervention of one actor to eliminate the identity of another. Assimilation of this kind is intimately bound up with the deployment of state violence. Through its special relation to a state, a dominant group uses state organs of coercion to force members of other groups into renouncing their specificity and identifying entirely with its own identity. The measures typically introduced to achieve this can include: forced name changing; the outlawing of the group's language; the alteration of place names in an area historically inhabited by the group; the official denial of the existence of the group; the revision and fabrication of history; and the criminalisation of expressions of the group's identity. In a society of this kind, the dominated group will be rendered communicatively defunct, as they will be denied the opportunity to initiate public debate on matters relevant to the group. The group is *non sum*, at least according to official dictates, leaving any discussion on its concerns redundant, illegitimate and illegal.

There is no shortage of examples throughout history that can be drawn on to illustrate this totalising form of assimilation. Two recent cases that stand out are those involving Kurds in Turkey and Macedonians in Greece.

In Turkey, the deeply unitary state has, since the 1930s, subjected Kurds to a number of oppressive assimilatory measures, the aim of which has been to alter the ethnic composition of Kurds such that they no longer conceive of themselves as a distinct group. While laws on this matter have more recently been relaxed to bring Turkey in closer conformity with European Union (EU) accession criteria, Kurdish had long been a forbidden language in Turkey, outlawed not only within schools and the bureaucracy but also within the informal and private spheres of society. For example, until 1991 it was illegal to broadcast and publish in Kurdish, even to simply write and utter the word Kurd, with those choosing to go in defiance of this law facing imprisonment on the grounds of inciting separatism (Hassanpour 1992). The presence of these severe restrictions made it impossible for Kurdish perspectives to gain access to the public sphere, to say nothing of opportunities available to Kurds for direct input in policy making.

Similarly, ethnic Macedonians in Greece are placed under enormous pressure to deny their distinctive identity and assimilate into the ethnic Greek population. This occurs through a variety of oppressive state policies aimed at maintaining a society with an exclusively Hellenic character. Of these, the official denial of a Macedonian minority in the country features most prominently. In Greece, the state accounts for Macedonians as 'Slavophone Greeks' (Human Rights Watch 1994: 11), while anyone who publicly declares themselves as Macedonian or insists that a Macedonian minority exists faces the prospect of being blacklisted from employment in the public sector.[5] Under these strict conditions of censure, Macedonians have found it extremely difficult to extend the scope of public deliberations to include matters relevant to their identity, as doing so exposes them to any number of legal and social sanctions from an intolerant judicial system and deeply hostile Greek public (Human Rights Watch 1994). At the same time, the lack of a Macedonian presence in Greek public life because of this censure has been used by authorities in self-serving ways to demonstrate the absence of Macedonians in Greece and therefore to deny the need to debate minority rights for them (Balkan Insight 2008).

Yet assimilatory domination does not always manifest itself as a desire for complete cultural annihilation. Indeed, many governments do not flout the human rights of their citizens in the tyrannical ways documented above, but instead impose assimilatory pressures by more subtle and selective means. In such instances, groups are permitted to maintain aspects of their cultural practices and identities, but are pressured into viewing their life-chances as bound up with the participation in common educational, economic, political, and legal institutions, which operate exclusively in the language and in accordance with the culture of the dominant group (Kymlicka 2001: 51). This process is commonly distinguished as 'integration', and is presented in a normatively favourable light by civic nationalists, since, unlike wholesale attempts at assimilation, integration entails a measure of reciprocity. Under an integrationist understanding of citizenship, a minority culture is expected to acquire some of the characteristics and practices prescribed by the majority culture. At the same time, the majority does not promote a social space that is exclusively its own cultural domain, but remains tolerant of the presence and maintenance of the minority's identity, provided this occurs within the private spheres of society.

Nevertheless, even the process of integration, despite freeing itself of much of the oppressive baggage of cultural assimilation, can also serve as a potent mode of domination, as not all groups expected to integrate consent to the process or to the privatisation of identity it demands. Despite providing ample room for manoeuvre in the private sphere, integration can still appeal to the unity of a single homogenous public, whose norms and institutions almost always end up being biased towards the dominant and more numerous group (Kymlicka 2001: 24–5; Young 1990: 185–7). Some minorities, as we witnessed early in this chapter, are happy to go along with this, seeing it as consistent with the realisation of their life-plans. Other minorities, however, roundly object to integration, taking it to conflict with a deeply felt conviction to maintain their own fully constituted and publicly expressed wills. Their situation can be characterised as one of arbitrary coercion when the state takes active measures to repress the expression of their identity through appeals to a supposedly common or civic good, as in reality, such appeals will be reflective of a particularistic perspective with which the group does not identify. Once again, to stand any chance of having its opinions converted into policy outcomes, the group is forced to assume the integrator's partial assumptions and priorities, and to put a lid on its own, as this is what affords them the greatest legitimacy and chance of having their preferences taken up in the empowered deliberative spaces.

The Bulgarian majority, for example, relies on a strategy of this kind to keep Bulgaria's Turkish minority in a position of political subordination. Turks in present day Bulgaria are no longer subject to the draconian policies of cultural assimilation that once featured under communism, being permitted to maintain themselves as culturally distinct in the institutions of private life, while also receiving a level of assistance from the state to carry out Turkish-language instruction in primary and secondary schools. However, while permitting Turkish self-identification as a matter of private consumption, the Bulgarian government has been deeply hostile towards attempts to make public institutions reflective of the Turkish identity. Not only has it flatly rejected any notion of institutional recognition for Turks, it has restricted opportunities for political deliberation along Turkish lines through the introduction of a law that forbids ethnically based political parties. In practice, this law is only loosely enforced, with the Movement for Rights and Freedoms (DPS) party emerging as the *de facto* representative of Bulgaria's Turks. However, the presence of such a law serves as a constraint on Turks to freely and equally participate in both public and empowered deliberative spaces, as the toleration of the DPS party by the country's major parties is premised on a condition that it will exercise 'self-restraint with regard to radical ethnopolitical demands' (Brusis 2003: 7). Therefore, far from being free to speak in a way that attends to their constituencies' concerns, DPS representatives must constantly be wary of not coming across as too Turkish when they contest issues for fear of having their party shut down by the constitutional court.

Conclusion

In this chapter, I assessed the extent to which three prominent ideals of multicultural social and political organisation align with the requirements of solidarity. I argued the deliberative ideal's emphasis on public reason-giving and critical reflection in the pursuit of preferences embodies a notion of collective organisation that most faithfully reflects the spirit of mutual obligation inherent to solidarity. At the same time, I pointed to the ways in which such a procedural framework risks becoming a smokescreen for subjugation when inequality and antipathy define human relations. In the chapter that follows, I begin the task of analysing how to ground deliberation under the hostile empirical conditions identified so far.

Notes

1. At times, Kymlicka refers to immigrant groups as 'ethnic groups'. To avoid ambiguity, I will use only the former label in the context of the current discussion.
2. It should be noted that Kymlicka's use of the term 'societal culture' denotes a pluralist, and not monist, ideal of community. The term is making reference to a community forged around 'a common language and social institutions', such as schools, 'media, law, economy and government', and not to a more demanding form of collective identity based on adherence to common worldviews, ideologies, religious beliefs, norms, mores, family customs, personal lifestyles, and so on (Kymlicka 2001: 25, 55, 263, 311). Some might still deem Kymlicka's understanding of community monist, given its focus on linguistic commonality. However, it is important to distinguish language from other focal points of collective identity, as the presence of a common linguistic medium does not limit people's freedom to adhere to different ideologies, moralities, traditions, and so on. For more on this point, see Bauböck (2001: 4).
3. For a spirited critique of deliberative democracy from a realist angle, see Shapiro (1999). For other sceptical accounts of deliberative democracy along the same lines, see Bell (1999: 73); Przeworski (1998: 140–1, 145); Stokes (1998: 123–4).
4. For a thorough account of these practices, see Laden (2000: 131–85). See also Tully (2002: 221–5)
5. For example, an ethnic Greek senior political communications advisor for the left-leaning PASOK party was dismissed from its ranks in 2008 for publicly stating that a Macedonian minority existed in Greece and that the neighbouring Republic of Macedonia, which Greece refuses to recognise under its constitutional name, had a right to use the name Macedonia. See Michas (2008).

3   Group Entitlements and Deliberation

Having outlined the conditions under which solidarity is constrained, we are now ready to explore the conditions under which it is expanded. A task of this kind calls for two types of questions. The first is remedial. Here we want to establish what kinds of corrective measures ought to be advanced to enhance the ability of the disadvantaged to influence deliberative outcomes. This involves an investigation into the political institutional arrangements required to ameliorate the exclusionary and assimilatory practices outlined in Chapter 2. It also involves an inquiry into the ways such changes are likely to create tensions between the various goals of deliberation and how these tensions can be eased. The second question is operational. How can the measures put forward to counter practices of oppression be implemented, given that the more powerful groups are likely to resist such changes?

In this chapter, I shall explore the remedial measures. In the chapter thereafter, I will turn specifically to questions of implementation, considering some of the obstacles parity-enhancing reforms encounter when attempts are made to institutionalise them, along with possible strategies that might be drawn on to overcome these obstacles.

There is general agreement among deliberative democrats that free and equal participation is best achieved through the elimination of structural inequalities that feed asymmetries in power. Yet, despite being united on this more general aspect of institutional reform, deliberative democrats diverge significantly on how it ought to be achieved. The main dividing line between them is drawn over the issue of whether taking explicit measures to include marginalised groups in the institutions of the state is the most appropriate way to rectify deliberative inequalities. On the one hand, those deliberative democrats who argue against group oriented measures, or at least advocate only a nominal role for them, take the view that such a remedy – while certainly empowering recipient groups to further their own ends next to the majority – can be self-defeating insofar as it does not lead to full participation and, over all, works to inhibit rather than enhance deliberative principles (Bohman 1996: 122; Benhabib 2002: 149; James 2004: 49). In view of this, they contend that groups should seek to influence political decisions from within the public sphere. The key to effective participation, they argue, rests not on the presence of group-specific institutional arrangements, but on the reform of democratic institutions and the public sphere itself, such that groups find it easier to initiate public deliberation about their concerns and needs, and their reasons become a tangible part of decisions.

On the other hand, those deliberative democrats who argue in favour of group remedies point out that such measures form an indispensable component of any polity seeking the achievement of political inclusion. They note that members of less privileged groups are currently underrepresented in most contemporary democracies, and as a result, do not have their interests and perspectives properly taken into account next to the better represented, and, as it turns out, more powerful groups (Phillips 1995; Young 2000; Laden 2000). If such exclusion is to be avoided and the distribution of power is to be made more symmetrical across groups, they argue that the introduction of measures designed to specifically increase the political presence of dominated groups is the only way we can hope to level the playing field during political deliberations.

In this chapter, I will present a set of remedies consistent with the latter perspective. While not wishing to present group entitlements as a solution for every instance of oppression, I will nevertheless argue that they remain the only plausible countermeasure in the bulk of instances of oppression. They do so, I will argue, by empowering weaker groups to make others acknowledge and respond to their core concerns in the decision-making process where they would otherwise be ignored.

I recognise, however, that a number of issues stand in the path of group entitlements fulfilling their task as a countermeasure against oppression. These relate to the concern that group specific measures will come at a cost to open deliberative communication; that they will not do justice to the level of diversity present within a plural context; and that they will, in the long run, work to freeze, even harden, social cleavages. In the course of the chapter, I will provide responses to each of these issues, pointing to the ways group specific measures can be brought in accord with the goals of ideal deliberation and pluralism, despite, at times, standing in tension with them.

Non-group approaches to deliberative inclusion

We can begin by turning briefly to some prominent deliberative designs that favour contestation in the spheres of civil society over group-based inclusion in the state. Exemplary here are the deliberative designs of James Bohman (1996) and Seyla Benhabib (2002). Each of these theorists presents their own unique set of prescriptions – developed in opposition to group specific prescriptions – for promoting deliberation where power disparities and hostility define ethnic relations. I will suggest that each fails in the task of offering a credible proposal for bringing practice into closer conformity with deliberative principles, as the non-group specific prescriptions they emphasise do not sufficiently guard vulnerable groups against the targeted modes of oppression outlined in the previous chapter.

James Bohman offers a set of deliberative designs that are particularly unwelcoming of group-based remedies, eschewing not merely the more sedentary forms of representation that ensure a permanent place for groups within the state (for example, reserved seats and veto powers), but more sweepingly, the relatively transitory and fluid ones in which groups gain representation on the basis of elected political parties under systems of proportional representation. Bohman's categorical rejection of group representation is premised on the assumption that represented groups are not motivated to deliberate with the rest of society, because in the possession of special representational rights their 'public reasons do not have to be generally convincing, nor do they have to be addressed to the public at large' (1996: 122). Effective participation by minorities can occur without recourse to group representation, argues Bohman, but it requires institutional reforms that encourage minorities to forge cross-cutting associations with one another and nurture 'a vibrant public sphere capable of correcting its own inadequacies' (1996: 138). On his account, this entails mobilising 'already existing informal networks among groups to create social movements' (1996: 133). It also requires more direct institutional changes designed to benefit those most disadvantaged in deliberation, involving such measures as campaign finance reform, changes in voting procedures and government regulation of market-oriented media (1996: 138–9).

Bohman's response, then, is to emphasise the valuable role voluntary associations can play in channelling the demands of ethnic groups. The underlying assumption in this approach is that whenever the demands of ethnic groups are not being acted on by the state, it is because the groups lack the resources necessary to articulate their interests forcefully enough to influence legislation and public policy. Once the economic inequalities that cause this are ameliorated, groups will supposedly be well placed to cogently articulate their interests, taking advantage of their capacity for more effective associational activity within civil society. This, consequently, is supposed to enable them to favourably change the political agenda without the need to be represented in decision-making bodies.

However, it is difficult to see how Bohman's focus on interest articulation through associational activity stands to be of much benefit to ethnic groups that are persistently ignored by an unreceptive state or are met with hostility whenever they attempt to mobilise on an issue which does not sit well with the powers that be. While he believes the formation of robust associational bonds among minorities and collective action in a reformed public sphere will make it difficult for the majority to act without taking the interests of democratically engaged minorities into consideration, the empirical account of interethnic politics presented so far tells a very different story (Chapter 2). It shows that majorities can, and often do, ignore minority concerns in the generation of policy when groups are insufficiently represented. This, we noted, was true even in instances where minorities had the resources to exercise robust agency in civil society and were successful at giving powerful public expression to issues concerning their community. Campaign finance reform, changes in voting procedures and government regulation of market oriented media, while desirable, do not, on their own, result in the thorough-going redistribution of decision-making power required to force the majority to act in a manner accountable to all.

Seyla Benhabib echoes Bohman's calls for a civil society approach to deliberative contestation without group specific institutional measures. But in contrast to Bohman, she focuses less on interest articulation to shape the political agenda and more on the ways oppressed groups can harness discursive powers to redefine and renegotiate their perceptions of one another. Her key to fostering greater inclusion and empowerment lies in 'having more faith in the capacity of ordinary political actors to renegotiate their own narratives of identity and difference through multicultural encounters in a democratic civil society' (2002: 104). This is deemed preferable to group representation, because, on her account, group representation embodies a form of 'cultural holism' and denies the ability of individuals within the group to exercise autonomy. Benhabib's deliberative encounters involve bringing the worldviews of distinct communities into contact with one another with the purpose of encouraging moral and political learning, and spurring on a process of resignification and renarration of cultural evaluations. Aside from creating greater inclusion and empowerment, it is hoped this will ward off the threat of destructive ethnic conflict, because it provides the means though which diverse people can 'learn to live with the otherness of others whose ways of being may be deeply threatening to our own' (2002: 130).

However, Benhabib's response seems to underestimate the difficulty of establishing understanding and cooperation from a starting point of conflict and intolerance. The problem is that she falls into the trap common within deliberative circles of assuming participants have prior commitments to reasonableness and respect for their opponents (Warren 2002: 182). Yet as already noted in the previous chapter, it is precisely the absence of such shared commitments that define many interethnic relations, and leave them prone to destructive, rather than restorative, transformations under processes of public deliberation. An awareness of this would lead one to question why further hostility, rather than mutual understanding, would not follow in a society that, in Benhabib's words, releases 'its conflictual and explosive potential in the public civil sphere through the dialogue, confrontation, and give-and-take of ordinary citizens' (2002: 129). As with Bohman's public sphere oriented reforms, Benhabib's leave too much to chance: there is simply nothing in it for historical oppressors to cease lording over the vulnerable, given that their position of structural advantage within the state is left intact, rather than dismantled.

Power-dividing

One way of confronting such structures of disadvantage without recourse to group specific measures could be to reconstruct institutions of government such that the power of the privileged within them is undercut. By diminishing concentrations of sovereign power in this way, the need for group rights and protections is made redundant, as the privileged lose the capacity to arbitrarily impose compulsory force over others via its control of the state's institutions of coercion and law making.

Philip Roeder (2005) advances such a strategy through the notion of 'power-dividing'. This model of ethnic accommodation gains its inspiration from the Madisonian idea of limited government and entails the allocation of 'governmental powers among separate, independent [state] organs constituted on the bases of multiple, cross-cutting majorities' (Rothchild and Roeder 2005a: 18). The idea is that members of the majority ethnicity will be incapable of forming a consensus among themselves to encroach on the rights of minorities, as majority members will be institutionally pitted against one another through their participation in organs of the state that are in mutual competition. Thus, if one of these organs were to make a move to expand its powers relative to an ethnic minority, the other competing organs would presumably come to the rescue of that minority, as it is in their interests that this competitor organ is blocked from usurping further power, regardless of the fact that it is composed of individuals of the same ethnicity. The concrete measures Roeder considers integral to a 'power-dividing' regime and the appearance of these competitively aligned 'alternative majorities' include: 'presidentialism with a real balance of powers between executive and legislature' in contrast to 'parliamentarianism in protecting democracy and human rights'; 'bicameral legislatures with competing based on representation' in contrast to 'unicameral bodies'; and 'independent judiciaries empowered with judicial review over the acts of legislatures and executives' in contrast to 'weak judiciaries' (Rothchild and Roeder 2005a: 17).

Relative to the naivety of proposals focused simply on reconstructing the public sphere, power-dividing provides a more credible response to how minorities might be protected without recourse to group-based measures. By making distributions of sovereign power its focal point, power-dividing responds to the injustices that frequently fuel ethnic conflict, namely, one group's control of the state to advance its own fortunes at the expense of another (Horowitz 1985: 194; Dryzek 2005: 226).

Nevertheless, there is much to doubt about the promise of such an arrangement to offer genuine protection to the most vulnerable in a context of intense rivalry and historical oppression. The success of power-dividing hinges on a hopeful assumption that intra-majority rivalries will reliably motivate just behaviour towards marginalised and despised minorities. Roeder draws on several case studies in support of this thesis, contending that power-dividing 'has been more successful than power sharing at preserving the rights of minorities' (2005: 52). However, his case-study analysis does not convincingly show this, as the societies he singles out as benefiting from power-dividing – Switzerland, Belgium and India – also embody the group specificity of power-sharing he eschews. There is, in other words, no clean separation between a power-sharing and power-dividing causal story in his analysis to make a definitive case for the latter over the former.

The problem with power-dividing is that it leaves minorities beholden to the goodwill of majorities, who will only come to the rescue of an oppressed minority if it is in their political interests to do so. This leaves too much to chance, as majority members can remain bitterly divided but continue oppressing minorities for whom they may have little regard or simply lack a perceived interest in siding with. The United States is a case in point. Roeder identifies it as an archetypal power-dividing system and claims the dynamics of competitiveness within the ethnic majority have functioned to protect the rights of ethnic minorities. As he asserts:

> in the United States when some members of the ethnic majority have attacked the religious rights of ethnic minorities, such as the right of Native Americans to use peyote in religious rituals, other members of the ethnic majority, such as members of mainstream Protestant denominations that share civil liberties with the ethnic majority have been the minority's strongest allies. (2005: 64)

Beyond this offhand statement, Roeder offers no systematic historical analysis of ethnic relations in the United States to marshal his views around power-dividing's justice-promoting superiority. This is surprising, given the country's exemplification of power-dividing and, unlike his other cases, the country's disentanglement from power-sharing. However, scholars who have examined ethnic relations in the United States, and have done so through a more careful consideration of historical details, reveal not only that Native Americans, and other ethnic minorities, have suffered immensely at the hands of the majority, but that the country's system of government was the very instrument of this suffering. As Will Kymlicka points out, the United States has a long history of coercive assimilation of Native American tribes, native Hawaiians and Puerto Ricans into the common American culture, carried out with the aim of eliminating the extent to which such groups see themselves as separate self-governing nations (2001: 98–101, 247). What is more, far from functioning as a balance and check on the government, as envisaged in a power-dividing world, the Supreme Court served as the 'court of the conquerors'. It legitimised the acts of colonisation and conquest that dispossessed these minorities of their property and political power, and it denied them individual and treaty rights on the basis of racist and ethnocentric assumptions (2001: 85).

In sum, power-dividing can provide a suitable accompaniment to a system of group rights, but cannot on its own serve as a basis for just interethnic relations. A conscious strategy of empowerment of the vulnerable, rather than division among the privileged, will better ensure freedom and guard against domination, as the former gain the ability to keep the latter accountable to their needs and concerns. Without increased access to state institutions, groups which are democratically inconsequential will remain at the mercy of the good graces of their more powerful rivals. This is a flimsy foundation for justice, as the powerful will continue to remain the primary gatekeepers of the policy-making process, retaining the capacity to decide, without the fear of sanction, which viewpoints can and cannot count in democratic decisions.

Group entitlements and political consequentiality

Non-differentiated systems of the kind discussed so far would not be such a problem if we could trust that citizens entered democratic encounters with a readiness to be swayed by each other's reasons in the pursuit of their goals. But such moments of genuine open-mindedness are in depressingly short supply in contexts of political conflict, and therefore cannot on their own be relied on to come to the rescue of vulnerable or oppressed groups. Once we acknowledge deliberation can never be achieved in its perfect form but is only ever approximated, we begin to appreciate why explicit measures that ensure a meaningful political presence become necessary. Group-based remedies providing guarantees of inclusion in the organs of the state compensate for the lack of high-quality deliberations occurring among partisans operating in high-stakes political environments.[1] On the one hand, such remedies protect the vulnerable, given that political outcomes are so often determined by one's ability to bribe and blackmail effectively. On the other hand, they serve to encourage the very reflectiveness towards the other that is constitutive of deliberation when a prior commitment to reasonableness and mutual respect is absent. There are several reasons for this, all of which point to gains in democratic consequentiality that group-based measures can generate for the democratically marginalised.

First, measures that ensure presence in decision-making bodies make it more difficult for the powerful to pursue their interests without reflecting on the interests of others. Group presence helps solve what Roberto Gargarella describes as 'the motivational problem': that is, 'even if we knew perfectly well the preferences of others, we might have no motivation to take these preferences into account' (1998: 262). The motivational problem, as we saw in the previous chapter, is a major impediment to the ability of disadvantaged groups to be effective deliberators, as those in power had no incentive to take them seriously, and could instead ignore their viewpoints without the threat of any repercussions. Group representation reduces the prospects for such non-accountability because it forces participants to respect, or at least acknowledge, others' claims. For a proposal to be persuasive and accepted by others, participants in political debate must transform their claims from mere expressions of self-regarding interest to ones that frame proposals in a manner that is sensitive to the interests and concerns of all those present (Young 2000: 115).

Second, group presence allows the diverse needs and interests expressed in public deliberations to be more accurately expressed in political decisions. There are at least two ways this applies. In the first, more structural sense, the inclusion of groups in legislatures provides an important conduit for reasons voiced in the public sphere to carry across to decision-making arenas, and therefore, to have a more direct bearing on policy outcomes. One commonly voiced criticism against a Habermasian conception of the public sphere is that it is too weak to influence public policy directly because the structural juncture separating the public sphere from the state is too wide to allow for the direct interflow of communication (Fraser 1997b: 134–6). Group representation provides an important linkage to bridge this gap, as we can expect representatives to be more receptive and accountable to the particular concerns voiced by the group constituency they are there to represent.

In the second sense, the benefits of group inclusion flow from the closer alignment it can achieve between the perspectives voiced by the representative and the represented. Even when members of a powerful and privileged group do not act with dubious intent, they cannot be trusted to represent the marginalised reliably because their social position may not allow them to do this properly, or simply because their position of privilege depends to some degree on maintaining the status quo. As Phillips notes,

> [w]ith the best will in the world (and all too often we cannot rely on this), people are not good at imagining themselves in somebody else's shoes. We may get better at such acts of imaginative transcendence when our prejudices have been more forcefully exposed, but this only happens when the 'other' has been well represented. (1995: 53)

The inclusion of groups in the empowered institutional spaces of a state, as such, can protect them from having their demands misconstrued, or overlooked entirely, in political decisions that are influenced by public deliberations.

Finally, group presence allows sovereign power to be shared, rather than remain concentrated in the hands of the few. This significantly undermines the ability of an actor to single out an opponent and to use the organs of the state to marginalise and control this opponent. Such measures as veto rights, proportional representation in legislatures and affirmative action in a country's security forces all redress the asymmetrical distribution of political power that feeds exclusions and assimilations. A majority will be much more constrained in its ability to pass legislation or policies that encroach on minority interests when the minority is present in the legislature in sufficient numbers and can block political decisions that potentially harm it. When ongoing asymmetries in power are narrowed in this way, minorities gain the teeth required to make the majority accountable to them, while the majority, for its part, will not be entirely free to determine the conditions of its own actions without reciprocation.

Group representation and deliberative reflection

The arguments raised so far make a principled case for the inclusion of marginalised groups in the state. But there are a number of practical and conceptual challenges that group-based measures encounter, and these will require greater exploration. This will be the task of the remainder of the chapter. The concerns I wish to take up will focus on: the threat group representation poses to deliberative communication; the view that group representation does not do justice to the radical plurality of societies; and the view that group representation leads to social fragmentation, rather than unity. All these concerns suggest that group-based measures can actually contribute to, rather than alleviate, the conditions of oppression and fragmentation. I will be responding to each of them in turn, offering ways around some of the dilemmas they raise.

While most deliberative democrats agree that group representation fosters inclusion, there are some who have nevertheless shied away from endorsing it on the grounds that it stands to create more problems than any worthwhile gains. The main objection lies, as noted earlier, with the potential of group representation to discourage deliberative reflection and openness between groups. If valid, this objection carries considerable weight because open and unconstrained dialogue is a cornerstone of deliberative democracy. It is, after all, what distinguishes deliberative democracy from other bargaining-based democracies in which participants engage with one another through strategic interactions. If it is simply this latter form of politics that is fostered by arrangements of group representation, then there is an issue of coherency in advocating both deliberation and group representation at the same time. There are two aspects to the assertion that group representation encourages bargaining over deliberative practices: the first relates to the incentive structures group representation nurtures, the second to the normative obligations it imposes.

Incentive structures

Group representation is sometimes criticised for fostering a mindset that discourages deliberative openness. It is held that once groups are formally included in the spheres of decision making, they will be less inclined to deliberate with others, as formal inclusion already ensures favourable democratic outcomes when previously this had to be achieved through persuasion in dialogue with others. That is, if a level of political efficacy is already assured, then there is no need for a group to persuade a wider public of the validity of its intentions. Their realisation is, after all, already guaranteed in advance.[2]

This criticism overstates the latitude groups have to ignore the concerns of others in the democratic process, even when they enjoy robust mechanisms of representation such as veto powers. While group representation involves group empowerment, it does not equate with group omnipotence. It is, rather, a strategy for generating parity of power for groups whose opportunities are lacking relative to others. Parity of power, however, does not raise the authority of a group to a level permitting it to ignore others or to always have its own way. A represented group will still need to be responsive to the concerns and interests of others and present reasons society at large is likely to find convincing, for failing this, they face retaliation from their democratic competitors. After all, minority proposals can still be opposed and ultimately rejected in a system of group representation. As a result of knowing this in advance, minorities will be constrained to act in ways that merely further their own interests and will still feel accountable to a broader section of society, if only for politically instrumental reasons. In this regard, group representation does not give minorities *carte blanche* to make decisions at will, but merely allows them to be taken more seriously in a majoritarian system where their reasons are all too easily ignored by the numerically dominant.

It could, nevertheless, be pointed out that even if represented groups must still democratically engage with others to influence political decisions in a differentiated polity, the democratic engagement fostered under such a system is likely to be strategic, rather than communicative, because participants are, as David Miller has charged, encouraged to focus on their own sectional interests as opposed to the common good (2000: 78). The contention here, as we noted in Chapter 1, is that good deliberation is more likely in a community whose members share a common identity that transcends their group identities, as this is when they are likely to be committed to a common good and seek to achieve consensus. As a result, we should aim to establish institutional arrangements that foster public homogeneity, and avoid ones that draw attention to difference, which apparently sow the seeds of disagreement and sectarianism (2000: 158).

Discouraging participants from airing their differences may create conditions conducive to consensus. But this risks introducing a form of politics so sanitised of conflict and disagreement that actors find it difficult to raise concerns relating to their own particularistic experiences of injustice (Mouffe 2000). In such cases, any consensus that arises is likely to be a product of exclusion, falling well short of satisfying deliberative demands of free and equal participation in dialogue. Indeed, there are often good reasons for groups to withdraw from consensually driven deliberations, or to articulate a viewpoint that deviates from the common good. A group may, after all, have an interest or value that is incompatible with the common good or is negated in the search for an all-encompassing accord. Contra to those democrats who place a high premium on consensus, it may not be possible to achieve an outcome that is to everyone's benefit on certain issues. Competing interests and the presence of value pluralism may simply not allow it (Chapter 6). Moreover, what is taken to be the common good may, in certain situations, have been constructed through historical exclusion and oppression. Under such circumstances, the process of introducing a partial perspective into a public discussion is what allows an entrenched conception of the good to be revised so that is more inclusive of wider concerns. These are all communicatively consistent outcomes that a group-differentiated polity fosters.

Normative constraints

Alongside the incentive structures encouraged, the other way group measures stand in tension with deliberation is normative in nature and relates specifically to the commitments that come with representation. If the normative force of group representation derives from its promise to democratically incorporate historically marginalised identities, then, it would seem representatives are not at liberty to behave in the open-minded manner desired by deliberative theory because, in doing so, they would be straying from their original purpose of acting for the group. Deliberation requires representatives surrender their preferences to the force of the better argument. But when a representative gives oneself over to such a calculus, the group specificity of their advocacy disappears, and with it, the promise to provide a tangible presence in legislatures for interests unique to the group.

The upshot is that in order to maintain a link with their constituencies, group representatives are compelled to enter democratic forums with the mindset of partisans, not as self-reflexive actors. They have committed agendas handed to them from groups, and therefore, to remain faithful to such agendas, they must be wedded to particular outcomes and enter 'the forum to convince, not to be convinced' (Hendriks et al. 2007: 369). Such obstinacy sits uncomfortably with the deliberative requirement that political judgement should be a matter of public reasoning and open to potential transformation (Hendriks et al. 2007: 362).

The tension between deliberation and group representation leaves us with two equally unattractive options. On the one hand, we could restrict the extent to which representatives can reflect on and revise group preferences in the course of legislative debate in order to raise accountability towards the group. Representatives would be permitted to make only minor alterations to their position in the course of discussions. Anything more would have to be referred back to the groups for approval. This would have the intended result of leaving representatives acting in a manner that is faithful to their initial mandates. However, the tight link between representatives and groups sought under such a proposal remains hopelessly implausible. Representatives would have to break off discussion in order to consult with their members on every decision. This remains an unrealistic expectation when one considers the sheer size of groups and the level of diversity within them, along with the vast number of decisions made by legislatures.

On the other hand, we could take from this the view that representatives must be given ample room to deliberate on their own terms in order to perform their ascribed functions. Such autonomy is, after all, a very condition of representation, for it frees representatives to engage in discussion, and crucially, to embrace the power of subsequent discussion (Phillips 1995: 155–6). However, in following this course, we have arrived at a conclusion that is potentially at odds with the purpose of group representation in the first place. Given enough free rein, there would be nothing stopping the autonomous representative from expressing a position that ignores, even goes against, the needs, preferences, interests and perspectives of the group. A level of accountability still remains important because, as Phillips has put it, 'representatives who are in no way accountable are not representative at all' (1995: 156).

How, then, can we coherently advance a notion of group representation that stresses flexibility and reflection on preferences pursued while simultaneously upholding a condition of accountability requiring participants to stay true to whom they are there to represent? Each ideal seems to pull in opposite and irreconcilable directions.

An appropriate starting point for answering this question is to consider representation broadly defined. After all, deliberation sits in tension with all forms of elected representation, not merely group forms, as it is only in a direct democracy that participants are ever free from any obligations to a constituency. As Hanna Pitkin explains, representation involves the paradoxical situation of 'being made present in some sense, while not being present literally or fully in fact' (1972: 153). If we take this to be true, any system of political representation is confronted with the dilemma of whether the representative ought to do what 'his constituents want, and be bound by mandates and instructions from them' – that is, to act as a *delegate* – or whether he should be 'free to act as seems best to him in pursuit of their welfare' – in other words, to act as a *trustee* (1972: 144, 145).

Herein, then, lies an important clue on how to circumvent the conceptual stalemate appearing to dog group representation. Representation is accurately conceived as a practice involving elements of *both* delegation and trusteeship, rather than being a matter of deciding between one or the other, as it makes no sense to talk of the practice without assuming it entails some level of autonomy over what one advocates, but also answerability for what one has advocated (Young 2000: 128–33). Formulating the conceptual dispute as a mutually exclusive choice between trusteeship on the one hand and delegation on the other makes a consistent answer to the dilemma impossible. As Pitkin noted, both practices are constitutive. In her words:

> The representative must have some freedom, some discretion to act, or it is difficult to imagine his constituency wholly present in him. If he is totally bound and instructed, we tend to think of him more as a tool or limb or puppet whose motivating or deciding power is elsewhere. (Pitkin 1972: 153)

But at the same time:

> The representative cannot be persistently at odds with the desires of his constituency, or else it is again too difficult to conceive the constituency as present in him. When they are at odds, we tend to think of him as a separate being acting on his own to pursue his own goals. (Pitkin 1972: 153)

Applying Pitkin's insights specifically to the representation of groups, we can say that representative practice should not be conceived in narrow terms as a delegate type role under which the representative is confined to relaying a specific group mandate. Rather, the act of representing is to be looked at more loosely as involving both group delegate and trustee roles. Conceived in this way, the group representative's role is not restricted to simply passing on pre-agreed programmes and ideas, as, for example, does a messenger, but rather, involves independent action and judgement to secure the best possible outcome in the course of politics. This brings the concept of group representation more in line with the requirements of deliberative democracy, as the group representative is now open to the possibility of developing, refining and changing his/her position during participation in discussions and debates with other representatives (Young 2000: 131; Phillips 1995: 159).

In more concrete terms, a deliberatively consistent conception of group representation would encompass, as Young has pointed out, a deferring relationship between the representative and the group constituency the representative is standing for (2000: 131–2). While the representative acts on her own when she speaks for the group, she is at the same time both *anticipating* a subsequent moment of being held accountable to the group and *recollecting* the prior moment she was authorised to act on behalf of the group. By recollecting the moment of authorisation, the representative is recalling the transaction that took place at the outset between her and the group, before the representing began, at which time she acquired the right to act and the knowledge of the limits and restraints of her acts. By anticipating the moment of accountability, the representative is apprehending the subsequent moment when she must answer to her group for what she has done (Pitkin 1972: 39, 55). This cycle of anticipation and recollection is what keeps the representative and group bound together and functions to restrain the conduct of the representative such that the autonomy she gains will not result in total independence. The representative is, like a trustee, acting for the benefit of those she represents. But unlike a trustee, this will require consultation and responsiveness to their wishes.

In practice, these desirable features of representation rarely attain in any notable degree, as mass societies are characterised by communicative, demographic and spatial complexities that impede the development of tight links between representatives and their groups. Politicians like to showcase their reach into constituencies by chatting with punters on a high road or rolling up their sleeves to visit workers on the factory floor, frequently with the media in full tow. However, the reality is that the majority of people they represent will be too numerous, too far removed in their daily lives, and spatially too scattered for the realisation of the wholesome representative reach such politicians wish to portray. As matters stand, elections are the sole substantive basis for linking political representatives with their groups. These occur every few years and are therefore an inadequate means through which the actions of representatives can be made to bear strong traces of prior authorisation and subsequent accountability (Young 2000: 132). Given the scant opportunities for authorisation and accountability in existing democracies, it is of little surprise that representatives sometimes end up behaving as elite rulers, rather than leaders who take an interest in the perspectives of their constituents. They simply lack the institutional channels to give due consideration to the full scope of concerns raised within the group, leaving them prone to stray from their ascribed role of formulating policy with the desires of their constituencies in mind.

There are, nevertheless, actions that can be taken outside elections to foster stronger ties between representatives and groups, and therefore to enhance distinct moments of authorisation and accountability. Where group representation is a salient feature of a democracy, publicity should be nurtured as a guiding principle in decision making, as this militates against the normalisation of elite politics (O'Flynn 2009). A societal expectation that representatives justify their actions to a broader public plays an important self-disciplinary function. It motivates representatives to think and act inside the boundaries of what they anticipate they will be held accountable for, and by extension, what they recollect they were authorised to do, as this is the very essence of political justification. Where publicity becomes a patterned mode of political behaviour, it supplies the moments of authorisation and authenticity lacking between elections, given that the terms of a representative's legitimacy are strengthened around these practices. His/her authority to act and speak for the group comes to be premised on their communicative responsiveness towards the range of voices and perspectives within it, along with the popular evaluations of the justifications that are passed.

There are, in addition, more formal institutional channels through which representational accountability and authorisation can be proliferated and strengthened. Some suggested by Young include civic review boards, implementation studies and periodic official participatory hearings following the policy-making process (2000: 132).

In sum, we can say that while group representation stands in an uneasy relationship with deliberative democracy, it is not necessarily a mutually negating one. The success of group representation in stimulating communicative dialogue depends on finding the right institutional mix suitable to a specific context, a point to which I shall return later.

Group representation and diversity

Even if we accept that group entitlements stand to increase the political efficacy of the numerically inferior next to the superior, it is still unclear who is to be prioritised for them in practice. Prioritisation becomes an important issue when one considers the myriad of groups and subgroups eligible for representation on the basis of being encumbered by a majoritarian system of rule. It will be practically untenable to include all groups institutionally in a highly diverse society. But a failure to do so leaves a theory of representation open to the charge of offering justice to some but not others. There needs to be, then, greater clarity on the precise nature of how group entitlements ought to be allocated if they are to be a mechanism for an expansion of political voice and not its confinement to the privileged few.

There are two main aspects to the above concern I now wish to address. The first relates to the practical difficulties involved in finding a system of group entitlements that can account for all groups present in a diverse society. The second relates to the issues around having a single representative or set of representatives acting for the diversity of standpoints present within a group.

Diversity across groups

There is a real problem in asserting that we should assign group entitlements to all collective actors sitting in an unequal relation next to others. Insisting on group-based measures solely on the basis of such a criterion is likely to lead to what Leslie Green has dubbed 'rights inflation'; that is, an uncompromising position in which we are forced to endorse endless rights entitlements for countless groups (1995: 261). Needless to say, proceeding along these lines is untenable, if only because it imposes massive constraints on policy making. A legislature in which every single group were represented would be left in a state of paralysis, where even the most basic of tasks would fail to get done.

Yet though it is impossible to include all minorities, an ethic is still needed to guide the process of group entitlements, as, in its absence, the process risks becoming a form of power-politics, where only the more assertive and numerous gain assistance, while the weak and marginalised are ignored and continue to remain subject to oppression.

In Chapter 2, we considered the possibility of representation through a distributive ethic centred on the historical origins of a group. Under this ethic, groups that had territorial borders non-consensually drawn around them to make them minorities in their own land had a claim to representation and other measures geared to enhance their sovereignty relative to the majority. By contrast, groups that made the voluntary choice to arrive in a new society and submit to its governing institutions had a duty to integrate into them, rather than to seek special powers of self-government. A distributive principle of this nature narrows down the scope of who can and cannot seek group representation to homeland minorities. But even then, it represents only a nominal advance, as societies are typically constituted by a multitude of homeland minorities that would in principle all have a claim to legislative presence that cannot practically be met. What is more, while forced incorporation into a political community by conquest and colonisation is undeniably unjust, it seems problematic to reason that this alone should count as the ultimate court of appeal in determining the justness of group representation into the perpetual future. After all, the genesis of many states took place generations, sometimes centuries ago, telling us little, if anything, about group fortunes, wants and opportunities in the present.

Therefore, if a distributive logic for representation is to avoid becoming a blunt instrument, it will need to prioritise groups expressly on the basis of exposure to oppression and disadvantage.[3] Under this ethic, the case for dedicated forms of representation strengthens with a group's inability to influence the rules, proceedings and policies of an institution that has authority over it, but constrains the realisation of its core objectives in a significant and arbitrary way. What makes a constraint on group agency arbitrary, and therefore normatively unacceptable, is that those behind it persistently fail to account for the interests and concerns of the group bearing its consequences (Pettit 1997: 55, 56). The group is treated as an actor not worth listening to, and a voice that can be dismissed without independent reason in the formulation of policies that diminish its relative opportunities.

There are numerous advantages in prioritising representation according to a group's exposure to such coercion, all of which provide practical and normative gains over a criterion of representation premised on historical incorporation. First, it is more responsive to the concerns of justice. An evaluation of a rights claim is made with reference to the circumstances under which cohabitation occurs, attuned to the levels of systematically reproduced, but contextually variable, patterns of oppression that leave some better placed than others to have their interests met. This permits sensitivity to variability in circumstances between groups, and therefore creates a basis for representation to be prioritised to those who need it most. Groups are not prejudged as deserving of assistance in virtue of belonging to this or that historically determined category, which is morally irrelevant, but are targeted in light of the empirically variable circumstances contributing to their subjugation.

Second, and as a result of this, we gain the means to deduce a workable range of groups eligible for representation, but without losing sight of the moral purpose of having such groups represented in the first place. In a society comprising a plurality of homeland groups, a form of representational triage must be exercised, given that we can expect many of them to face certain barriers to participation next to a majority. A distributive criterion oriented towards group disadvantage offers the basis for such a programme of triage, as those most worthy of dedicated representation are ranked according to their subjection to what Petit calls 'mastery by others', that is, another's constraint on one's agency without justification or fear of penalty (1997: 22). Looked at this way, representation departs from the notion that legislatures must mirror society's composition of homeland minorities in order to be fair. Instead, fairness attains when legislatures encompass those groups which are most vulnerable to the excesses of others, and when they are encompassed in such a manner as to acquire the democratic power to make others answerable to them.

Finally, at the same time that a criterion premised on oppression narrows the quantitative scope of representation, it broadens it qualitatively. Once we recognise that powerlessness at the hands of another does not end at homeland groups, but extends beyond them, we are ready to consider a broader spectrum of identities as eligible for representation. This brings into the fold groups which do not owe their origins in a society to conquest by another, but which are nevertheless subject to another's active part in gaining control over them or worsening their life chances. Examples of such identities include the descendants of: immigrants who now resemble homeland minorities (Chinese in Southeast Asia, Germans and Greeks in Central Asia); colonisers (Turks in the Balkans, Russians in the Baltics); indentured workers (Indians in Fiji and the Caribbean); and slaves (Africans in the United States), among others. The representation of such groups would help accomplish the aim of equality, even though each has vastly different historical roots in a territory not reducible to the non-consensual act of territorial dispossession.

Diversity within groups

When representation is considered in relation to diversity existing *within* a group, two important concerns arise. The first is analogous to that raised in the above section: by committing ourselves to the idea that only those who share our experience can legitimately speak on behalf of us, we also necessarily accept that the representative will be unable to represent those experiences and identities he/she does not share within the group itself. That is, if members of the majority cannot speak for members of an ethnic minority, then neither can men of an ethnic minority speak on behalf of women in the group, nor can individuals of one religious persuasion in the ethnic group speak on behalf of individuals of another religious persuasion, or a member of the middle class on behalf of the working class, a member of the rural, peasant class on behalf of the urban class, and so on. Individuals present within each of these social cleavages share alternative experiences and perspectives that, it could be argued, only they can best represent. Needless to say, we are once again led down a slippery path of having to recognise all aspects of diversity one is likely to encounter within an ethnicity if we are to remain true to the goal of bringing about parity of participation for underrepresented groups. Given the considerable divisions and sub-groupings present within an ethnicity, this would entail political representation for endless lists of groups and interests, ranging from women and the disabled to 'pensioners, beekeepers, and people with blue eyes and red hair' (Phillips 1995: 46).

The response to this dilemma is the same as the response identified for representation in general: fair representation does not require mirroring every aspect of difference in society, and in this case, mirroring every aspect of difference within the group represented. We know already that representation does not have to be defined in terms of accurate resemblance, reflection or correspondence, but should occur with the intention of redressing historical exclusions and protecting vulnerable members from the harmful actions of others. This means that within an ethnic group, there will be certain sub-groups that are entitled to various forms of targeted assistance in virtue of being exposed to subordination at the hands of others (women are an obvious example here, religious minorities are another).

The second issue relates specifically to the concern of essentialism: if the person representing the group must in some strong sense share his/her constituency's identity or experiences, then surely this is an illusory aspiration, as in practice, each individual is distinguished by a multiplicity of cross-cutting, and at times contradictory, identities, interests and experiences. We are, in Kirstie McClure's words, 'complexly constituted not only through categories of gender, but of race and sexuality, ethnicity and class, and perhaps of religion and nationality as well'. In light of this, it is misleading to speak of ourselves as singular and unitary in composition. We are in fact 'socially located, temporally specific and potentially riven within a series of other relational differences' (1992: 122). Taking this into account, insisting that only those who share our own identity or experience can represent us reliably is at best misguided, and at worst simply another form of domination, since it puts forward a totalising and singular narrative of the subject that constrains one to act and self-define independently of what is laid down as institutionally relevant.[4]

The concern of essentialism frequently arises in discussions on group entitlements. But the causal relationship that informs this view is somewhat misleading. Empirical evidence suggests that factors outside group entitlements have an influence on hybridity, and that group entitlements can in fact heighten, rather than allay, the prevalence of hybridity. For example, drawing on the findings of an Anglo-Canadian study on the sociological effects of multicultural programmes, Tariq Modood highlights how South Asian adolescents in Vancouver felt much more hyphenated and mixed, and more readily identified with the values and lifestyles of their White peers than did South Asian adolescents in Birmingham, who tended to identify strongly with the norms and mores of their communities, despite the fact that there is much less official multiculturalism in Birmingham than there is in Vancouver (1998: 388). The key implication here is that much more than political recognition of difference and assimilationism influences hybridity. There are a number of socio-economic and cultural factors that shape the character of communities and the attitudes of their members, with Modood highlighting the important, if not primary, role played by familial and communal influences on such matters.[5] At the same time, when introduced properly, group entitlements can do more to facilitate hybridity than measures that force individuals to participate in society exclusively on the terms of the majority, because the logic of differentiated citizenship is much more consistent with the idea of mixed and hyphenated identities than a unitary notion of citizenship.

Types of group entitlements and their impact on deliberative reflection

The guidelines for group entitlements I have put forward so far may come across as somewhat non-committal, for beyond the need to tie them to exposure to disadvantage and oppression, I have offered very little on what kinds of measures ought to accompany them. Yet there are good reasons for choosing to approach group entitlements in this way. Determining the appropriateness of specific measures is best judged on a contextual basis, because the variation in local conditions makes recourse to any detailed universal principles problematic.

That said, while context will ultimately determine which arrangements are best suited to overcoming oppression, we can still make some general points on several prominent arrangements of group entitlements in anticipation of issues likely to arise in situations of inter-group disadvantage and hostility.

Flexible or dedicated group representation?

Some theorists have emphasised the desirability of modest guarantees of political presence over decisive ones, because this allows for greater fluidity in identification and makes representation more amenable to deliberative reflection. Phillips, for example, argues that the goals of group representation are best served when members of an excluded group can establish a political presence without strict notions of representation, as this frees them up from strict notions of accountability (1995: 155–6). Similarly, in her later work, Young retreated from the entrenched notions of group representation that she originally advocated – reserved seats in legislatures and veto powers – in favour of more ephemeral ones. Her main concern with the former measures was that they had the tendency to freeze group identity and make representatives less responsive to their own constituents (2000: 149).

However, modest forms of representation may not be possible in many settings, even though they are in principle more desirable. They may permit more fluid forms of representation, and therefore better appreciate the state of constant flux identities are in. But during severe cases of hostility and division, such as those encountered in post-conflict settings, more explicit guarantees of representation may be the only way to establish peaceful coexistence and foster a sense of attachment to the state by groups formerly oppressed and alienated by it. Under such circumstances, explicit action to establish equitable representation in the state bureaucracy, and quite importantly, in the police and security forces is often the only credible route to fostering acceptance of these institutions, and restricting the capacity of the majority to use them as objects of arbitrary coercion (Valadez 2001: 237).

In Northern Ireland, for instance, affirmative action programmes aimed at raising the proportion of Nationalist police officers has been crucial for fostering greater acceptance of the police force in the Nationalist community (Hays 2012). Once a much maligned tool of oppression for Unionists, the Northern Irish Police has acquired a greater level of legitimacy among Nationalist residents to enforce the law in neighbourhoods formerly exclusively controlled by IRA militia. The creation of multiethnic security forces through proportional group representation has been crucial in fostering acceptance of these forces by local communities in a number of other conflict-ridden countries, including Macedonia, Bosnia and Kosovo.

Moreover, far from simply being anti-deliberative, fixed representational measures can, under the right conditions, induce deliberative openness across group boundaries. In their empirical analysis of grand coalitions, Baechtiger et al. (2007: 84) observed that the appropriation of relatively secure positions of power in legislatures through fixed seats opened up an additional deliberative space for parties to democratically engage in a less partisan way. This was because electoral competition among the parties was reduced and parties were freed from stricter notions of accountability to their electorate. This, they noted, stood in contrast to more competitive systems, where the party in government no longer required the support of a broader coalition to introduce policies, and could therefore safely ignore the opposition, and where the opposition had to define itself against the party in government and not appear as overly cooperative in order to gain the support of voters.

By the same token, the prospective benefits brought about through such measures will have to be weighed against the potential problems they may pose down the track. In the presence of rigid representational measures which guarantee predetermined seats in governing bodies, any demographic shift leading to an increase in one ethnic group's population vis-à-vis another's can have a destabilising effect, in some cases, resulting in a renewal of conflict, as was illustrated in the case of Lebanon. When Lebanon's power-sharing arrangement was introduced in 1943, representational arrangements closely reflected the ethno-religious composition of society. However, as the Muslim share of the population increased, many Muslims saw the fixed Muslim–Christian ratio as unjust. The dissatisfaction this stirred among Muslims led to the collapse of power-sharing in 1975 and a civil war that lasted 15 years. To avoid such a scenario, rigid representational measures can be accompanied by provisions that allow for a planned transition towards more fluid forms of representation as the society progresses beyond post-conflict and divisive conditions. One good instance of this is offered by the cases of South Africa and Sierra Leone, which both had transitional forms of power-sharing that allowed for a reversion to more flexible distributions of sovereign power across belligerents once conditions better suited to it were established (Jarstad 2008b: 121–2).

Another downside with immutable representational measures is their propensity to encourage citizens to more strongly identify with group identities in order to make political or economic gains against each other. This kind of strategising becomes more likely leading up to and during the divvying up of seats and positions of authority among competing ethnic groups. Given such distributions occur relative to an identity's proportion of the population, groups are tempted to exaggerate their own presence as a way of capitalising on the share of guaranteed seats up for grabs and, therefore, overall influence in governing bodies and institutions. This kind of zero-sum behaviour can become entrenched even once ethnic ratios have been recorded and seats allotted, as groups will be mindful that these guarantees could be revised at a future point in time should demographic shifts occur.

Some flexible forms of institutional inclusion not carrying the baggage of this incentive structure are systems of proportional representation. Under a proportional system, ethnic presence in a legislature is not necessarily preassigned, but alters with the preferences of citizens at elections, as the number of seats ethnic parties acquire is proportionate to the votes cast for them. Thus, if citizens come to conceive of themselves in non-ethnic terms, this will be passed on at the ballot box, and subsequently reflected in legislatures through the seats won by parties championing interests other than those tied to ethnic identities. In this way, proportional representation does not come with the drawbacks of freeze-framing a specific pattern of group representation and assuming the interests of all ethnic co-members necessarily coincide. Rather, citizens determine for themselves whether or not to have a politician with a shared ethnicity standing for them, leaving the composition of legislatures responsive to the identity shifts taking place among the population. Some prominent examples of flexible proportional representation are electoral systems involving the party-list system, the single transferable vote (STV) system, and cumulative voting.[6]

Proportional representation gives citizens the opportunity to adopt a political orientation outside of an ethnically defined one. But whether or not they end up doing so in practice will still depend on the intensity of social cleavages present. Indeed, where they are deep and where individuals continue to interpret issues through the lens of ethnicity, we can still expect ethnically defined parties to prevail over ones that prioritise non-ethnic affiliations and interests. Under such circumstances, the outcomes of flexible systems of representation will merely emulate those of more rigid ones based on ethnic ratios.

Other more fluid measures that may be useful include those that focus on the redrawing of district boundaries so that oppressed groups either become the majority, or are present in numbers sufficient to allow them to project their perspectives into public debate where they would otherwise be absent (Young 2000: 151). This is more responsive to future demographic shifts, and so avoids the prospect of conflict when fixed ethnic ratios of representation must be altered in light of ethnic population shifts. Of course, districting, like territorial autonomy, presupposes that the group is spatially concentrated, and so it too has a limited application.

Veto rights

Group veto rights are another frequently encountered representational measure, particularly in the context of deeply divided societies. The possession of a right to veto provides a group with robust powers to protect its vital interests. Whenever these interests are at threat, the group can block a political decision on which it would otherwise be outvoted or overruled. Veto provisions are a 'safe' form of representation, and are therefore open to the types of criticism levelled at fixed representational measures. But like other fixed measures, they can also induce deliberatively consistent behaviour among representatives under the right conditions. In anticipation of a minority veto, the majority will be less inclined to unilaterally advance policies that adversely affect the veto-wielding minority, and more inclined to formulate policies in conjunction with the minority, anticipating it will stand a greater chance of getting them through the legislature if it behaves cooperatively.

Nevertheless, minority vetos have a potential for deadlocking political decisions, especially in contexts where a strong political ethos of restraint and compromise is absent. In such contexts, it may be wise to institutionalise a minority veto in a more restrictive sense; that is, to apply to policies that directly affect an ethnic group's vital interests, rather than in the more general sense to any governmental policy (Valadez 2001: 241).

A promising middle path between a fully-fledged veto right and no veto right at all is a double majority principle. For a decision to pass under this principle, two levels of majority support are required: a majority of all legislators present; and a majority of legislators declaring themselves to represent a minority community. In this sense, a double majority rule is an indirect veto mechanism. No minority wields individual veto power that it can put towards blockading decisions unilaterally. Instead, decisions are vetoed only when they fail to attract the support of the bulk of minority representatives. At the same time, minorities retain a presence in legislatures that is politically consequential. They have the ability to protect their interests under voting procedures, given that the passage of law is dependent on a quorum of approval emerging from their quarters. This procedural rule has proven to be an attractive innovation in Macedonia, where its introduction as a power-sharing measure is seen to strike an appropriate balance between the need for effective government on the one hand and the democratic empowerment of marginalised ethnic minorities on the other (Bieber 2008: 24–5).

Multination federalism

Multination federalism (which also comes under the banners of pluri-national and multiethnic federalism) is a group entitlement involving self-government defined on a territorial basis. It is suited to societies where ethnic groups are regionally concentrated, with self-government being promoted by the drawing of sub-unit boundaries such that ethnic groups form a democratic majority within these boundaries. Through their status as a majority within a sub-state jurisdiction, ethnic groups can make decisions in certain areas without being outvoted by the larger society, and consequently, can develop their identities alongside the broader identity cultivated by the central government and majority ethnicity (Kymlicka 2001: 94–5).

Multination federalism guarantees extensive powers of self-government, and owing to this, comes with a potential cost to across-group deliberation. This trade-off arises as a result of the institutional separation along ethnic lines inherent to a multination federation. Each sub-unit will be diffusing a territorially concentrated language and set of norms, based on the dominant ethnicity's identity, which is intended to guide interactions in schools, the media, law, the economy and the government (Kymlicka 2001: 25). This creates a discursive disjuncture with the broader federation, which will have its own corresponding public institutions and associated spheres of socialisation and public deliberation.

Moreover, the possession of self-government powers can nurture a sense of entitlement among ethnic groups at the expense of duty-boundedness to the rest of society, further compounding the conditions hostile to deliberation. In a self-reinforcing manner, participation in a multination federation tends to strengthen the perception among minorities that they have 'inherent rights of self-government' and that their 'participation in the larger country is conditional and revocable' (Kymlicka 2001: 115). This perception is inconsistent with the legal reality of federations: members of federal subunits are still bound to the broader polity and the central government still has authority to govern over all citizens wherever they may be in the federation, despite not having the authority to unilaterally revoke the powers of self-government delegated to the sub-units. Nevertheless, the ethnic groups in control of the subunits still commonly maintain a much looser interpretation of what their obligations are to the rest of society. They often perceive themselves as participating in a *de facto* confederation, rather than federation, and their own political community as primary, with the value and authority of the broader federation as derivative (Kymlicka 2001: 115). Under this frame of mind, the ethnic groups concerned feel absolved of much responsibility to justify themselves to the rest of the federation, considering it an act of generosity, rather than a legal or moral duty.

Some analysts have been at pains to point out that the independence of will that multination federations foster among ethnic minorities is to blame for secessionism and political violence observed in such systems. Roeder (2009: 208), for example, contends that multination federal arrangements 'shape the agenda of politics and distribute power in ways that create or keep alive conflicts among competing nation-state projects' because the significant freedoms of self-government that ethnic groups enjoy relative to the central authority allow them to constantly use the threat of secession as a bargaining chip. By contrast, in the absence of ethnically based federal sub-units, 'ethnic entrepreneurs are far less likely to have the support, resources and opportunities to press their claims successfully against a common-state government' (2009: 208–9). In defence of these assertions, Roeder provides a comprehensive catalogue of ethnic conflicts that have ensued on the territories of multination federations, painting a rather incriminating portrait of the system of government.

However, notwithstanding the tendency of multination federalism to keep alive perceptions of ethnic distinctness that can impede deeper unity across the state, it is an exaggeration to conclude that multination federalism is simply bound to cause conflict and disunity. The empirical evidence to make this claim is assembled through spurious case selections, as what are documented as federal failures are in fact sham or pseudo-federations, propped up by authoritarian systems that deny opportunities for self-rule and shared rule (McGarry and O'Leary 2009: 9). The various failed post-colonial and communist federations – which feature prominently in Roeder's analysis – are such examples. Mindful that these societies make for misleading comparisons, a restriction of the data set to democracies – that is, to societies permitting ethnic groups to compete actively and freely in the spheres of politics – would reveal that multination federations are in fact remarkably resilient: to date, no established democratic multination federation has fallen apart, despite the presence of active and popular secessionist movements within these territories (Kymlicka 2001: 116; McGarry and O'Leary 2009: 18).

The success or failure of multination federations must be judged relative to the plausible alternatives. If the alternative put forward is a unitary state or a single nation federation that denies ethnic groups the ability to self-govern – the institutional pathway favoured by Roeder – it is utterly implausible to claim that this will provide a credible basis for a stable and cohesive democracy. Unitary states and single nation federations are not an option in the resolution of ethnic conflicts: the choice is simply down to some form of self-government or the continuation conflict, as such conflicts originate due to the minority's rejection of assimilatory rule (for examples, see McGarry and O'Leary 2009: 10–12). Thus, an appreciation of the part played by unitary and single nation systems in fuelling interethnic antagonism would bring us to understand multination federalism as not merely a cause of conflict, but also its symptom and typically its solution. Ethnic minorities make claims for self-government as a means of protecting themselves from further subjection to the majoritarian policies of dominant groups. Multination federalism is one of few credible measures available to achieve such protection and to sublimate conflicts by channelling them into the democratic arenas of the state.

One response to the anxieties around multination federalism is to adopt John McGarry and Brendan O'Leary's (2009: 14–18) proposal of coupling multination federalism with consociationalism at the state centre. Under this proposal, a territorially compact minority would still maintain its status as a voting majority in a federal subunit, but would simultaneously exercise self-government by being incorporated into the broader governing institutions of the federation through a combination of the representational measures noted above. The advantage of combining multination federalism with consociationalism in this way is that answerability across ethnic lines is more firmly incentivised. To the extent that the minority will be a political player with the potential to thwart the majority in the central institutions, the majority will be motivated to seek its approval when advancing policies of common concern and will be deterred from passing such policies unilaterally. Similarly, to the extent that the minority will be included in the central governing institutions, it will have an increased stake in them, regarding them as a vehicle for the realisation of their own interests. However, as with the majority, the minority will have to pursue its interests through a process of justification to others potentially impacted by them if the realisation of these interests is to stand any chance of success.

One potential obstacle to the cohesion-generating potential of such a proposal is that it is still dependent on a minority's wishes to participate in the central institutions. Where the minority does not accept the authority of those institutions and has no desire to see them function effectively, the federation will continue to remain unstable and fractious. This course of events has characterised the Bosnian state since its inception at the conclusion of the Yugoslav wars. Ethnic Serb politicians have taken every opportunity to undermine the country's central institutions from functioning properly, despite enjoying generous representation within them through a shared multi-member presidency, allocated seats in the legislature and veto powers. The determination to discredit these institutions has stemmed from the Serb perception that they are a property of the Bosniak majority and therefore predatory towards Serb aspirations to remain autonomous inside their own federal subunit, Republika Srpska (Bieber 2006: 21; Vasilev 2011: 61–2, 66).

Nevertheless, while a consociational dimension to multination federations may not always be sufficient to generate constructive relationships, it is still preferable to having no consociationalism at all. The institutional presence of ethnic minorities lays down the incentive structures for cooperation at some future point by minimising the risk of severance between the centre and subunits, and by establishing discursive connections across ethnic lines that would otherwise be non-existent.

Conclusion

In this chapter I have argued that group-specific institutional arrangements are an indispensable ingredient of deliberation, even though they sometimes stand in tension with it. This is because they empower vulnerable groups to bring the privileged sections of society into a tracking relationship with them. With these concluding remarks, we are brought to the next task of the book, namely, how we are to implement the institutional arrangements defended so far in the face of resistance by those who stand to lose out from them.

Notes

1. For an insight into the negative relationship between partisanship and deliberation, see Williams (2000) and Hendriks et al. (2007).
2. Bohman uses the case of Israel in support of this view, arguing that proportional representation has allowed the religious right to remove, without adequate public justification, certain topics of discussion from the public agenda, such as who has the right of return (1996: 122).
3. The following analysis draws generously on the ideas of Young (1990: 184–8).
4. For further articulation of this perspective, see Benhabib's critique of Will Kymlicka and Charles Taylor in Benhabib (2002: Chapter 3).

5. In the above case, Modood observes that more of the Birmingham sample came from poor homes, were more residentially concentrated and were exposed to greater levels of parental/communal conservatism, all of which functioned to have a greater influence on adolescents than the official multiculturalism they were exposed to in schools (1998: 388).
6. For a detailed discussion of these 'flexible electoral systems', see Valadez (2001: 201–8).

4 Transnational Advocacy Networks and Conditionality

We have noted so far that politics guided by deliberative tenets represents the most faithful practical embodiment of solidarity, as preferences under this framework must be justified to a socially interconnected constituency in order to count as legitimate. We also noted that if deliberative behaviour is to stand any chance of becoming patterned under conditions of inequality and disrespect, democratic practice requires the incorporation of group entitlements, as the institutional presence they guarantee for the disadvantaged motivates others to take their claims seriously.

This, however, remains an incomplete picture as far as the institutionalisation of solidarity is concerned, as it still leaves untouched the issue of how such reforms can be promoted when those small in numbers and strength must mobilise from a starting point of democratic marginalisation. To turn to deliberative theory for answers is to risk descending into the circular logic outlined in Chapter 2, as deliberation under conditions of inequality and disrespect can replicate the status quo, rather than bring about the reforms necessary for an expansion of relations of mutual responsibility. Put differently, we may know what reforms are required to deepen democracy and cultivate mutual answerability. But the presence of injustices means we cannot rely on democratic channels to implement these reforms, as the powerful will be in a structural position to withstand political pressure for change that threatens their status of privilege.

This chapter explores how actors in positions of strength can be influenced to adopt proposals that move society in the direction of solidarity by actors in positions of weakness. It is argued that democratic channels can be plausible routes for the disruption of circuits of domination, but that they require a combination of external influence and strategic action in order to be effective.

Strategic action, in the context intended here, refers to behaviour guided by a cost-benefit calculation, which, ideally, brings those in power to perceive intransigence on demands for reform as costly and responsiveness as beneficial. External influence refers to the involvement of parties beyond the nation-state where the struggle for reform is ensuing, which, owing to their superior material and discursive capabilities, have the capacity to amplify pressure for just institutional change already coming from within. These two dimensions of political mobilisation do not sit comfortably with deliberative theory or, indeed, with the concept of solidarity outlined in this book. Each, after all, implies 'weighing in' on people and a reliance on instrumental transactions to achieve a desired outcome. This represents a significant departure from the deliberative tenet that political outcomes should emerge through an assessment of what everyone could reasonably accept. However, I argue that strategic intent and external influence can be justified from the standpoints of solidarity and deliberation whenever they are oriented towards enhancing an oppressed group's ability to participate effectively in democratic politics, and moreover, whenever deliberative appeals to reason consistently fail to initiate just institutional change.

In the final part, the chapter focuses on two models of reform that combine strategic action and external intervention, assessing their suitability for policy change specifically under the sociologically challenging conditions of divided societies. They are conditionality and transnational advocacy networking. Conditionality involves the provision of material incentives by an external agent to achieve compliant behaviour, while transnational advocacy networking involves the use of discursive power by a conglomeration of domestic and international actors towards the same objective. Both modes of influence tend to be analysed in isolation of one another, or are sometimes presented as competing pathways for reform. However, I argue that when a reform campaign is waged on elements of both, it stands to make gains both from a functional and normative perspective, as each process performs roles complementary to the other. Transnational advocacy networks bring norm violations to the attention of materially capable actors and therefore facilitate the activation of conditionality, keep the practice of conditionality principled, and frame reform measures in ways that make their uptake a more attractive proposition for targeted actors. Sponsors of conditionality, by contrast, provide transnational advocacy networks with teeth. The array of material incentives they bring to the intervention can prove decisive in making it unbearably costly for a targeted actor to continue resisting demands for reform.

Strategic action

Following Jürgen Habermas (1984), the two forms of influence we might wish to identify in our analysis of democratically enacted reform are those involving strategic and communicative action. Reform efforts inspired by strategic action are those in which influence is sought through the invocation of instrumental calculations around the costs and benefits of acting or failing to act on demands being made, and not a reflection of the rightness of the demands being made. Accordingly, an agent that responds to a set of demands on instrumental grounds has done so not because he/she believes it was the normatively appropriate thing to do, but because he/she took it to be the most effective way of maximising core interests in light of the available opportunity structures.

Whereas strategic calculation refers to a 'logic of consequences', communicative action implies a 'logic of appropriateness' (Checkel 2005: 804) and a 'logic of arguing' (Risse 2000: 1–2). That is, agents choose to act a certain way not because it will maximise self-interest, but because it is perceived as the most rightful and justifiable thing to do from the standpoint of all affected parties. This type of reform process involves argumentative discourses in the deliberative sense, whereby actors accept or reject the normative validity of proposals through communication, argumentation and persuasion. It thus stands independent from the instrumental structure of reasoning in which actors weigh up the costs and benefits of material and symbolic incentives when making choices. For example, in an arrangement of multicultural coexistence born of communicative reasoning, majority members are compliant with minority rights norms because they actually regard such norms as ethically or morally appropriate, and not because they are a means to fulfilling a self-interested objective – the majority has, so to speak, consciously and reflectively internalised the norms of multicultural coexistence put before it in the course of a communicative discourse assessing the rightness or wrongness of institutional designs for the accommodation of minorities.

Though communicative action represents the desired mode of influence in deliberative models, it is not, on its own, a sufficient tool for the facilitation of reform in divided societies. In such contexts, mere exhortations to the moral appropriateness of proposed reforms are likely to fall on deaf ears, as the cost of their adoption is likely to be too high for the group in power to interpret proposed changes from a principled perspective. Measures geared towards the elimination of unjust conditions involve redistributions of power and privilege, a scenario that can cause considerable angst among groups benefiting from existing inequalities, as they are likely to be fearful of what their opponents will do once they become newly empowered. Under such circumstances, receptiveness to principled arguments will be minimal, as principles will be overshadowed by a desire to maximise one's position vis-à-vis rivals. Even when the group in power accepts that the reforms being demanded are consistent with prevailing views on human rights and are the correct thing to do, there is no guarantee this will be followed by compliance, as the perceived risks involved are ones the group will be loath to take. Group actors may feel that new measures are a prelude to secession, that they increase their vulnerability at the hands of opponents, or they may simply fear being subject to a backlash from within their own constituency for bowing to pressure from rival groups. In sum, when a group takes its very well-being and collective survival to hinge on the continued subordination of others, there is simply too much at stake for an orientation of mutual understanding to emerge in the course of politics.

Whenever these are the defining conditions of social life, reform has a far greater chance of success through the treatment of the group in power as a utility maximiser, and not merely a communicative agent, as change sought in this way better responds to the factors that are contributing to the group's intransigence. Insofar as privileged groups are resisting change on the grounds it is too risky, creating openness towards change requires presenting a set of alternatives that reduce the costs and increase the benefits of moving beyond the status quo. As will be noted shortly, this involves influencing the group to act on calls for reform through material and social incentives in the form of financial assistance, trade opportunities, increased status through membership in intergovernmental organisations, enhanced security, among other things, all of which can be provided by capable external agents with a stake in seeing through principled reform. Quite crucially, creating openness to change through the invocation of a cost-benefit calculus must also involve measures that make the social and political contexts in which reform is being sought appear less risky for the group ceding power. This requires establishing some kind of physical or political presence for influential external agents, the role of which would be to act as security guarantors during the adoption of new policies. It also requires bringing about interpretive change over reform measures such that citizens come to perceive them as enhancing social stability and being mutually beneficial, rather than a zero-sum game.

Yet an approach to reform that has a prominent role for strategic action sits uncomfortably with the deliberative requirement that influence is sought through an orientation of mutual understanding. This tension is highlighted by Seyla Benhabib (2002), who considers the bargaining behaviour and egoism of strategic action coercive and improper for the enactment of policies that are of moral significance (see also Habermas 1998: 4). Making this point in relation to human rights, she insists we must be prepared to argue for their validity from the standpoint of all human beings, given that human rights are supposed to constitute the moral foundation for democracies everywhere (Benhabib 2002: 143–4). In these terms, it would be inappropriate for American leaders to say, 'We accept human rights because from our point of view, they are the best way to spread our way of life throughout the world,' or Chinese leaders to say, 'We accept a minimum list of human rights because, from our point of view, they permit us to gain international credibility and to access international markets' (2002: 143–4).

However, if moral justifications on their own are doing little to ameliorate human oppression, there is nothing to be gained by dogmatically adhering to them. A just arrangement arrived at on strategic grounds is still far more desirable than no just arrangement at all. In reality, this is the stark choice reformers are confronted with. To demand that we pursue reform only on the basis of reasons we think can be justified from the standpoint of all human beings is utterly utopian and loses sight of the moral purpose of such reforms, namely, to alleviate human suffering. Instead, we are led down a self-defeating path of logic where we must condemn, for example, the abolition of apartheid on the grounds that it was motivated by self-interested reasons, rather than moral conviction on the part of Whites to accept a multiracial democracy. Were it not for the emergence of pragmatic and opportunistic motives for reform among White rulers – arising in reaction to growing resistance by Blacks in townships, along with the crippling effects of sanctions and disinvestment in the country – it is almost certain that the situation in South Africa would not have turned in the dramatic fashion that it did (Goodwin and Schiff 1995: 141). It was, in other words, self-interest that made change possible in South Africa where decades of moral persuasion had failed.

A similar point can be made in relation to the international spread of minority rights norms. This process reflects a mixture of motivations, all of which are not moral in nature. For example, the United Nations (UN) introduced norms and standards for the protection of Indigenous people on moral and humanitarian grounds, driven by a joint desire to atone for the historical injustice of colonialism and to prevent a return to racial segregation. By contrast, European international organisations endorsed the protection of national minorities for instrumental and geopolitical reasons, fearing the mistreatment of minorities by national governments would threaten international peace and security through the spill-over of intrastate violence (Kymlicka 2007a: 268–70). However, that the global spread of minority rights norms was not always moral by intention does not translate into outcomes that are any less moral by justification. It was, after all, self-interested calculations that motivated a shift towards egalitarian state–minority relations where mere appeals to communicative reason did not.[1]

The strategic course of action advocated here can be further justified from a moral standpoint when one considers that reforms initially adopted on self-interested grounds can subsequently be accepted on principled grounds. Theorists of socialisation point to the way cooperation starting off as incentive based can subsequently undergo a shift to encompass reasoning more reflective of a logic of appropriateness (Risse and Sikkink 1999: 11–16; Johnston 2005: 1014). In these situations, actors initially change their behaviour consistent with a set of norms with the intention of maximising some material payoff, but over time internalise such norms through an evaluation of their ethical soundness. Some observers point out that this pattern of socialisation underlies the policy changes on minority rights observed in the Baltic States as they integrated into Euro-Atlantic institutions. Initially, state actors behaved in a highly strategic manner, carefully calculating how to change laws to ward off sanctions and opprobrium from the EU, the Council of Europe (CE) and the Organization for Security and Co-operation in Europe (OSCE). However, following the formal alteration of law, deeper socialisation effects emerged, evidenced through changing domestic practice and sustained compliance (Kelley 2004; Checkel 2005: 814). Insofar as strategic reasoning has the potential to work synergistically with, and is often a prerequisite for, communicative reasoning, it remains a plausible and defensible component of a deliberative strategy of reform.[2]

Involvement of external agents

Alongside strategic action, an additional element requiring theoretical acknowledgement and normative acceptance in conceptualisations of just reform is the part played by agents external to the society in question. External agents are pivotal to the success of attempts at establishing more egalitarian institutional transformation because they can disrupt the circuits of domination keeping oppressed groups from being politically consequential. The involvement of an external agent can tip the balance dramatically in favour of subordinated groups, because they gain the capacity to impose far greater costs on their oppressors than if they merely acted on their own. External agents comprise international actors such as intergovernmental organisations, human rights organisations, donor institutions, powerful nation-states and non-government organisations (NGOs) applying pressure in ways that increase the costs of inaction and the benefits of action on democratically voiced demands for reform. Such pressure is applied through the provision or retraction of incentives considered important by a target agent – such as aid assistance, membership to international organisations, security measures, trade privileges, diplomatic relations, economic benefits, and so on – carefully carried out with the express purpose of eliciting enhanced receptiveness towards reform proposals ordinarily ignored (Vachudova 2005: 106).

However, external actors do not merely offer material rewards and punishments to influence positive domestic transformations. They, in addition, offer social inducements, which can also have far reaching effects on target agents. Social inducements include rewards in the form of international recognition, public praise and invitations to join intergovernmental meetings, while corresponding punishments involve exclusion, shaming and shunning (Schimmelfennig 2005: 832). Accordingly, when such pressure has been successful, the norm-violating agent alters its behaviour towards compliance for the instrumental purpose of wanting to avoid the unpleasant experience of being constructed as an outcast among a community of international actors by whom it wishes to be held in high esteem (Risse and Sikkink 1999: 15).

The following section will explore how strategic action and external influence combine in the resistance of interethnic domination. Two models of reform that involve the coupling of strategic action and external agency will be analysed – conditionality and transnational advocacy models – noting the circumstances under which these models are most likely to succeed and most likely to fail as drivers of domestic reform.

118

Conditionality

Conditionality refers to behavioural change through the prospect of tangible rewards. This practice corresponds most clearly with a rationalist set of assumptions just noted that define actors as utility maximisers (Kelley 2004: 428). Actors are presented with concrete incentives in the form of political, economic and security benefits to alter their behaviour and policies in the direction of international norms. As such, under the conditionality approach one would expect the level of compliance with international norms to correlate with the size and the credibility of the international organisation's conditional incentives (Schimmelfennig and Scholtz 2007: 6) – that is, if the tangible benefits of compliance outweigh the costs of non-compliance, we can expect the domestic agent to adapt its behaviour to norms.

One context where conditionality has achieved notable results has been that of Central and Eastern Europe. Since the early 1990s, European organisations such as the CE, the OSCE, North Atlantic Treaty Organisation (NATO) and the EU have been pursuing a strategy of political conditionality to compel governments of transition states in the region to alter their policies in line with normative requirements set by these intergovernmental organisations. This strategy has been credited for bringing about sustained domestic change in a number of Central and Eastern European states that were initially norm violating and unresponsive towards socially imposed pressure for conformance in the area of minority rights (Vachudova 2005).

Indeed, the international actors that were most successful in inducing compliance to supranational norms were those that were capable of offering and withholding the most tangible material benefits. This is witnessed most strikingly through the success of NATO and the EU in bringing about compliance where other non-resource based intergovernmental organisations such as the Organisation for Security and Co-operation in Europe (OSCE) and Council of Europe (CE) struggled. Though all European organisations have played an active role in monitoring the development of democracy and human rights in Central and Eastern Europe, it was only NATO and the EU that were able to achieve thorough-going reform in these areas in the face of initial intransigence. This success can be attributed to their strategy of pressure involving the extension and retraction of security, political and welfare incentives to steer reform when other European institutions were relying merely on social modes of pressure involving the bestowal of praise and disapproval.[3] The material incentives offered by the EU and NATO had greater motivating capacity because they were highly desirable in the eyes of target agents and outweighed the perceived costs of adapting to normative demands (for example, costs associated with opposition from domestic publics and the reduction in state power relative to rival actors) (Schimmelfennig 2005).

Thus, in Latvia, government officials were subject to intense criticism by the OSCE and CE in the period following independence from the USSR for introducing a citizenship law that discriminated against the country's Russian speaking minority. This criticism, which was backed by visits to the country by the OSCE and CE, along with policy recommendations by them for egalitarian naturalisation requirements, was ignored by Latvian officials intent on maintaining exclusionary laws. However, matters changed once membership to the EU became tied to the citizenship issue. Officials weighed their options in light of these new circumstances, and decided in the end that missing out on EU membership would be more costly than making amendments to the law as demanded by the country's Russian speakers and European organisations (Kelley 2004: 445–6).

In Slovakia, conditionality played an important part in defeating an amendment to the country's penal code that was targeted at undermining the Hungarian minority's ability to criticise the government. Following his return to power in 1995, the populist Slovak prime minister Vladimír Mečiar led a coalition that pushed through an amendment to the country's penal code that could ultimately see people jailed for organising public rallies judged to be subversive, a measure that affected all citizens, but was motivated by the underhanded intention to placate Hungarian activists. Slovak officials were initially unfazed by OSCE and EU criticism of the amendment and the accompanying calls to respect minority rights and freedom of speech. However, when the EU indicated the amendment could compromise Slovakia's chances of membership, debate about the amendment returned to parliament. This culminated in a number of defections in the coalition that originally passed it, and ultimately in the amendment's defeat (Kelley 2004: 447–9).

We can witness in a number of other Central and Eastern European contexts a similar process of initial intransigence in the face of social pressure, followed by compliance when social pressure was supplemented with tangible material incentives involving membership to the EU and NATO. Examples include the reformulation of citizenship laws that discriminated against Russophones in Estonia and the introduction of policies protecting the human rights of Roma in the Czech Republic, Slovakia, Bulgaria and Romania. In each of these cases, conditionality, tied to the extension or retraction of material benefits, proved more effective in motivating minority rights reforms than strategies of influence relying solely on criticism, shaming and acts of persuasion.

Conditionality beyond the EU

Despite being highly effective, it is only in Europe that conditionality remains a consciously implemented and regularly practised policy for the promotion of equitable terms of interethnic coexistence. This has raised questions about conditionality's applicability in parts of the world where a deeply integrated set of regional institutions is not available to serve as its vehicle. Indeed, some have posited that Europe is a *sui generis* case, and that what has been witnessed there cannot be readily emulated elsewhere (Johnston 2005: 1036). Europe, it is argued, has a depth of integration, level of political community and pooling of sovereignty not present anywhere else, making it difficult to envisage a successful application of conditionality beyond its highly institutionalised confines. Thus, while the EU has clearly stated criteria for membership in the *acquis communautaire*, which includes provisions for minority protection that aspiring states are required to follow, Southeast Asian institutions such as the Association of Southeast

Asian Nations (ASEAN) and the ASEAN Regional Forum (ARF) are deliberately under-institutionalised and founded on informal, elite-based, consensus-driven deliberation, from which questions of domestic governance are intentionally avoided. The same applies in Latin America, where institutions rely on informal elite interaction, rather than on principled procedures, to resolve disputes within them (Johnston 2005: 1037; Acharya 2004: 256).

The divergence in the quality and intensity of institutional practice between European and non-European supranational contexts cautions against a direct extension of the insights gained from the European experience to the rest of the world. But though the presence of a regional state-analogue like the EU offers clear functional advantages, it is not a necessary ingredient for the successful application of conditionality. Indeed, a glance at the broader international system reveals that conditionality remains at the heart of the coordination of much political action that bears no direct association with EU membership carrots and sticks. It is just that the language of conditionality is not always utilised to describe such coordination, even though it embodies the manipulation of behaviour through rewards and punitive measures by external actors seeking to achieve specific objectives.

The practice of power mediation by influential nation-states is one such example. In a manner akin to how European institutions operate, power mediators draw on their economic, military and political resources to steer the preferences of conflicting parties in a direction that achieves a desired objective, in this specific case, the resolution of conflict. Power mediation has been central to the attainment of a number of notable peace agreements (for example, the Dayton Peace Agreement in Bosnia, the Ohrid Framework Agreement in Macedonia and the Good Friday Agreement in Northern Ireland), and its success as a peace-making instrument lies with the mediator's use of carrots and sticks (alongside communicative processes) to heighten belligerent perceptions that continued conflict will be mutually hurting, and that flexibility and compromise is an instrumentally more attractive option (Zartman 2001: 9; Svensson 2007: 232).

Sanctioning is a related form of conditionality also practised outside the sphere of supranational governments. Nation-states frequently, though often tardily, coalesce into international sanction regimes in response to violations of human rights, imposing material pressures on non-compliant governments to alter their behaviour. Such pressures involve withholding and extending foreign aid, trade privileges, diplomatic ties and membership in regional organisations, among other things. Again, the assertion of material leverage in this fashion has been highly productive when appropriately timed, pushing norm-violating agents towards making tactical concessions in order to regain material privileges, but, in the process, also opening up spaces for more discursive modes of norm adaptation thereafter (Risse and Sikkink 1999: 25).

To this list one could add the practice of kin-state advocacy. This involves the exertion of pressure by a state sharing a cultural affinity with a minority in a neighbouring state, carried out with a view to curtailing its repression. Such interventions take the form of diplomatic pressure, the renegotiation of terms of trade, the financial sponsorship of the minority, or the amplification of official statements condemning human rights violations. Some analysts justifiably express reservations about kin-state advocacy, seeing it as a cover for irredentism and an operation that can only lead to an escalation of conflict. John Dryzek, for example, cites Nazi Germany's invasion of Sudetenland, Turkey's of Cyprus and Serb dominated Yugoslavia's of Croatia to conclude there can be no civilising force in the opening of channels between a minority and a neighbouring state of shared ethnicity (2005: 232). More recently, Russia's annexation of the Crimea Peninsula and its support of separatists in Eastern Ukraine have once again drawn negative attention to the practice of kin-state advocacy. However, despite the murderous violence associated with these specific cases, they remain outliers in a broader scheme of kin-state politics. Military intervention by kin-states has been the overwhelming exception, rather than the rule, in the post-Second World War period (Waterbury 2008: 219, fn. 1), pointing to a more complex picture of the practice than might initially be perceived.

Indeed, kin-state interventions do not simply lead to an escalation in conflict, and nor are they merely an embodiment of jingoism, but can remain measured and guided by humanitarian intentions (Wolff 2006: 114–15). Russia's intervention in the post-communist Baltic states to end the discrimination of the Russian-speaking minorities there did not involve acts of aggression, but rhetorical appeals directed at the international community to bring more pressure to bear on Baltic governments. It also played out as Russia's conditioning of its withdrawal of Soviet era troops from Baltic lands and concessions on the delimitation of Russian–Baltic state territorial borders on the improved treatment of Russophone citizens (Chen 2012: 58). Turkey's interventions at the height of Bulgaria's tyrannical cultural assimilation and mass expulsions of the Turkish minority in the late 1980s and early 1990s were diplomatic, rather than military in nature, involving direct communication between prime ministers, official denouncements of Bulgarian policy, and Turkish threats to sever interstate relations if the persecution of its ethnic kindred continued. This pressure proved decisive in swaying the Bulgarian government to overturn its repressive policies without arousing Turkish secessionist movements on Bulgarian soil (Koinova 2008: 383–4). Similarly, though the Albanian state has at various times supported Macedonian Albanians in their struggle for greater collective rights, it has done so in a manner that has limited the attraction of secession and tempered radical elements with moderation by encouraging Albanians to redress their grievances within Macedonia's political institutions and in accordance with EU norms (Koinova 2008: 380, 381; Vasilev 2011: 71). In sum, kin-state activism can be motivated by, and can achieve, humanitarian ends, even though it is the particularism of cultural affinities that draws attention to a specific group's plight in the first instance.

The lesson in this is that in regions lacking well-integrated intergovernmental bodies prepared to use conditionality to redress injustices, it is influential states, be they great powers, regional powers, kin-states or patron states, but also intergovernmental bodies operating at a distance from their traditional geographic homes and multinational corporations seeking to boost their ethical credentials, that can use a strategy of extending inducements and amplifying pressure to encourage reform where the initiatives of oppressed domestic reformers are met with resistance.

Conceived along these lines, conditionality has a much broader application, becoming plausible in contexts where interstate relations are not tightly mediated by supranational institutions, where intergovernmental organisations in the region are only able to offer modest material incentives to influence target agents, or where a norm-violating agent is itself already a member of the intergovernmental organisation sponsoring conditionality (in which case, the practice serves a tool of arbitrary coercion). The contingent factor for the functional efficacy of conditionality is not the presence of a deeply integrated supranational institution, but any materially capable actor prepared to elicit norm conformance through the extension and retraction of prized benefits and costly punishments.

The shortcomings of conditionality

There are two crucial questions prompted by this reconceptualisation of conditionality. First, what will motivate materially capable parties to sponsor conditionality? Second, how can the process remain principled rather than become an outlet for arbitrary interference?

The success of the expansive notion of conditionality outlined here hinges on providing satisfactory answers to these questions, for even though drivers of conditionality already exist beyond Europe, they do not always observe the norms they are supposed to promote. Indeed, in an international environment lacking a central authority that coercively coordinates action, those possessing the material capabilities to sponsor conditionality are free to pay no mind to norm violations. After all, they do not shoulder any formally sanctionable duty to protect the vulnerable. Worse still, they have the capacity to enact conditionality in a manner that goes against the interests of the vulnerable, extending carrots and sticks to further their own narrow ambitions at the expense of others.

Thus, we witness powerful nation-states and international organisations acting decisively in one instance of injustice, but dithering in other, sometimes more egregious ones, washing their hands of the responsibility to intervene despite possessing the means to put an end to human suffering (the international community standing idly by during the ethnic cleansing in Rwanda and Bosnia being the most abominable cases of such inaction in recent times).[4] We also witness kin-states coming to the aid of their mistreated ethnic kindred while turning a blind eye to the fate of other oppressed minorities in the same norm-violating state, which are sometimes subject to injustices far graver than those experienced by the kin minority itself (e.g., the Roma in Europe); the International Monetary Fund (IMF) and the World Bank utilising conditionality to entrench the authority of the global corporate market, with the process being subject to very little democratic oversight by those who must bear the heaviest consequences of such actions (Tully 2002: 211, 213–14); and multinational corporations making pledges of 'corporate social responsibility', while using the threat of capital flight to exploit minority populations and to escape accountability for their actions (e.g., oil companies in Timor-Leste and Nigeria, mining companies in Bougainvillaea and Sierra Leone). The problem, then, is that conditionality, in its various guises, remains a double-edged sword. Sometimes it embodies the exercise of material capabilities in the performance of a responsibility to act rightfully. At other times, it involves the exercise of compulsory power to get others to behave according to one's own will (Bukovansky et al. 2012: 68–9).

While conditionality currently suffers from motivational deficits and misappropriation by unscrupulous sponsors, there is nothing intrinsic to the practice that should make this unavoidable. The challenges raised by these shortcomings can be met. But what is required is the empowerment of sources of political mobilisation centred on transnational advocacy networks.

Transnational advocacy networks

TANs are alliances of domestic and international activists working across territorial boundaries to pressure states and powerful global actors to alter their procedures, policies and behaviour (Keck and Sikkink 1998: 12–13). They are quintessentially 'discursive orders', exerting leverage and coordinating action through the force of ideas, norms and social influence and therefore embodying a mode of power that stands independently of that which is exercised through the mobilisation of armies, control over governmental bureaucracies, massive wealth and a large citizenry (Dryzek 2000: 121, 131).

To be sure, TANs are not purely discursive in their influence and sponsors of conditionality are not purely resource based. TANs supply money and goods to domestic allies to increase their leverage relative to their oppressors (Keck and Sikkink 1998: 23), while intergovernmental bodies and nation-states engage in activities of social learning alongside the provision of material inducements to spread values beyond their borders. Moreover, TANs do not simply draw on the force of reason to bring opponents around to their cause. They also engage in behaviour that is highly strategic, disrupting and inconveniencing, rather than simply cooperating and searching for common ground.

Nevertheless, TANs are defined by their relative lack of material capital and their reliance on the force of communication to coordinate action, while the extension and retraction of prized resources is definitive of how sponsors of conditionality pursue behavioural change. Furthermore, the highly strategic behaviour of TANs is typically only a stage in a broader campaign of initiating public reflection and opinion shifts towards a desired policy. In systemic terms, TANs are behaving strategically in one location in order to ignite processes of persuasion across other dialogically interlinked sites – be they the media, legislatures, executive branches, international organisations, universities, scientific research establishments, schools, private institutions or informal spheres of talk, among others – with the intention of raising global awareness around an issue and garnering widespread support behind a favoured policy response (Mansbridge et al. 2012: 8–10). For these reasons, it still makes analytical sense to treat the assertions of power behind transnational networking and conditionality as distinctive, despite the degree of overlap existing between them in practice.

In what follows, I argue TANs hold the key to understanding how conditionality can be strengthened in functional and normative terms. This is the case in at least two respects that correspond with the shortcomings identified with conditionality so far. First, TANs serve as a vehicle through which material orders are roused into action when they sit on their hands during instances of oppression. Second, TANs are the means through which the behaviour of intervening agents is kept at bay by subjecting it to the constraints set by international norms. Let us turn to the first of these points before moving to the second.

Motivation

We have noted that material orders very rarely take the lead in redressing injustices across territorial boundaries when it does not serve an immediate interest. The exception is cases of severe human rights violations, which, in the words of Michael Walzer (1977: 107), 'shock the moral conscience of mankind'. Extreme instances of human suffering are usually met with international condemnation, sanctions and in some cases military intervention, the motivations of which cannot be reduced to a straightforward cost-benefit calculation. This poses an important motivational question: what is it that will compel material orders to activate conditionality in the presence of not-so-extreme forms of injustice such as the institutional discrimination and exclusion of minorities? After all, though unpardonable, these kinds of injustices might not leave enough at stake (morally or strategically) in the eyes of the materially capable to make it worthwhile to expend resources abroad and to potentially make enemies of other states in the pursuit of what is just.

TANs play an important role in filling this motivational gap, as their reform campaigns stand a far greater chance of success when material orders are mobilised into fighting the same cause alongside them. Network actors seek to forge links with materially well-endowed actors because they are mindful of the limitations of their own discursively oriented mode of pressure involving shaming and framing. Shaming is effective only when norm-violating agents are sensitive to what others think of them. Where norm violators are invulnerable to such pressure, network actors must draw into the campaign material orders, as reinforcement by reward and punishment adversely impacts on the welfare of the target agent and therefore its capacity to continue along the path of non-compliance.

For example, shaming proved a potent weapon in bringing the Mexican government to end its military operation against the Zapatistas in 1994. This is because the government had a strong economic interest in ensuring its reputation was not damaged abroad. Concerned that global protests by INGOs, Mexican diaspora communities, and anti-globalisation associations sympathetic to the Zapatistas was generating adverse publicity in the United States – the main source of Mexico's foreign investment and trade revenue – the Mexican government backed down from its military intervention after nine days and entered into negotiations with the Zapatistas to address their grievances (Martinez-Torres 2001). By contrast, shaming activity on its own was ineffective in bringing the Nigerian government to end its persecution of the Ogoni people. The Ogoni had built a robust international support network made up of INGOs such as Human Rights Watch, Amnesty International, Greenpeace and Friends of the Earth in the mid-1990s, which disseminated information globally on the human rights abuses and environmental exploitation occurring around Shell's oil operations in Ogoni lands. However, this international attention did little to impede the regime's brutal clamp-down on Ogoni activists, as the regime was willing to bear significant reputational costs in order to maintain its policies. In the face of this reputational insensitivity, network actors sought out the interventions of resource strong states and IOs, resulting in Nigeria's suspension from the Commonwealth and the imposition of diplomatic sanctions by many countries, among which was the United States.[5]

Similarly, framing activity does not always achieve the resonance behind the new meanings discursive orders desire, especially when mistrust and insecurity defines ethnic relations. To stand any measure of success under such conditions, framing activity must ensue against a backdrop of security assurances provided by material orders, as such assurances nurture the disposition of openness necessary for new interpretive frames to gain credence.

This was witnessed in the interethnic struggles that took place in Macedonia during the 2000s. Increased acceptance of the Ohrid Framework Agreement (OFA) and the power-sharing it entailed for the Albanian minority was achieved through the reconceptualisation of Albanian political autonomy as a matter of peace and social stability, and not, as it had previously been framed, as a matter of human rights and minority justice. The peace and stability frame proved more effective in generating openness towards power-sharing because it allayed the widespread fear among the ethnic Macedonian majority that their country would eventually dissolve in the wake of devolved power to Albanians (Vasilev 2011). However, the ascendancy of this new frame was not merely a consequence of the free play of discourses by network actors. It was, in addition, aided by the presence of materially capable actors such as the EU and NATO, which situated bureaucrats and military personnel on Macedonian soil and influenced popular understandings of power-sharing by tying it to the security benefits that would supposedly follow through eventual membership in their ranks (Illievski and Taleski 2009). As a result of these security assurances, the terms of discourse on power-sharing were altered, and wider credulity was generated behind the notion that political autonomy for Albanians was a gateway to Macedonia's territorial integrity, rather than its very threat.

This dependence on material orders makes TANs ideal points of departure for thinking about how to respond to the motivational deficits around conditionality. Insofar as the realisation of their campaign goals is bound up with involvement of resource rich allies, TANs have a strong incentive to muster material orders to their cause. For this reason, they remain important initiators and catalysts of conditionality where materially well-endowed actors fail to respond to injustices. Such acts of initiation are achieved through the same methods of reputational enforcement and framing activity directed towards non-compliant domestic governments, but this time deployed in the direction of suitable sponsors of conditionality. This takes the form of TANs making material capable actors aware of, or socially constructing, their stakeholder status in a situation of minority oppression by drawing to their attention the benefits of action and the costs of inaction on a minority's plight. Such heightened awareness around the stakes of intervention is typically predicated on: damaged economic and geopolitical interests caused by communal violence or its very threat as minorities resist the rule of zealous central authorities; large-scale population flows as minorities migrate to neighbouring states or Western democracies to escape ill-treatment; the growth of organised trans-border crime in the form of people smuggling and human, arms and drug trafficking when the rule of law or a state's legitimacy deteriorates in regions where an oppressed minority is concentrated;[6] terrorism, which typically has regional, but also international flow-on effects; and reputational gains that could be made through efforts to end human rights abuses or the conflicts they spawn (which, for example, Norway has enjoyed in its role as peacemaker) (Svensson 2007: 233; Zartman 2008: 159–60). Furthermore, network campaigns of consciousness-raising and stakeholder construction to prompt assistance towards a mistreated group have also encompassed a more morally oriented discourse (Risse and Sikkink 1999: 22–3). Under such circumstances, TANs turn the screw on influential nation-states and international organisations (IOs) by reminding them of their identity as promoters of human rights and the duty they have to live up to this self-ascribed and widely accepted role.

This mutually beneficial interplay between transnational politics and conditionality can be observed in the European context. NGOs were pivotal in highlighting minority oppression in accession states well before European institutions began to rely on conditionality to drive reform on minority issues and well before the Copenhagen Criteria were developed as guidelines for minority treatment. The greater visibility of minority oppression generated through network information flows was pivotal to raising the resolve of European intergovernmental organisations, but also individual European nation-states, to prioritise the improved treatment of minorities as a precondition for accession. By persistently bringing acts of oppression to their attention, network actors stirred the conscience of powerful European actors, frequently reminding them of the immorality of not intervening. Quite importantly, however, they also evoked a strategic calculus among them by creating a greater awareness of the potentially destabilising effects continued minority abuse could have in Europe. This latter factor has been particularly salient in making the need for action on minority abuse seem more real in Europe, as it has resonated strongly with the EU's driving logic of advancing peace and security, and expanding the common market.

For example, human rights NGOs such as Helsinki Monitor, Amnesty International and Human Rights Watch, and the advocacy group European Roma Rights Centre played a vital part in raising awareness of Roma oppression in Central and Eastern Europe (CEE) prior to and during NATO and EU enlargement. They did this by investigating and uncovering instances of political and economic discrimination, along with targeted violence towards Roma, and subsequently disseminating information on these matters to a wider European and global audience through the publication of regular reports.[7] European institutions, in turn, came to look at such abuses increasingly through the lens of stability, as the oppression of Roma in Central and Eastern Europe was linked to the rise in undocumented immigration of Roma individuals to Western member states (Bakker 2003: 166; Kymlicka 2007a: 220).

A similar lesson can be drawn in the case of Turkey. The EU's present day conditioning of Turkey's membership on the improved treatment of Kurdish minority members was preceded by years of campaigning by local activists, diasporic Kurdish communities and human rights organisations like Amnesty International to bring to attention rights abuses towards Kurds and to pressure external agents to intervene. The information politics of these network actors not only highlighted to a wider European audience the extent to which Turkey's behaviour is out of tune with EU norms, but moreover, also created a heightened awareness among European publics that they would have to inherit the security issues stemming from continued Kurdish oppression were Turkey to become a member state.

Another example of the synergies between networking and conditionality is found in South Africa. It may have been great power intervention that was critical in the demise of apartheid through the imposition of sanctions that hurt South Africa's economy and eroded the regime's authority. However, such intervention only emerged in the wake of the transnational mobilisation of anti-apartheid network groups. These comprised development and human rights NGOs, church groups, trade unions and third world governments, which channelled increased resources to the domestic opposition and spread popular awareness of apartheid internationally. The effect of this action was to transform leading Western states into 'latter day converts to the anti-apartheid cause' (Black 1999: 106). The negative attention and popular outrage network actors were generating globally raised concern among Western leaders that their legitimacy would be compromised were they to be perceived as 'defenders of the apartheid state' (95). This concern, along with the desire to preserve Western national interests in the region that were threatened by a violent revolution in South Africa, compelled Western leaders to eventually take a more forceful response towards the regime.

Principled pressure

An additional way transnational networks improve the practice of conditionality is by providing normative guidance to interventions. We have noted that conditionality is misappropriated when powerful actors use it to achieve objectives at the expense of weaker, more vulnerable actors. However, room for such misappropriation is narrowed when agents of conditionality act as a part of, or in close association with, TANs, because unlike material orders, TANs have principled, and not instrumental, sensibilities at the heart of their desires for social change. As Margaret Keck and Kathryn Sikkink highlight, TANs are 'organised to promote causes, principled ideas, and norms, and they often involve individuals advocating policy changes that cannot be easily linked back to a rationalist understanding of their "interests"' (1998: 8–9). While actors relying on conditionality can also have principled concerns at heart when seeking domestic reform, their intentions are nevertheless overshadowed by instrumental objectives, centred on the promotion of market, geo-political and security imperatives first and foremost.[8]

In virtue of this, TANs are likely to more genuinely reflect the

interests of oppressed groups than are sponsor agents of conditionality. Unlike the states or clubs of states sponsoring conditionality, the civil society actors typically coordinating TANs are
not, in Dryzek's words, 'bound by reasons of state, by the conventions of diplomatic niceties, by the fear of upsetting allied or rival
states, or (more important) fear of upsetting actual and potential
investors in one's country, or the financial markets' (2000: 131).
Given this, they are better adapted to function as a moral check
on the excesses of intervening actors, having the latitude to make
it known when they are behaving irresponsibly and to apply pressure to keep them on the straight and narrow.

This politics of accountability was evident in the examples cited
so far to the extent that TANs exerted pressure on material orders
to take action on norm breaking when they otherwise remained
reluctant interveners, or in some cases, actual allies of pariah
governments (for example, the Reagan and Thatcher administra-
tions' support for the South African apartheid regime). It has also
been evident in the EU's eastward enlargements, where TANs not
only work with European institutions to bring pressure to bear
on norm-violating governments, but also against European institutions by highlighting their passivity towards existing member
states falling short of the human rights standards demanded of
aspiring member states.

For example, the human rights NGO Greek Helsinki Monitor,
Rainbow (an ethnic Macedonian political party in Greece), and
various Macedonian diaspora associations have worked together
to amplify public awareness around the hypocrisy of the EU's
commitment to minority rights in Central and Eastern Europe,
but its feeble stance on the decades long minority oppression
in Greece, an EU member state which denies the existence of
ethnic minorities on its territory and curtails their freedom to
self-identify. The network's activism has gained the attention
and sympathy of representatives in the European Parliament,
who have called for a sterner response to Greece's draconian
policies (Greek Helsinki Monitor and Minority Rights Group –
Greece 1998; McDougall 2009). It has also initiated trials in the
European Court of Human Rights, which ended in convictions
against Greece, and prompted a UN fact-finding mission urging

the Greek government to honour core international human rights treaties. These developments have been a major source of embarrassment for the EU and eroded its credibility as a principled actor on ethnic issues by highlighting the gulf existing between its proclaimed standards and the behaviour of a long-standing member state.

Similarly, the perennial supply of reports and publications by the European Roma Rights Centre has played an important role in highlighting the unaltered, if not deteriorating, situation of Roma communities after more than a decade of sustained EU funding and assistance for Roma programmes in new member states. The organisation's sober assessments of Roma integration have functioned as a counterweight to the European Commission's tendency to selectively publicise 'good news' around EU initiatives on Roma affairs. They have also been a rallying point for compelling the Commission to move from mere facilitator to enforcer of EU policies so that member states are confronted, even punished, for their inaction on Roma injustices (Guy 2011).

More broadly, we observe that the lead in the global promotion of civic sensibilities is taken by TANs, which push nation-states, intergovernmental organisations (IOs) and multinational organisations to behave more responsibly whenever they fail to stay accountable towards those who are vulnerable and harmed by their actions. This leadership role is so significant that when Western donors begin coordinating foreign aid, or the World Bank attaches 'good governance criteria' to their structural adjustment programmes, or debt forgiveness for the most indebted poor countries is given serious consideration, we can be confident it is in large part the outcome of public action initiated by networks of NGOs campaigning for a principled cause (Risse and Sikkink 1999: 36; Dryzek 2000: 130; Young 2000: 274–5).

While accountability politics is at the heart of how TANs bring normative direction to the interventions of material orders, it is by no means the only route. No less important is the educative role TANs play, whereby they convey to IOs what is appropriate interethnic conduct and how corresponding norms should be inscribed into international law. Indeed, while the recent evolution of standards around ethnicity is the outcome of IOs formulating norms and standards to advance their own institutional agendas, the part played by network actors in this evolution cannot be overlooked, as IOs have been deeply dependent on their expertise and practical experience to determine what are acceptable solutions to ethnic issues, and in a more prior sense, to identify what are interethnic problems requiring attention to begin with. This dependence arises from the lack of staff in IOs with specialised knowledge on ethnic matters, leaving their decision making reliant on the input and wisdom of civil society actors with a better awareness of the historical and social complexities of particular societies (Kymlicka 2007a: 13–14). It is for this reason, as Kymlicka points out, IOs frequently 'recruit academics, think-tanks, philanthropic foundations, and professional advocacy groups to sit on advisory groups, serve as consultants, write working papers, and act as partners in joint projects and programmes' (2007a: 13–14).

Of course it would be naive to assume all network actors are committed humanists. Many maintain goals that are inconsistent with human rights and respect for diversity. As such, they will have no part to play as facilitators of justice and sociability between ethnic groups. For example, diaspora communities can be a force for moderation, but also extremism when they fund militants engaged in political violence (Wolff 2006: 116). More generally, global civil society has an underbelly of crime syndicates, terrorist organisations and religious fundamentalists engaged in borderless exchanges of arms, organised violence and fanaticism. These transnational actors also work together as a network for the purposes of mutual gain. However, far from promoting civic goals, their activities foment social instability and contribute to injustices by eroding the rule of law and undermining the authority of governments to rule over their territories (Wolff 2006: 119–20).

Nevertheless, it remains an empirical fact that the most determined activity for the elimination of injustices arises in the associational spheres outside states or state-like entities. While we must guard against being enamoured by a heady view of such spheres, this does not detract from the reality that they remain crucial sources of principled social change. It is with this insight in mind that the final section considers possible pathways for empirically embedding the beneficial interplay between conditionality and network advocacy.

Strengthening the synergies between material and discursive influence

What kinds of institutional modifications would strengthen external interventions from the functional and normative perspectives emphasised so far? There are two modifications worth considering owing to the appropriate balance they strike between plausibility and justifiability: first, the enhanced differentiation of international legal norms on minority rights; second, the inclusion of network actors in the decision-making arenas of material orders. In what remains, I will defend their suitability while pointing to potential issues they raise.

Differentiation of international legal norms on minority rights

A notable characteristic of the evolution of multiculturalism has been the appearance of an international legal code specifying what constitutes acceptable and unacceptable behaviour towards cultural minorities (Boulden and Kymlicka 2015 forthcoming). This legal code remains, for the most part, judicially unenforceable. However, it still has notable effects on the regulation of interethnic relations, as states are monitored and critiqued against it, and frequently adapt their behaviour in line with its associated norms, despite their non-binding character. While some states continue to behave in defiance of these norms, they nevertheless feel compelled to justify their non-compliance to an international audience. That such justifications tend to be couched in the language of exceptionalism, rather than being round rejections of the validity of these norms, points to the latent social power residing within them, and their relevance as instruments for the regulation of interethnic relations.

However, as Kymlicka (2007a: 274–5) argues, this internationalised legal code would more potently perform its critical and disciplinary functions were it to take on a greater degree of prescriptive detail and specificity. In their current state, international norms on minority rights have a generic composition, either failing to make any clear-cut distinction between the various cultural groups they are designed to protect, or where such distinctions are made, lacking the prescriptive depth necessary for unambiguous and decisive guidelines on what groups can and cannot legitimately claim against the state. This is evident in the context of Europe, where international declarations and conventions have been formulated around an all-encompassing 'national minorities' category, which disregards or conflates the profoundly distinctive experiences and perspectives of other minorities, such as immigrants and Roma. The same goes at the level of the UN, where a wide range of documents address the specific needs and aspirations of Indigenous people, but remain reticent on those of national minorities and immigrants, which are problematically lumped under a broadly based minority category.

The effect of this generic treatment of diversity is an international legal code with depleted rhetorical force. To the extent that international declarations and conventions fail to acknowledge that different minorities have different needs and aspirations, they remain too blunt to adequately signal what constitutes appropriate or inappropriate state policy on matters of cultural diversity. Furthermore, those campaigning for the improved treatment of minorities are deprived of an effective source of social power, as the international system lacks a normative referent fine-tuned enough to be attentive to the specific needs and aspirations of different minorities. As such, the discursive force of any activism geared towards criticising and overturning state policies encroaching on minority interests remains untapped.

A differentiated set of legal norms would help address this problem by lending greater legitimacy to the claim making of minorities on issues sitting within the realm of what such norms sanction. Under this proposal, the international institutional structure would catalogue multiple categories of ethnic groups, along with a detailed set of corresponding entitlements tied to their varied circumstances. The effect would be an altered field of legitimate behaviour that better protects minority interests, as answerability to minorities becomes more clearly articulated and more widely sanctioned through its enshrinement in an internationally endorsed legal code. Put differently, the international codification of differentiated rights globally embeds a set of responsibilities for the protection of minorities that give other actors 'the right to hold the ordained answerable for the performance of those responsibilities' (Bukovansky et al. 2012: 69). Actors can shirk these responsibilities where they are not binding. But they would do so at a cost to the legitimacy they command, given that they will be acting in defiance of an authoritative benchmark of what is rightful.

It is for similar reasons that the practice of conditionality would be strengthened under refined and expanded legal norms on minority rights. The presence of targeted norms provides enhanced clarity on when and to what ends material orders can *rightfully* assert their coercive powers, while at the same time offering a fine-tuned critical vantage point for TANs to pressure material orders to respond to minority oppression when it is met with inaction.

That said, the enhanced legal prescription of norms comes with a set of drawbacks that need to be weighed against resultant gains in social power when considering how far the process of prescription should be carried through. Any attempt to articulate what are the specific needs and aspirations of groups will be fraught with reification, as immense diversity in social characteristics exists within national minorities, immigrants, Indigenous groups, Roma, and so on. We have already witnessed in Chapter 2 that ethnic groups have wants and needs that vary geographically and alter with time. Therefore, to expressly codify minority wants and needs, along with the institutional designs they supposedly entail, risks locking minority socialisation into a specific path by shutting down spaces for debate and contestation over alternative institutional modes of coexistence which may be just as, if not more, appropriate in a given context. For this reason, generic norms are not necessarily counterproductive, and according to some, a feature of the international system that should be embraced, rather than overcome. After all, their under-elaborated and open-ended nature permits domestic actors to be authors of the process of change, giving them the freedom to tailor reforms specific to their concrete needs and to localise foreign norms so that a better fit is achieved with prior domestic ideas and beliefs (Acharya 2004; Kelley 2004: 452–3).

Of course, the extent to which essentialisation and deliberative censorship are likely side effects of legal prescription will vary with the depth of detail going into norms – the greater the specificity of who is entitled to what, the higher risk of such unwanted effects. At the moment, the prescriptive detail of international norms remains too sparse to pose any such danger. As such, a deeper level of legal differentiation would arrive at a more appropriate balance between social empowerment on the one hand, and space for deliberative interpretation and contextual adaptation on the other.

Inclusion of network actors in international organisations

Another system change that could improve external interventions is the proliferation of institutional channels of participation for non-state actors inside intergovernmental organisations. Such inclusion dilutes the grip of member states over these organisations by exposing intergovernmental policy making to a wider array of affected parties. This not only extends the scope and depth of accountability of international organisations that are shaped by the narrow agendas of the more powerful member states funding them. It also provides opportunities for progressive policy making by enhancing the flow of information on an issue normally not available to decision makers weighing up various proposals.

This form of political presence has been introduced, yet remains underdeveloped, in a number of IOs attempting to combat widespread perceptions that they lack standards of accountability. For example, the EU funds, consults and provides policy-making access to NGOs engaged in trans-border activism in issue areas ranging from immigration and Roma rights to environmental policy and humanitarian aid. Similarly, the UN arranges parallel civil society forums at its global summits, provides access for NGOs to the programmes of some of its agencies, and considers 'alternative reports' from civil society actors during some of its intergovernmental meetings (Young 2000: 273; Wild 2006: 13–14). The intention of this institutional channelling is to address the democratic deficit of these institutions and to elevate their legitimacy, with the inclusion of civil society actors in their decision-making arenas bolstering their claims of representativeness.

Contemplation over how to build on this trend requires keeping a wary eye on co-option, a looming threat to the accountability and epistemic gains formal institutional inclusion promises. Co-option occurs when the interests of one entity are absorbed into the leadership or policy-determining structure of another entity, but without the attainment of shared power.[9] In these terms, network actors undergo co-option when their migration from the oppositional sphere of civil society to the formal institutional spheres of intergovernmental bodies is achieved through the assimilation of their defining principles and the erosion of their autonomy to support divergent policy paths. The result is network actors stripped of an insurgent character, symbolically, if ever, confronting institutions acting against the very interests network actors purport to represent.

Empirical experience tells us that co-option is not an inevitable outcome of formal institutional inclusion, even though it remains an ever-present danger. For example, studies across policy domains in the EU reveal a mixed picture on the extent to which accredited NGOs retain or lose their independence to promote constituent interests. In the domain of immigration, Andrew Geddes shows that pro-immigrant groups that have been most successful at gaining inclusion are those that have, to the detriment of immigrants, aligned their stated objectives with the EU's preference for maintaining restrictions on the movement of people across its external borders (2000: 645). By contrast, Ondřej Císař and Kateřina Vráblíková (2012) show that the Commission's funding of Roma advocacy NGOs has not depleted their ability or resolve to campaign on behalf of the Roma in the Czech Republic. If anything, this funding has had the opposite effect by contributing to the professionalisation of NGOs and empowering them to withstand domestic public opinion that has been deeply hostile towards the expansion of rights for the Roma.

One way to minimise the risk of co-option is to follow Dryzek's (2000: 136–8) proposal of favouring 'passive' channels of inclusion over 'active' ones. Active inclusion involves the IO's sponsorship of civil society groups and the promotion of their power within the organisation. By contrast, passive inclusion occurs when civil society groups are situated outside the IO, but the IO remains receptive to their lobbying and policy advice. The advantage of the latter arrangement is that NGOs are not beholden to the agendas of IOs nor weighed down by their authority structures, given that they have not opened themselves up to substantive inclusion. This is conducive to the maintenance of civil society's democratic vitality, which in turn, is a gain from the perspective of accountability.

Of course, there is a point when passive inclusion becomes too passive to meaningfully perform an accountability function. Where that threshold lies will vary from one IO to the next, depending on how determined it is to see through its preferred policies to the exclusion of opposing voices. In organisations with a history of unresponsiveness towards actors affected by their policies, active rather than passive inclusion is the more plausible strategy for enhancing accountability. This is because passive inclusion permits proximity to the centres of power within the organisation, thereby disrupting the decision-making monopolies that enable it to be unresponsive to a wider array of concerns. Such responsiveness is notoriously difficult to accomplish when political mobilisation is restricted to outside the organisation, because, for reasons already outlined in Chapter 3, the hostile interests which have captured the decision-making process will remain neither motivated nor obligated to act on the claims of others.

Conclusion

In this chapter, I considered pathways for the introduction of institutional arrangements conducive to solidarity where such arrangements are likely to encounter resistance by powerful actors. Such reform, I argued, is met with the greatest chances of success when it is underpinned by strategic forms of action along with pressure by external actors, as this enables subordinated groups to have a tangible influence on a political process in which they are normally too powerless to be taken seriously. I also suggested that a coupling of conditionality with transnational advocacy networking could offer a credible vehicle for such action, with agents of conditionality providing the material incentives to bring about compliance and transnational networking offering the motivational, principled and discursive basis along which such pressure can be applied. Having analysed formal structural changes that promote solidarity, we are now ready to focus on informal ones. In the following chapter, I examine potential pathways for the generation of mutual answerability at the everyday level of social interaction involving shifts in interethnic attitudes.

Notes

1. Similar critiques are offered by Monique Deveaux (2003), Mark Warren (2007) and Aubin Calvert (2013), who also argue against excluding self-interest and strategic intent from the boundaries of legitimate political action.
2. See also Mark Warren's analysis of the potential for strategic action to enhance communicative action within a domestic context (2007: 284–5).
3. These material incentives included military protection, full access to the EU's internal market and economic subsidies, and full participation in the spheres of decision making in both organisations.
4. For a compelling defence of a cosmopolitan ethic that assigns responsibilities according to material capability, see Bukovansky et al. (2012: 213–63).
5. Shell, on the other hand, was more sensitive to the global visibility network actors generated towards the Ogoni's plight and the hand it was playing in it. During the network campaigns, it implemented new policies on environmental and human rights issues in its overseas operations, and took measures to improve its operations in the

Niger Delta (although some Ogoni members have described these changes as merely symbolic). See Clifford (2002).
6. For a discussion on the links between ethnic conflict, weak states and organised crime, see Wolff (2006: 117–22).
7. For an example of such reports, see Bakker (2003).
8. The EU offers a relevant example here. It seeks norm conformance on minority rights primarily because it perceives such norms to promote the vitality of the common market, social cohesion, and peace and security, rather than simply because norm conformance protects vulnerable minorities in and of itself. See Kymlicka (2007a: 45).
9. This definition borrows from Dryzek, who builds on Selznick's earlier formulation of co-option (2000: 88).

5   In-group Deliberation and Integration

So far, I have focused on the formal institutional arrangements that best meet the demands of solidarity. In this chapter, I turn specifically to matters of behavioural and attitudinal change at the everyday level, offering routes for fostering mutual answerability whenever misconceptions, disparaging stereotypes or a history of violence leave groups harbouring dehumanising images of one another. This shift in the analysis is driven by a concern that formal arrangements of accommodating diversity stand little chance of enduring unless active measures are taken to foster an expansion of relations of obligation in the informal spheres of association. Indeed, many societies that have undergone post-conflict reconstruction reflect the lack of impact institutional renovation within the state can have on improving interethnic relations throughout society. In places like Northern Ireland, Bosnia, Lebanon and Macedonia, power-sharing has made democratic politics possible where formerly violence was the chief medium through which competing goals were pursued. Nevertheless, relations between groups at the everyday level and within civil society have largely remained in stasis, mirroring the social divisions and bad blood present at the time power-sharing agreements were conceived.

The response to the challenge of fostering solidarity that I wish to develop and defend in this chapter is somewhat unusual, for it draws on practice that is looked upon with a level of disdain by democrats. In contrast to the normally advocated path of seeking to build relationships through deliberation *across* group boundaries, I posit this goal can be plausibly achieved through a focus on deliberations *within* groups, among socially *like* members.

Across-group deliberations are preferred by democrats on the grounds that they break down stereotypes and provide opportunities for commonalities to emerge, while in-group deliberations are discouraged on the grounds that they intensify adherence to viewpoints that stoke hostilities and preclude the possibility of sociability between groups. I agree with these theorists that heterogeneous and porous public spheres are a precondition for healthy group relations, and that institutional architects ought to continue thinking of how integrated notions of coexistence can be fostered where deep social cleavages divide citizens. However, I do not share the conviction that in-group pathways are either inconsequential or necessarily inimical to the realisation of these goals. On the contrary, rather than simply being a source of extremism and belligerence, in-group deliberations can attenuate conflict and foster acceptance where across group deliberations fail. For this reason, I argue they can play a more compelling role than they are currently given credit for in how we might favourably alter societies marked by inter-group hostility.

I approach this argument in three stages. First, I draw attention to what can be considered an overly pious view of across-difference encounters within deliberative theory. Second, I explore how in-group deliberation presents itself as a promising, yet underappreciated, vehicle for the cultivation of mutual understanding and openness. Finally, drawing on these insights, I add flesh to a normative notion of in-group deliberation, which I refer to as 'integrative leadership'. This concept alerts us to the ways in which social influence and already-established channels of communication within groups are not simply mediums for breeding intolerance, but can also be harnessed to transform negative out-member images into positive ones.

Across-group versus in-group deliberation

Deliberative theorists have long favoured engagement across group lines to resolve conflict and dispel negative inter-group emotions, taking it to be a presumptively more wholesome practice than its in-group counterpart. This bias is informed by the established view within democratic circles that dialogue among like-minded

individuals intensifies prevailing stereotypes and negative sentiments, while engagement with differently situated others exposes
the arbitrariness of prejudices and aids in the construction of more
accurate and positive re-evaluations of others. Specifically, inter-
group conversations are regarded as a self-evident pathway for
the generation of reciprocal bonds, even morally desirable traits,
as such conversations impel participants to adopt the standpoint
of the other, and thereby alter their interpretation of a situation in
a fashion promoting toleration, understanding and cooperation.
By contrast, in-group deliberative spheres do not have relevant
outsiders present, and are therefore deemed less universalising,
and by extension, more vulnerable to the spread and intensification of conflict. In such settings, the boundaries of the relevant
constituency of the affected will be more narrowly drawn, for in
the absence of outsiders, participants have few incentives to give
reasons non-members are likely to accept.

The foregoing assumptions are grounded in much contemporary analysis of deliberation. Cass Sunstein, for example, argues
that 'heterogeneous groups are often a far better source of good
judgements, simply because more arguments will be made available' (2002: 192). By contrast, 'enclave deliberation' is prone
to 'widespread error', 'social fragmentation' and even 'fanaticism', as it draws on limited argument pools and is subsumed
by parochial influences (2002: 177, 186). David Miller regards
deliberations among sub-national groups as corrosive to civic solidarity, because such interactions orient participants away from
the common good towards narrowly held sectarian interests. As
a consequence, he believes deliberation 'that serves the cause of
social justice' is most likely to occur at the national level, as such a
forum is encompassing of all the diversity, and therefore interests,
present within the political community (2000: 151–2, 158). On
a slightly different note, Katherine Walsh claims people receive
little practice in understanding the concerns and practices of
others in society when they congregate with individuals they perceive to be like themselves. Given this, she believes homogenous
spheres of association hold 'little potential for improving connections among people' (2007: 48). Roberto Gargarella, on the other
hand, implicates unrepresentative deliberative forums in what he

calls the 'motivational problem'; that is, an unwillingness to take the preferences of others into account, even when participants know perfectly well what is the nature of these preferences. To circumvent this problem, he calls for deliberative spheres which are fully representative of a constituency's diversity, as this impels participants to treat others' preferences as if they were their own (1998: 262).

In all these accounts, across-group deliberations are seen to encourage participants to adopt George Herbert Mead's celebrated perspective of the 'generalised other'; in other words, the act of imagining what is expected of oneself with reference to the intentions and thoughts of wider society (1934: 154). In-group deliberations, by contrast, are synonymous with the narrow-mindedness John Stuart Mill was referring to in his metaphor of 'one eyed men'; that is, people who are unable to orient their minds and efforts beyond a singular course of inquiry (2003: 67).

Deliberative theory, to be sure, does not entirely dismiss in-group discursive arenas of any normative value. Some theorists regard them as sites in which marginalised and silenced groups can articulate and sustain viewpoints that do not get a fair hearing in mainstream publics (Karpowitz et al. 2009: 578–9; Sunstein 2002: 177). Others regard them as important sources of interpersonal trust that nurture well-being and expand people's capacity for agency (Putnam 2000: 22). However, the emancipatory benefits of in-group environments are typically advanced with the caveat that they come with undesirable side effects in the form of social instability, social fragmentation, parochialism, even violence (Karpowitz et al. 2009: 580; Sunstein 2002: 177; Putnam 2000: 23; Uslaner 1999).

Yet there is much to suggest that the foregoing portrayals of across-group deliberation are constructed on overly optimistic assumptions about the practice's tolerance-enhancing potential. The main issue, no less, is that they take for granted the very background conditions necessary for empathetic imaginings to get off the ground, namely a disposition of reasonableness and mutual respect among interlocutors. Indeed, what characterises disputes in contexts of deep division and intolerance is not mere disagreements over competing viewpoints, but a desire to eradicate the viewpoints, even identity, of a despised or mistrusted rival (Dryzek 2005: 219). In the face of these sociological realities, there is every possibility that recourse to inter-group deliberation, despite the best intentions of its advocates, will actually reinforce the negative sentiments and injustices it is supposed to remove by bringing out the worst in people rather than the best. Far from adopting the standpoint of the other, people will, in Mark Warren's words, 'want to win, often even if that means wilful misunderstanding of opponents, distorting their claims, questioning their motives and attacking their character' (2002: 182). Likewise, there are few reasons to feel confident that repeated interactions with individuals of a maligned identity will necessarily lead to a positive re-evaluation of it. We can expect an intensification of stereotypes and prejudices if those individuals behave in ways that correspond to preconceived views.

Theorists writing with deeply divided societies in mind demonstrate greater sensitivity to the potential pitfalls of across-difference deliberation (Fishkin 2009: 159–96; O'Flynn 2006; Dryzek 2005). The emphasis in this branch of inquiry is on the design of institutions that increase the perceived rewards of reasoned exchange, or at least make it less risky, where the starting point of politics is deep antipathy. In this vein, James Fishkin (2009: 168) advances deliberative polls as key to nurturing an environment where participants can 'get over the initial lack of mutual trust and respect that applies to a deeply divided society'. In a deliberative poll, the availability of accurate information and expert knowledge, the exposure to a diversity of opinions, and the facilitation of debate by experienced moderators serves to improve the quality of deliberation by countering the tendency of severe divisions to blind participants 'to the merits of some arguments or even prevent them from considering anything but their own group's advantage' (2009: 161).

The controlled discursive environments of deliberative polls have consistently demonstrated the capacity to nurture understanding and reflection across ethnic divides, as examples of such polls in Northern Ireland, Bulgaria and Australia have shown (Fishkin 2009: 161–9). Yet, on their own, they cannot be the solution to nurturing tolerance and understanding insofar as they are too costly, too time consuming and virtually impossible to replicate on a grand scale. Deliberative polls can accommodate, at most, 500 participants at one time, and take months of organisation, which means that only a highly select proportion of the population can ever have the opportunity to benefit from them. Sometimes, deliberative polls are televised, allowing for mass, though vicarious participation. Yet, even then, any opinion changes that take place can soon wear off as individuals re-immerse themselves in unfacilitated, everyday discursive environments. Here, they are once again exposed to the pernicious influences of not-so-perfect information and the dominant attitudes that led them to view others in an unfavourable light to begin with.[1]

A complementary, though more widely adaptable, alternative is offered by John Dryzek (2005: 226) through his notion of a 'semi-detached public sphere'. Here, reflection across difference is generated by re-structuring the very sites of politics such that the moments of discursive engagement remain separate from the decision moments tied to the state – in other words, situating deliberation in a public sphere that is at some distance from, but not completely unconnected with, the state. By maintaining this separation, Dryzek argues that an environment is created that is much more conducive to reflection, since deliberation is no longer overwhelmed by decision. Decision can overwhelm deliberation because participants are more likely to regard the discursive process as an all or nothing game and therefore resort to strategic behaviour. This, as Dryzek notes, is especially the case when decision is tied to sovereign authority, as groups are involved in a deadly numbers game to secure a hold over the state, and therefore the rest of society.

A semi-detached public sphere is a plausible strategy for encouraging an orientation of mutual understanding where interactions normally occur on the basis of strategic intent. Yet, little attention focuses on how it can be enlisted to moderate politics within groups through the same decoupling of deliberative contestation from sovereign power, this time targeting ethnically like rivals engaged in the commonplace practice of 'outbidding' in the pursuit of ethnic votes. The goal of conflict transformation is simply taken up from the perspective of inter-group interactions, demonstrating the broader tendency within scholarship to under-state, or simply overlook, the part in-group deliberative spheres can play in the facilitation of attitudinal shifts consistent with solidarity.

Although dialogue among like-members has a propensity to lead to a polarisation of viewpoints, it does not follow that the viewpoints gaining wider and more intensified adherence will necessarily be intolerant ones. They can also be ones that show greater acceptance of, and respect for, the other. Take the process of reconciliation. While it rests on a degree of across-difference dialogue to express forgiveness for past wrongs and acknowledge-ment of complicity in them, this comprises only a fraction of the intersubjective exchanges that are contributing to the alteration of mindsets. The bulk is taken up by the conversations occur-ring within the belligerent groups in the stages leading up to the moment of reciprocal exchange and in the periods follow-ing it. In the lead-up stages, resistance to reconciliation is often strong, both among victims who have experienced trauma, but also among perpetrators who find it difficult to acknowledge that their actions were wrong (Staub 2006: 873). To create openness towards the notion of reconciliation, a process of debate and negotiation must occur within the group, whereby individuals inclined towards reconciliation persuade those resistant to it of its merits. Likewise, while the reciprocal exchange of apology and forgiveness is a deeply cathartic experience for those taking part, it is the frenzy of critical conversations it spawns thereafter that determines whether or not a more positive relationship will emerge between groups. Once again, a great deal of these conver-sations occur within, rather than across, group lines, involving ethnically like individuals debating the significance of the recip-rocal exchange and what it ought to entail for their collective futures.

Thus, in South Africa, we witness that the goals of restorative justice were pursued against a backdrop of intense deliberations among Blacks reflecting on the legitimacy of a mode of recon-ciliation that demanded refraining from vengeance and forgiv-ing transgressors for past wrongs. The acceptance of this mode of reconciliation by significant sections of the Black population (Amstutz 2005: 198) cannot simply be put down to the impact of interracial dialogue, as such encounters were few and far between in the immediate aftermath of apartheid. Though the Truth and Reconciliation Commission's (TRC's) hearings did provide opportunities for such dialogue, the details of which were made widely available via the media's extensive coverage, they tended to leave Blacks feeling offended, rather than satisfied that a proper reckoning with the past had occurred. This is because many Whites seeking amnesty from punishment displayed a lack of contrition in their apologies, while the most influential members among them either failed to admit responsibility for complicity in crimes or simply refused to appear at the hearings altogether.[2] Rather, the widespread acceptance of the tenets of restorative justice is better understood in the light of the reflective discourse generated by Archbishop Desmond Tutu and Nelson Mandela, both of whom sought to rebuild society on the basis of Christian values of forgiveness and redemption, and the Bantu ethic of *ubuntu* (see below). Though this discourse was national in scope, it was predominantly in-group in character, as each leader devoted considerable attention to persuading Blacks of the wrongness and futility of seeking to settle scores with former persecutors (Frost 1998: 1–27).

An in-group pathway of conflict transformation has also underpinned the reconciliation process in Rwanda, where the legacy of genocide has been confronted through hearings in *gacaca* courts. Gacaca are traditional Rwandan institutions of participatory conflict resolution founded on the principle that the community should reintegrate the individuals it punishes (Clark 2005: 14). The remarkably high degree of public participation in gacaca and limited violence that has accompanied them, coupled with the intermingling of hundreds of thousands of mass murderers with the families of victims at every level of society, represents a bittersweet realisation of this principle (Gourevitch 2009: 25). However, the uneasy coexistence that has emerged in Rwanda is not attributable in any meaningful sense to the deliberations between Hutu genocide suspects and Tutsi victims in gacaca hearings. These hearings have frequently been the site of acrimony and reawakened trauma as participants recount conflicting versions of events and are once again forced to recall harrowing experiences at the hands of *génocidaires* receiving significantly reduced sentences in exchange for confessions (Clark 2005: 20).

A more plausible explanation is found in the critical conversations that have taken place among Tutsi members contemplating how to reconstruct their devastated communities. Central to these internal reflections has been (Tutsi) President Paul Kagame's appeal to victims to accept the reprieval of Hutu *génocidaires*, with many Tutsi members reluctantly concurring with him that reintegration offers the most pragmatic way to deal with the genocide (Gourevitch 2009: 31). Also of central importance in these deliberations has been the role played by the Christian ethic of forgiveness, inspiring the predominantly Catholic Tutsi to forgive on the grounds that they are fulfilling a moral duty (Clark 2005: 18–19).

This form of limited across-difference communication, followed by extensive in-group discussion to reflect on what has been said by the other, is characteristic of how identity-based conflicts are dealt with more generally. However, though the across-communication aspect receives generous theoretical attention, the in-group component largely goes unnoticed, despite featuring prominently in cases of favourable attitudinal transformation.

Social division and in-group deliberation

It is plausible, perhaps self-evident, that far from declining, the relevance of in-group discursive environments as sites of favourable conflict transformation grows with increasing social divisions. Where divisions are stark, people will talk more with members of their own identity and less with members of others. In this way, in-group environments already have the discursive infrastructure in place through which mindsets can be altered. By contrast, across-group communicative conduits are liable to be weak, ephemeral and in some cases entirely absent in the presence of deep social cleavages. This places additional burdens on processes of attitude change, for not only must one be attentive to the quality of communications taking place, one must ensure that some level of communication is taking place to begin with. Where there is no communication, there can be no reliable way of effecting attitudinal shifts.

Apart from already having in place the discursive infrastructure through which viewpoints can be exchanged, in-group environments are, from a psychological perspective, more amenable to the uptake of new viewpoints in contexts of deep division. It stands to reason that the deeper the social divisions, the greater will be the level of mistrust between groups. In turn, the greater the level of mistrust, the harder it will be for members of opposing groups to be persuasive to one another.[3] In virtue of being mistrusted, out-group members are inclined to be perceived as bad sources of information, lacking not only factual accuracy but also sincerity. People will be left unpersuaded by their utterances, because they will have little desire to place themselves in their shoes and to see things from their perspective. By contrast, like-members conveying the same message stand to be greeted with a greater level of empathy and persuasiveness. Their in-group status automatically lends them a sense of trustworthiness not available to members of opposing groups, and leaves them less prone to suspicions of having motives that are deleterious to the group's interests when they advance viewpoints that challenge conventional wisdom.

In-group pathways, thus, seek to make use of existing networks of trust to disseminate and generate legitimacy around new information and ideas, while across-group ones embark on the notoriously difficult task of establishing trust where it is lacking in order to achieve the same result. Though trust in the case of the former is in the less favoured 'particularised' form, as opposed to the more desirable 'generalised' form[4] – that is, it is among like as opposed to unlike members – it does not follow that this will automatically be inimical to the goal of fostering toleration and acceptance. As with intra-group discursive channels, it all depends on what one is seeking to promote through such networks of trust. Furthermore, much like intra-group discursive spheres, particularised trust presents itself as a ready resource through which mindsets can be transformed. Failure to make use of it – as parochial as it may seem – in favour of generating generalised trust – which, in any case, is too difficult to establish in any substantive sense – is to miss an opportunity to influentially disperse new information and ideas that could change attitudes and nurture confidence towards people beyond one's own ethnic confines.

All this is not to suggest that intra-group encounters can entirely supplant inter-group ones as a means to restore damaged relations. Some form of intersubjective engagement is integral to this task, for we cannot know for certain how people different to ourselves wish to be recognised or, indeed, what types of practical relations they find injurious unless we enter into dialogue with them to find this out. Moreover, any process of reconciliation must be an inter-group one, requiring, as it does, mutually hostile groups to acknowledge the humanity of one another, to demonstrate acceptance of each other, and, where appropriate, to direct to one another symbolic gestures of apology and forgiveness for past wrongdoings.

Nevertheless, dialogic encounters among like-members do play a highly significant, though insufficiently acknowledged, part in the generation of tolerance, both qualitatively and quantitatively. They constitute the greater proportion of individuals' intersubjective experiences, and are the means through which viewpoints exchanged across group boundaries reach those not present at such encounters. It is with these assumptions in mind that I now explore how interpersonal dynamics within, rather than across, divided communities can bring about conflict-abating shifts in inter-group perceptions.

Social influence and in-group deliberation

An appreciation of why in-group spheres can and sometimes do moderate conflict requires closer scrutiny of the modes of persuasion commonly invoked to deny them this quality. In his classic study of the interpersonal dynamics of deliberative bodies, Sunstein (2002: 179–80) identifies two modes of persuasion that typically drive the polarisation of group opinion and potentially cultivate a disposition of hostility towards non-members. The first involves social influence. Insofar as people want to be favourably perceived by group members, they are likely to adjust their position in the direction of the dominant position. In so doing, they preserve their image, both to others and themselves, but in the process, direct the group towards homogeneity in opinion, as their judgements are moving towards what others in the group think. The second explanation centres on processes of argumentation. In a group containing members already inclined a certain way, argument pools will be limited, as a disproportionate number of viewpoints will be circulating on a given issue. This means members will be exposed to some, but not all, relevant arguments, similarly moving the group further in the direction of initial inclinations.

For Sunstein, these mechanisms of opinion change are implicated in the intensification of some unsavoury behaviours and dispositions within ethnic groups and nations. As he sees it, it is the very 'reputational' forces of social influence and the 'informational' forces of limited argument pools that fuel and amplify the outrage of feuding groups, and solidify their impression of the events surrounding the conflict. Members of such groups tend to talk only to one another, thereby producing cascade effects that can lead individuals to increasingly extreme positions (2002: 185). In the face of the serious dangers in-group deliberation poses, Sunstein 'makes a plea for ensuring the deliberation occurs within a large and heterogeneous public sphere, and for guarding against a situation in which like-minded people are walling themselves off from alternative perspectives' (2002: 186).

Sunstein's concerns about the potential dangers of in-group deliberation are certainly warranted. However, they risk leading us astray when they are taken as the complete picture of what we can expect from the practice. First, we might wish to recall that polarisation simply involves the intensification of a certain group preference. To say that a group polarises is to say nothing of the quality of the specific polarisation it has undergone, meaning that the intensification of a set of preferences can be of the conflict-stimulating but also conflict-abating type, along with the hate-promoting, but also respect-generating type. This fact is not lost on Sunstein. At a certain point in his analysis, he observes that sometimes 'the more extreme tendency is better' and that 'group polarisation is likely to have fuelled the antislavery movement and many others that deserve to meet with widespread approval' (2002: 188). However, Sunstein attributes little normative potential to these insights. They remain mere qualifications to his broader argument that polarisation is a predominantly perilous practice, particularly in the explosive settings of multiethnic societies.

Second, and perhaps more crucially, the very forces Sunstein identifies as vehicles of polarisation and bad deliberation can also function to get a dysfunctional deliberating body out of its malaise. If we consider social influence, it is not the case that it simply produces bad deliberation. It can actually enhance deliberation by serving as the means through which new arguments reach an insulated group. Such outcomes can be expected where high status members contribute to deliberations through the expression of dissent, the defence of non-normative, or the introduction of previously absent views. Their influence over minds can prove more powerful than the disapproving gaze cast by the majority, especially if they are individuals held in high regard or have vested in them some kind of political or moral authority to prescribe for the group. The increase in heterogeneity that results from such influence can either depolarise the group by eroding the hegemony of any narrow set of assumptions that have governed opinion up to that point, or it can polarise the group in a normatively favourable direction by amplifying human qualities vital for good deliberation. For example, when tolerance and openness to difference become socially preferred characteristics in a group previously inclined towards xenophobia and blind patriotism, we can expect deliberation to improve rather than deteriorate, as being perceived favourably will require approaching that which is foreign with an open mind as opposed to prejudging it as illegitimate.

The most obvious manifestation of social influence tied to prominence within a group, as Max Weber explained, involves the power of charismatic individuals to change minds by inspiring loyalty from their followers in virtue of displaying traits and qualities they hold in high esteem. Attitudinal congruence with such individuals reinforces our convictions that we are right about the way we think, while dissimilarity with them constitutes

a punishing interaction that raises the possibility that we are
to some degree wrong in our judgements (Collins 1970: 120).
However, as we shall see shortly, charisma is by no means a
prerequisite for persuasiveness. Individuals lacking charisma, but
who nevertheless occupy some prominent or esteemed role within
the group, can also influentially shape mindsets. Though lacking
a loyal followership, such individuals still have the potential to
exercise influence over people for the very reason that they will be
regarded as credible sources of information and will have authority to criticise and prescribe for the group. For, as we just noted,
the credibility of speakers is likely to be greater when an audience
looks up to them, and in divided contexts, when the audience
considers them to be ethnically proximate.

It might be objected that the exercise of such influence is incompatible with deliberation. For one, it sits in defiance of the core
deliberative tenet of symmetry in participation, whereby the
cogency of arguments is supposed to win the day and not the
status of the person behind them. This raises serious questions
as to what exactly is deliberative about the phenomenon. For
another, there is the risk social influence sets a dangerous precedent by encouraging patterns of persuasion that stoke, rather
than abate, conflict. After all, a contributing factor of conflict
is the willingness of the masses to uncritically accept the ready-
made opinions of demagogues intent on sustaining interethnic
animosity for their own aggrandisement. In addition, one could
point out it is the same disposition of non-reflection towards
influential group members that has the propensity to reinforce
the oppression of vulnerable members. Deference to a speaker
in virtue of who they are, rather than what they say, can nurture
an environment where traditionally marginalised voices, such as
those of women, go unheard unless they are an ostensible feature
of what the influential speaker hopes to promote. Given this, a
strategy of opinion change reliant on the force of character might
seem like an odd place to locate our hopes for favourable conflict
transformation.

Yet the force of such objections can be disarmed by pointing to the complexity of the relationship between social influence and argumentation. First, although social influence implies

a certain asymmetry, the kind of social influence that can be endorsed by deliberative theory is associated with asymmetry of the non-coercive type. Participants are not manipulated, deceived or threatened into siding with the influential deliberator. Instead, his/her elevated status or charisma is put to the task of garnering attention towards arguments normally suppressed by polarisation. Interlocutors weigh up rather than slavishly side with these arguments, and they are free to reject them without the fear of repercussions should they fail to be persuaded by their content.

Second, it is not merely the case that social influence subjugates; it also liberates by exposing and challenging the very people who hide behind unexamined myths and facts to pursue objectives that adversely impact on others. Indeed, it is often the case that what is required to ignite wider reflection on ingrained traditions and dogma that coerce people into oppressive conformity is the expression of public opposition towards them by an influential member of the group. Foreknowledge that social influence cuts both ways means we do not have to throw the baby out with the bath water. It allows us to distinguish the potential of social influence to emancipate from its potential subjugate.

Looked at in these terms, social influence is consistent with deliberative practice and functions as a counterweight to extremism and oppression when, on the one hand, it compels hitherto conforming group members to re-examine their own thoughts and, on the other hand, fortifies dissenters to 'come out' and express independent judgements they would otherwise suppress for fear of subjection to social disapproval. These processes of reflection and dissent take on a normatively desirable quality when they challenge entrenched views within a group that have some members of society as less than equal and therefore less worthy of being treated from the moral point of view.

Related back to Sunstein's analytical insights, social influence can work to redress, rather than simply sustain, skewed argument pools, as the affinity and affective ties an influential dissenter has with group members allows him/her to be a proficient disseminator of alternative arguments. This can function to bring to the group's attention information and perspectives members are unaware of or simply fail to take seriously because they are associated with an ethnicity they distrust or disrespect. The result is improved deliberation from a functional perspective when participants begin weighing up a more wholesome sweep of arguments, but also from a normative perspective when the circulation of new arguments stimulates enlarged thinking and a reconsideration of one's negative preconceptions towards outsiders.

Once again, Sunstein is not blind to the capacity of social influence to serve such deliberative goals. We find intimations to this effect in his observation that 'groups may even shift away from their original tendency and in the direction held by few or even one' if 'the outliers are especially convincing' (2002: 180). He also concedes that 'social influences need not be inconsistent with the effort to produce truth and understanding', as the perseveration of one's image might in some instances be tied to supporting a standpoint that is consistent with these goals (2002: 188). Yet even so, Sunstein still believes social influence is too risky to function as a trusted route for good deliberative outcomes. In his view, the safer way of increasing the likelihood that deliberation will 'lead in sensible directions' is to ensure that 'polarisation, if it occurs, will be the result of learning, rather than group dynamics' (2002: 188).

Sunstein's prioritisation of learning ahead of social influence is one deliberative democrats cannot in principle reject, given their emphasis on reflection and argumentative exchange for establishing the validity of a position. However, a normative hierarchy of this kind runs into difficulties when it serves as a touchstone for judging what is and is not legitimate practical deliberation. By precluding a normative role for social influence in a process of opinion change, Sunstein risks setting standards for deliberation that are empirically unattainable. After all, opinion shifts rarely, if ever, take place purely through an examination of the content of arguments. Whether we like it or not, there is almost always some kind of reference to who is behind arguments when judgements are made about their merits (Zaller 1992: 45–6). Rather than seeking to resist these tendencies, deliberative democrats would do better to work with them, using appeals to the force of character to engage people's capacity for practical judgement, and to spark thoughtfulness and active reasoning among them

(Chambers 2009: 335–6). Such appeals are justifiable from a deliberative standpoint, as they are oriented towards the achievement of reciprocal understanding, and are 'essential in reaching others when simple argument cannot' (Dryzek 2000: 70).

In the face of the empirical obstacles to deliberation, it would be more instructive to approach the task of institutionalisation along consequentialist lines, accepting temporary deviations from ideal practice provided this serves as the basis for its promotion in the long run. If our goal is good deliberation, it should matter less how we get there than getting there at all. Non-deliberative interventions may be the only plausible route for achieving an orientation of mutual understanding where material inequality, misrecognition and deep mistrust blunt the transformative potential of appeals to reason. Alongside the exchange of logical arguments, persuasion under such circumstances requires appeals to emotion, the evocation of symbolism, shaming, threats, pressures and sanctions (Risse and Sikkink 1999: 15), as this is what compels indifferent and privileged individuals to reflect and act on the appeals of others. Conceived along these lines, deliberation would be welcoming of social influence, but also additional non-communicative interactions involving bargaining and rhetoric, provided they were, as Dryzek (2007: 241) has counselled, 'non-coercive, capable of inducing reflection, and capable of connecting particular points and experiences to more general questions and principles'.

Examples

The role of social influence in stimulating deliberation is not only a theoretical possibility; it has a precedent in the real world. This will now be demonstrated with reference to some prominent conflicts. In each of these examples, influential co-members are expanding argument pools and bringing to attention the standpoint of a rival group where severe social division does not permit iterated deliberation across group lines to achieve this.

South Africa offers a striking illustration of conflict transformation through in-group deliberations involving such leadership acts. Owing to the enormous stature they enjoyed among Blacks, Nelson Mandela and Desmond Tutu were able to influentially shape Black opinion away from seeking retribution for wrongs suffered under apartheid and channel it towards support for multiracial democracy. Integral to this transformation were Desmond Tutu's captivating speeches, which, in a manner consistent with ideal deliberation, encouraged Blacks to adopt the standpoint of Whites when contemplating the country's future. 'We must remember', he once told a Black audience, 'that white South Africans are not demons with horns and tails. No, they are human beings, most of them very frightened human beings. Wouldn't you be if you were outnumbered five to one? And remember, that quite a few have opposed apartheid and paid heavily for that stand' (Frost 1998: 21). Through his sharp wit, animated delivery and use of metaphors that drew on aspects of people's daily lives, Tutu was able to deliver a message of tolerance that resonated far more strongly than would have been the case had the same message been delivered by a White person or an obscure figure speaking in the cerebral style typical of a logician or a philosopher.

Mandela's and Tutu's public invocations of the Bantu humanist ethic of *ubuntu* also played a part in making multiracial coexistence a more compelling alternative among Blacks. The ideal *ubuntu* seeks to promote is a society in which a heightened awareness exists around the unavoidability of human interconnectedness and the constitutive role it plays in bringing people to realise a meaningful existence (Krog 2008: 355). Both Tutu and Mandela drew on this ideal to depict the bitterness South Africans felt towards each other as an ethical problem, and one which could only be resolved through reconciliation and forgiveness, as this, in their view, offered the means through which society could once again regain the humanness ascribed by *ubuntu* and therefore the very basis for a fuller realisation of life plans (Frost 1998: 1–2). Their strategy of linking reconciliation and forgiveness to *ubuntu* (but also to Christian theology and spirituality) was influential in shaping how Blacks responded to the legacy of apartheid rule. This is evidenced by the ethic's prevalence in both the testimonials of the TRC and the extensive public deliberations generated by TRC hearings in the years that followed (Krog 2008: 362).

A lesser-known fact is that prominent White South Africans also played a noteworthy, though much more modest, part in nurturing tolerance within their own communities. This occurred through an analogous process of lending credibility in public deliberations to Black perspectives that Whites were either unaware of or simply dismissed due to ingrained prejudices. Illustrative here are the events surrounding the so-called 'Trek to Lusaka'. Starting in 1985, respected members of the White social, economic and political elite of South Africa travelled to Lusaka in Zambia every year to meet with the exiled African National Congress (ANC) leadership. The main purpose of these meetings was to discuss what the government and economy would look like in South Africa were apartheid to end one day. However, the meetings also served the more immediate purpose of elevating the social status of Blacks, heaping honour upon the ANC and reconstituting supporters of apartheid as bearers of morally suspect and anachronistic visions of society. This led at least some Whites to reconsider their support for apartheid and to reinterpret the ANC as a political actor with legitimate aspirations (Price 1991: 239).

Examined from a deliberative vantage point, the trek owed much of its success to the social influence wielded by its participants and their strategic use of symbolic acts to bring out in concentrated form the arguments for racial equality they sought to reinforce in White public spheres. Only a tiny proportion of the White population undertook the trek. But those who did were respected members, comprising clergymen, academics, politicians, journalists, farmers and sportsmen (Price 1991: 239). As a result, they were able to stimulate far greater reflection on the immorality of apartheid than Blacks were in their situation of social subordination and legal exclusion.

South Africa represents a special example of conflict transformation, owing to the presence of leaders with personal qualities and public admiration rarely paralleled elsewhere. As such, we must be careful not to overstate what can be generalised from it to contemplate future efforts at moderation. By the same token, the success of social influence does not depend on the presence of leaders with the calibre of Mandela and Tutu, even though this is a clear advantage. Lesser figures in other societies have been equal to the task of inspiring shifts in opinion towards toleration and moderation in virtue of occupying positions of prominence within their groups.

In the struggle for formal equality in Australia during the 1960s, the Aboriginal rights groups which succeeded in pushing governments to repeal racially discriminatory laws were in fact established and administered by non-Indigenous people seeking out Indigenous viewpoints (Chesterman 2005: 20). During this early period of the struggle, non-Indigenous activists were functioning as surrogates for Indigenous people, relaying their viewpoints in public spheres from which they were absent, and impelling wider society to interpret public policy and historical events from an Indigenous standpoint.

The one-sided view of victimhood among Serbs in representations of the war in Yugoslavia was challenged through the reports of conscionable Serbian journalists and Serbian human rights activists as opposed to international actors or members of ethnic groups subjected to violence, both of whom were considered too biased by the Serbian public to be trusted as credible sources of information. This started with the publication of an article in a local newspaper revealing that state authorities had covered up the discovery of a freezer truck laden with human corpses found in the depths of the Danube River, and was followed by a series of further reports on the discovery of burial sites of massacres in Kosovo, which commanders in the police, the military and Slobodan Milošević, Yugoslavia's then autocratic ruler, had attempted to hide from the public. The effect of these information flows was dramatic in that it marked a break with a period of 'reflexive denial' among Serbs, forcing them, for the first time, to re-examine their collective responsibility for war crimes (Gordy 2005: 93–5).

In Turkey, progress towards the normalisation of minority rights, a deeply controversial topic in the unitary nationalist state, was given dramatic impetus through the activism of Orhan Pamuk, the acclaimed Turkish novelist and Nobel Prize winner. In an attempt to demystify historical facts zealously policed out of mainstream discourses, Pamuk publicly remarked in 2005 that 'one million Armenians and 30,000 Kurds were killed in Turkey' (BBC 2005). The effect of Pamuk's statement, along with the criminal case that followed it (opened on the grounds that he insulted the Turkish Republic) was palpable. It stimulated a national debate on free speech in which the treatment of Kurds was considered with a level of frankness not witnessed since the state's conception.

In Muslim communities, it is religious leaders, rather than non-believers, who generate receptivity to arguments condemning extremism. This is because the position of authority religious leaders inhabit enables them to more legitimately specify for their constituents what actions sit inside and outside the ethical parameters set by religious doctrine. The very same attribute also empowers them to more forcefully discredit violent interpretations of Islam as inconsistent with Islamic principles. In practice, such appeals have taken the form of moderate Islamic leaders emphasising the enjoinment of human rights norms to the Quran, and any violation of them as *haram* (Parekh 2006: 183–4).

There are, needless to say, further examples one could draw on. However, these are sufficient to make the point that in-group deliberation can, and sometimes does, elicit favourable shifts in the quality of group relationships by unsettling entrenched opinions and giving voice to outside perspectives where social division does not permit sustained and constructive deliberations across group lines.

Integrative leadership

What the above examples all have in common is the presence of individuals who take a leading role in bringing their group to develop a more enlarged and considered understanding of its relationship with another. Such individuals can be referred to as 'integrative leaders', as their deliberative interventions are driven by a desire to enhance the social proximity of estranged groups, be it through the renouncement of negative emotions, the accomplishment of reconciliation, or in a fuller sense, some form of positive affirmation of another's identity. They are described as leaders not because they pursue and exercise power as an end in itself – as in the Machiavellian sense of a leader – but because they give direction to a community of citizens in the management of their common affairs (Tucker 1995: 3).

To appreciate what kind of social environment is conducive to the habituation of integrative leadership, a brief insight is required into the constraints and motivations governing the behaviour of actors best suited to the practice. At first glance, one could reason that political representatives make the most suitable integrative leaders. Through their occupation of public office, they have at their ready disposal a wide and potent array of discursive platforms through which to reach populations and bring about mass opinion change (Zaller 1992: 311–12). Yet while highly expedient, political incumbency comes with a set of constraints that frustrate attempts at fostering acceptance of outsiders. The most inhibitive of these is the risk posed by unscrupulous political opponents wishing to electorally cash in on attempts at conciliation. Through a strategy of 'outflanking' (McGarry and O'Leary 1994), they can poach a moderate politician's supporter base by portraying openness to the claims of a rival group as a sign of weakness, even betrayal, and their own hardline stance as evidence that they are the more trustworthy custodians of community interests. Under these circumstances, the moderating intentions of elected representatives count for little, as the structures of electoral competition punish leadership that chooses to take a conciliatory path.

The situation of such formal integrative leaders can be contrasted to that of informal ones. These are actors situated outside the institutions of the state and inside the discursive arena of the public sphere, who, as a result, have greater autonomy to promote ecumenical viewpoints. Informal integration leaders come from a variety of backgrounds, encompassing such diverse public roles as religious officials, actors, artists, musicians, intellectuals, writers, human rights campaigners, social critics, journalists, members of royal families, businesspeople, philanthropists, socialites, and the like, the persuasive power of whom increases with their prestige, social status, or charisma. Strategies of discrediting and 'outflanking' are a less effective constraint on the agency of such individuals, for they do not have their livelihoods and careers threatened in the dramatic fashion formal leaders do when they express views that contravene group wisdom. They are not burdened by partisan commitments, and nor are they subject to the whims of a nationalistically aroused electorate. The lower stakes of failure mean informal leaders have latitude to voice opinions that a formal leader would only dare express in private for fear of going awry with his/her formal constituencies.

By the same token, the autonomy informal leaders enjoy is won at a cost to efficacy in influence. Insofar as they will lack ready or reliable access to the media, they will not receive the extensive and regular coverage afforded to formal leaders. In comparison to formal leaders, whose very location in a legislature automatically affords them a high degree of publicity, informal leaders are more likely to receive episodic and fleeting public attention. This means they will have to campaign more tenaciously, creatively and smartly if they are to have any success influencing what viewpoints get taken up during group deliberations.

There are nevertheless institutional arrangements that attend to the deficiencies of each form of integrative leadership, and potentially bring the practices into a synergistic relationship with one another. One such arrangement involves the redesign of a divided society's electoral system to incorporate the alternative vote (AV) (Horowitz 2004; Reilly 2001). Electoral institutions are a crucial component of a strategy of conflict transformation, as they have a profound impact on the calculations political leaders make in their behaviour towards one another. The attraction of AV from the perspective of integrative deliberation is that it alters incentive structures in the direction of moderation by removing the advantage of outflanking and making the promotion of out-group viewpoints electorally rewarding. Under the AV's preferential system of voting, electoral success can depend on securing second or subsequent preferences cast by voters of ethnic groups other than the representative's own. The outcome of such recurrent exchange is reciprocal moderation, as representatives will not want to appear hostile and disparaging towards the ethnic outsiders on whose very votes they depend. Accordingly, those wishing to promote the viewpoints of an outside identity will have enhanced opportunities to do so, as they will be in a structurally better position to withstand the assaults of populist hardliners on their character and conciliatory policies. The effects of AV are also friendly towards informal integrative leaders. By taking the venom out of political rhetoric, and thereby nurturing a social environment that is less intimidating for anyone wishing to express an independent opinion, AV can prise open spaces for critical examination of taken-for-granted assumptions in the currents of deliberation flowing outside the state.

Opportunities for integrative leadership can be further opened up through the interventions of external third parties, especially those who are capable of extending and retracting inducements prized by domestic politicians. The EU offers a positive example of such influence. Its strategy of extending domestic politicians material and symbolic rewards to bring their behaviour in line with EU rules and norms has been consequential in curbing ethnonationalist rhetoric and checking extreme tendencies in a number of Eastern European societies (Kelley 2004; Vasilev 2011). Similarly, the security assurances provided by the United States, the United Kingdom and the Irish Republic in the Northern Irish peace process were pivotal in allaying the perceived risks of power-sharing sufficient to transform ethnic leaders into drivers of moderation (McGarry and O'Leary 2006: 48–52, 57). Under the altered incentive structures that followed external involvement, ethnic leaders began extolling to their divided communities the virtues of choosing peace and co-existence over continued violence and separatism, advancing this as consistent with the protection of community interests where it was once presented as an impediment.

Finally, any attempt at expanding the integrative horizons of deliberations cannot do without a pluralised and independent mass media. Where ownership of the media is in the hands of the many rather than the few, and where the media understands itself as detached from social and political pressure and is committed to taking up issues impartially (Habermas 1996: 373–9), there is a greater likelihood that the viewpoints expressed by integration leaders will be amplified and more widely disseminated within the group. Under a plural and free media, the diversity of information and arguments flowing within the public sphere will be broadened, allowing a greater share of the alternative perspectives projected by integrative leaders to reach group members and influence their preferences during deliberations. It also helps to expose the contingency of power relations within a group, thereby guarding against the spectre of ideological hegemony and discursive domination by extremist forces. Such group reflexiveness is likely to be diminished where media ownership is concentrated and where the media is not committed to holding to account the exercise of power by public officials. Group publics will be less heterogeneous and therefore less likely to resemble a 'marketplace of ideas' in which ill-founded arguments and nationalist myths are discredited 'by revealing their factual inaccuracies, their logical contradictions, or the hidden costs of acting on their implications' (Snyder and Ballentine 1996: 12).

Conclusion

Deliberative theorists have given in-group deliberation short shrift, taking it to be a practice that is at odds with conflict transformation in the direction of solidarity. I have argued that this need not necessarily be the case. While in-group deliberation can be implicated in the intensification of hostile attitudes towards outsiders, it also serves as the very means through which openness and an orientation of mutual understanding can be fostered in societies lacking a meaningful interethnic public. Indeed, where antipathies run deep and where groups are additionally divided along linguistic lines, transformative deliberation must begin inside the group, as this is where one finds the psychological and communicative infrastructure to facilitate the kinds of identity shifts that presuppose iterated across-group deliberations and lead to the institutionalisation of an overarching public sphere. Given this, deliberative theory would benefit from a re-examination of its normative subordination of in-group dynamics, recognising their potential to serve, and not simply impede, communicative goals in the sociologically challenging settings of deeply divided societies.

Notes

1. Consider, for example, the way popular attitudes on the issue of republicanism changed in Australia following the nationally televised deliberative poll on the issue, to once again return to their pre-poll status when the national referendum on the issue was held two weeks later. See Fishkin and Luskin (2000: 24).
2. For example, though F. W. de Clerk apologised for certain injustices committed under apartheid, he asserted he had committed no crime, and therefore did not require applying for amnesty. On the other hand, P. W. Botha refused to appear at the TRC hearings altogether, describing them as a 'circus'.
3. This conclusion stems from the empirical observation that people find it difficult to empathise with members of an unfriendly group. See Collins (1970: 136–7) and Sunstein (2001: 28).
4. For more on the distinction between particular and general trust, see Uslaner (1999).

6 Consensus Across Deep Difference

A guiding contention of this book has been that deliberative principles provide the most suitable framework for the expansion of relations of solidarity. In this chapter, I reflect on and defend this position in response to assertions that deliberative democracy is incompatible with solidarity due to its emphasis on the attainment of consensus.

Deliberative democracy, as we have noted, is a normative theory that provides criteria for collective action based on the generation of mutual convictions. It is easy to see how this focus on the attainment of mutually acceptable solutions can be both an expression and violation of solidarity. It can be an expression of solidarity insofar as decision making through mutual assent is an embodiment of collective freedom: by aspiring to win others' support for a decision, one is respecting their autonomy, seeking to rule with them and not over them. But consensus can be a violation of solidarity insofar as the pursuit of consensus risks imposing unjust conformity pressures. Disputed values, beliefs and preferences can clash so intractably that they defy reconciliation under a single horizon of agreement. Parties pressured to arrive at a common position under such circumstances are parties pressured to give ground on their deepest commitments. This leads deliberations astray of solidarity's normative imperative that attentiveness is shown to the needs and interests of people different to us.

Some theorists have responded to the tension between consensus and democracy's pluralist aspirations with the conclusion that the former needs to be dispensed with in order to guarantee the latter. The most thorough articulation of this viewpoint in recent times has come from agonists. In their view, democracies need to uphold conflict as an end in itself, rather than strive for the closure of a consensus, as a domain of interaction devoid of an expectation of agreement best nurtures the open-endedness in human relations necessary to secure freedom and the integrity of diverse actors (see, for example, Mouffe 2000; Little 2003; Tully 2004; Schaap 2006). This perspective has emerged as highly influential. As Simone Chambers (2003: 321) concludes in a survey article, even deliberative theory, with its origins in an ideal of consensus, 'has moved away from a consensus-centred teleology – contestation and indeed the agonistic side of democracy now have their place'.

In this chapter, I reflect on the agonistic turn in democratic theory, and argue that a complete rejection of consensus is unsustainable from the very pluralist perspective agonists seek to uphold. In place of viewing consensus as unattainable and undesirable, I put forward a conceptualisation that conceives it as a matter of degree. I contend this understanding not only better captures the complexity of human relations, it also allows us to distinguish the potential accomplishments of aspiring towards consensus from the potential hazards.

To make these points, I begin by charting competing interpretations of consensus that characterise it as either an embodiment or threat to democracy. Following this, I turn to the agonistic understanding of consensus as always impossible and always coercive. I argue this one-sidedly negative characterisation is misplaced, as it is founded on semiotic insights that lack causal and explanatory relevance with how concrete actors embedded in empirical situations agree and disagree with one another. I then go on to demonstrate how consensus and conflict exist along a continuum of comprehensiveness. I do this by building on John Dryzek and Simon Niemeyer's (2006) typology of consensus to introduce the concepts of an 'active' and 'passive' consensus. In the final part, I consider the normative implications of these findings. I spell out how a norm of consensus can be consistent with the egalitarian expression of diversity, and offer reasons for favouring it over a norm of dissensus, even where the complete resolution of conflict appears remote.

Consensus as a democratic ideal

Consensus has long occupied a central place in democratic thought. In classical Athens, *homonoia* – literally 'same-mindedness' – was upheld as a primary virtue, as a citizenry acting of one mind was seen to be contributing to the welfare of the city (Ober 1989: 297). *Homonoia* implied social and political differences had been overcome in a unified community of interest, and that the threat posed to the city by narrow interests had been contained by a citizenry willing in common.

Centuries later, Rousseau revived this thinking, refashioning consensus to meet the challenges of representative government in mass societies. For him, the appeal of consensus lay with its ability to function as a bridge between individual and collective freedom. While these ideals can pull in opposite directions, Rousseau understood consensus to come to the service of both, as individuals desiring the same thing remain free when subject to collective decisions (Dryzek and Niemeyer 2006: 634). Consensus, according to Rousseau, would ideally be generated by a unifying 'legislator', who would bring individual wills into alignment with the common good (Markell 1997: 380).

In contemporary times, consensus has been put to the task of processing conflicts over value pluralism. For Jürgen Habermas (1998: 7–10), consensus functions as a 'postmetaphysical' condition for legitimacy in decision making among people no longer worshipping the same God. Previously biblically transmitted prophetic doctrines imbued public decisions with legitimacy. However, with the historical transition to secularism and a pluralism of worldviews, religion has disintegrated as a public basis of morality shared by all. In a world where human beings have been 'forsaken by God', rational argumentation steps up as the final arbiter of legitimacy. The attainment of legitimacy now depends on the extent to which acceptance behind a norm is generated through justification from the perspective of all relevant interests and value orientations (Habermas 1998: 42).

John Rawls (1997) echoes these themes through his notion of an 'overlapping consensus'. Modern societies might be constituted by religious and philosophical worldviews fundamentally at odds with one another. However, in Rawls' view, these 'comprehensive moral doctrines' (or at least the 'reasonable' ones among them) overlap enough to permit a consensus over the values that ought to underpin the shared political system. Key to the discovery of such a consensus is the exercise of 'public reason'; that is, adherents of each comprehensive doctrine 'explain the basis of their actions to one another in terms each could reasonably expect that others might endorse as consistent with their freedom and equality' (Rawls 1997: 97).

While philosophically minded theorists have sought to link consensus to theories of justice, pragmatically minded ones defend it as a matter of practical benefit. In Arend Lijphart's (1998: 105) view, a 'culture of consensus' better fosters the institutional inclusion of historically marginalised voices than a 'culture of competition'. 'Consensus democracies', that is, democracies ordered around a 'coalitional and consultative style of decision-making', are supposedly highly receptive to a society's spectrum of diversity, as policy-making success in such systems depends on winning the assent of actors outside one's immediate political affiliations. By contrast, majoritarian systems, with their absence of a unanimity requirement to pass decisions, lack the incentive structure that would motivate participants to track the interests of differently defined others, leaving such systems ill-equipped to fulfil the inclusion criterion of democracy (Lijphart 1998: 105).

Consensus might predominate in philosophical models of the ideal society and in institutional designs on how to produce justifiable policies in a context of conflict. However, it has not been embraced by all as a self-evident good. Indeed, as far back as classical Athens, the ideal had its detractors, perhaps the most famous among them being Plato, who viewed agreement among the deliberating masses as a product of rhetorical cunning. As he saw it, anyone versed enough in the art of persuasion could steer an ignorant crowd towards a particular viewpoint through group-think and words that gratify (Sharples 1994: 51–2).

Much later, in the course of the nineteenth century, J. S. Mill expressed similar reservations about consensus at a time when the expansion of political rights was opening up governing power to an ever-increasing proportion of the population. Mill believed dissenting voices would be cowed by the weight of public opinion in a system that vests political judgement in 'the people', as individuals would be tempted to blindly defer to the views of the person next to them, and to believe that 'an opinion is better if other people hold it too, and best if shared by everyone' (Moore 2014: 8). The association of consensus with the urge to follow the crowd led Mill to ultimately dismiss it as dangerous. Not only did it lead to poor judgement, it was how society could exercise despotism over free-thinking individuals (Moore 2014: 5–6).

Consensus as an anti-democratic ideal

In recent times, these historical objections have been raised with renewed vigour by agonists questioning the compatibility of consensus with democratic ideals of inclusion and equality. Agonists join hands with liberals like Mill in highlighting the threat consensus poses to the autonomy of individuals and minorities by constraining the expression of viewpoints that deviate from those receiving popular acceptance. However, while liberals have conventionally conceptualised the impediments to consensus as a matter of ethical incommensurability, agonists have held that this focus on a clash of ethical commitments leads to a rather superficial understanding of conflict and a misguided belief that conflict can be overcome under the right empirical conditions (Mouffe 2000: 8). For agonists, the attempt to manipulate the empirical world in order to make it more amenable to full inclusion and harmonious relations is a futile endeavour, because the impediments to consensus are not the lack of motivation among people to reconcile their competing visions of the good life, but more fundamentally, the semiotic reality that representations of the good life, however inclusively they may be formulated, always leave traces of exclusion that stimulate antagonism.

This refutation of consensus has been profoundly influential. It has compelled democratic theories to defend and revise themselves in full view of how they potentially impact on identities that only figured marginally in earlier thinking due to a preference for abstract theoretical analysis or an overreliance on hypothetical subjects that all too often projected the biases and oversights of the philosophers behind them. I believe this trend has taken theorisation in beneficial directions. However, I am also of the view that a wholesale rejection of consensus is incompatible with the very pluralist goals agonists and other democrats hope to advance. In what follows, I support this view with two arguments: first, that agonists have a misplaced theory of social relations that leads them to erroneously conclude consensus is *always* unattainable and its pursuit is *always* implicated in antagonism; second, that the inclusive solidarity agonists hope to achieve is actually dependent on a norm of consensus, rather than something it can dispense with.

The semiotic refutation of consensus

Agonists establishing a link between semiotics and politics typically draw on Jacques Derrida's (1976: 33–65) concept of the 'constitutive outside'. According to this concept, meaning is a factor not of any relation a signifier bears with an isolatable and stable referent, but rather, its relation to other signifiers, which similarly acquire meaning through their relation to other signifiers, and so on. This perpetual postponement of complete meaning, or *différance*, where every meaning is a meaning of a meaning, implies a quasi-exclusionary quality, as what is being represented is never fully internal to the signifier. Rather, it remains an always as yet to be realised representation.

The key move of agonists is to apply these insights beyond the realm of language – the context for which Derrida originally intended them – to account for conflict and exclusions occurring in the empirical world. Insofar as totality in signification remains unattainable, it is reasoned that ethical confluence and harmonious relations must remain unattainable. Every attempt at unity will be accompanied by exclusion, as the 'constitutive outside' tells us that such exclusions are a very precondition for the emergence of unity. In the words of Mouffe (2000: 21), '[s]ince the constitutive outside is present within the inside as its always real possibility, every identity becomes purely contingent'. Owing to this, we must, in Mouffe's view, 'abandon the very idea of a complete reabsorption of alterity into oneness and harmony'. A 'non-exclusive public sphere of rational argument where a non-coercive consensus is attained' will forever remain an impossibility for the fundamental reason that 'consensus is a *conceptual* impossibility' (Mouffe 2000: 33; original emphasis).

For agonists, the inability of discursive structures to produce final closure has two implications. First, it reveals that a consensus is a hegemony, and not an inclusive confluence of ideas divorced from the effects of power. If no instituting act is fully encompassing, and if decision occurs along 'an undecidable terrain', it follows that a consensus is simply a form of symbolic displacement and a repression of structural possibilities (Norval 2004: 143). As Aletta Norval (2004: 144) puts it, the 'fullness of community is constructed in its absence'. This incomplete fullness results from a competition between different groups 'to temporarily give to their particularism the function of a universal representation' (Laclau 1996: 35).

The second implication is that antagonism will be an unavoidable constant in social life. Insofar as all representations are hegemonic, and insofar as all identities are forged in the absence of full inclusion, it follows that conflict will be an eternal feature of societies, as people who are marginalised by prevailing hegemonies and contingent notions of community will respond with defiance. In the words of Mouffe:

> the constitutive outside allows us to tackle the conditions of emergence of antagonism . . . If collective identities can only be established on the mode of an us/them, it is clear that under certain conditions, they can always be transformed into antagonistic relations. (Mouffe 2000: 13)

The implications are that antagonism can never be eliminated, only transformed into more desirable forms. That is, it can manifest itself as a relationship between 'enemies', what Mouffe calls, 'antagonism proper', or as a relationship between 'friendly enemies', what Mouffe calls 'adversaries' (2000: 13).

However, a closer inspection of these implications reveals they are premised on a rather shaky line of justification. First, there is no reason why semiotic indeterminacy should prevent empirically constituted actors from seeing eye to eye with each other. At its most basic, a consensus is a mutually held perception of sharing something in common with another, and incomplete signifying activities can coexist side by side with such a convergence of consciousness. Indeed, it would be odd to tell a collection of people that the common standpoint at which they have arrived is false simply because systems of signs cannot yield a stable representation of the world. People agree (and disagree) on values, beliefs and preferences regardless of what assumptions a semiotic methodology might have about the stability or instability of signifying elements.

Put differently, a semiotic refutation of consensus is inadequate for the very reason that it is divorced from the lived experiences of people for whom it is accounting. A consensus conceived simply as an order of signification misses the critical interplay between the interpretive horizons of its actual authors. It relies, instead, on a dehistoricised insight into opinions that reduces them to configurations of signs. This window on the situation makes no appeal to an epistemic subject at all in order to make sense of the epistemic object. Instead, as Seyla Benhabib (1992: 209) has pointed out, the 'subject is replaced by a system of structures, oppositions and differences which, to be intelligible, need not be viewed as products of a living subjectivity at all'. Yet no theory of consensus can be complete unless it addresses knowledge from the perspective of the participants themselves (Habermas 1994: 22–5, 50). It is, after all, their underlying knowledge that brings them to see their commitments as mutually compatible and it is their understanding of what binds them together that gives rise to a consensus.

The second reason why the semiotically based implications raised by agonists are misplaced is that there is no reason why a consensus is destined to be accompanied by antagonism just because it is not universally inclusive. Even if we accept the view that a consensus is unavoidably forged as a 'we' in relation to a 'them', it does not follow that this contrastiveness will automatically produce in its wake a Schmittian friend/enemy configuration, or for that matter, even a more benign adversarial configuration involving 'friendly enemies' (Abizadeh 2005: 58). This is because people are not hell-bent on gaining inclusion into every sphere of association, and nor do they consider every act of social differentiation some kind of existential threat. People value goods differently, and for this reason, are content to be included only in those decisions that have direct bearing on the share of goods they value most or to remain members of only those communities which matter to them most.

Thus, the flaw with the agonistic line of reasoning is that it presents the relationship between exclusion and antagonism as 'before the fact', contending that the latter aprioristically follows in the wake of the former. In reality, antagonism bears no logical relation to exclusion – the relationship is in fact an empirically contingent one. Whether antagonistic relations arise in the wake of exclusion can only be ascertained on a case-by-case basis, depending on how people react in the face of social differentiation. It is not a matter that can be determined independently of observation and experience. Indeed, were a relationship of conceptual necessity to hold true, the social world would be characterised by what Jeremy Valentine (2001: 90) describes as a 'complete and irreparable randomization of everything'. Insofar as individuation itself is based on exclusion and social differentiation, antagonism would have to define every social interaction, right down to the level of individuals, leaving no grounds for human relations to emerge, and no basis for collective agency and cooperation, only anomie and atomisation.

The agonistic dependence on consensus

We have noted that the agonistic position is defined by its rejection of consensus, at both a conceptual and a normative level. However, the force of these objections is undermined by the observation that agonists actually depend on, rather than dispense with, consensus to promote their idealisations of an inclusive society. This dependence is evident in two ways.

First, agonists introduce caveats to qualify their opposition to consensus. Despite railing against consensus, agonists accept its possibility and express sympathy for it in various understated ways. Consensus retains its place within agonistic theory because it plays an indispensable circumscribing function on diversity, ensuring diversity remains consistent with the goals of community and avoids descending into an 'anything goes' relativism (Dryzek and Niemeyer 2006: 637). Thus, Mouffe (2000: 55) asserts that a layer of 'commonality' is necessary to bind together the radically plural polity she envisages. The nature of this commonality is left undefined. But whatever its basis, it is at odds with Mouffe's core contention that antagonism is 'inerradicable' (104). She also argues for 'some common ground' and 'a shared adhesion to the ethico-political principles of liberal democracy: liberty and equality' (102). Yet these principles bear an uncanny resemblance to the very procedural principles she objects to in Habermas' model of deliberation, which on her account, self-servingly 'eliminate those positions which cannot be agreed to by participants' (86).[1] The tenor of this vocabulary is not merely descriptive. It is also normative. Mouffe is not only *describing* sites of consensus, she *wants* consensus to materialise and sees it as having a certain value.

In a second, less direct sense, agonists depend on consensus for the attainment of the inclusive solidarity they envisage. Andrew Schaap (2004: 524, 538) has summed up agonistic solidarity as the inauguration of 'civic friendship', whereby 'enmity' is transformed into an 'integrative and ethical' relationship, and a 'shared horizon' emerges on the basis of 'shared understanding'. This specification of solidarity does not necessarily imply the *attainment* of a consensus, as it is possible for parties to express the civic friendship necessary for an integrative relationship without sharing the same views on a matter. Such a relationship would emerge through mutual acceptance of the other's position as legitimate despite its incompatibility with one's own position (see below). Nevertheless, the objective of moving from enmity towards this desired endpoint does imply an *orientation* of consensus, as parties must enter their encounters with a preparedness to accept something valid about each other. Where this readiness to be persuaded by the other is missing, there is little hope for the kind of inclusive and open-ended solidarity desired by agonists. Parties will not be searching for a shared horizon, they will not be seeking any insight into each other's positions, and nor will there be, in Patchen Markell's (1997: 390) words, a 'foreswearing of the mechanisms of coercion'. Instead, desired outcomes will be pursued strategically, whereby the intent to win and advance one's own objectives will predominate over the intent to learn and question one's objectives from the standpoint of the other.

Consensus as a matter of degree

I have argued up to this point that a conceptualisation that reduces consensus to systems of signs is inadequate due to its detachment from human experience. I have also argued that a characterisation of human relations as always adversarial is too sweeping, for it fails to account for the empirical reality that humans agree and cooperate, and not only quarrel and struggle. In what follows, I will respond to these conceptual shortcomings by providing a counter-theory of consensus rooted in empirical practice and social psychology. The aim is to show there are degrees of consensus, and that it is not an unattainable absolute whose pursuit is simply implicated in coercion. Understanding human relations in this way allows us to appreciate the subtle and beneficial ways a norm of consensus can inform democratic practice even where the complete attainment of consensus appears remote. It also helps us appreciate how falling back on an antagonistic model of democracy as a response to deep difference is drawing the institutional possibilities too narrowly. Just because *absolute* reconciliation is an empty hope does not mean movement towards reconciliation will be an empty hope or, indeed, that aspiring towards reconciliation has no normative merit.

To develop these arguments, it is instructive to move along the tracks laid out by Dryzek and Niemeyer's (2006) typology of consensus. The refined portrait of consensus this paints serves as an ideal starting point from which to further build on a theoretical answer around the possibilities of consensus and the normative benefits of its pursuit.

Dryzek and Niemeyer (2006: 638) distinguish between, on the one hand, qualities that a consensus can take and, on the other hand, levels at which consensus can attain. On matters of quality, a consensus can take the form of a normative, epistemic or preference agreement. A *normative* consensus refers to agreements over values; *epistemic* consensus to agreements over the validity of the systems of knowledge relied on to make sense of the world (e.g., competing scientific paradigms, or more fundamentally, competing scientific and non-scientific paradigms); and *preference* consensus refers to agreements over what should be done (e.g., competing policy options).

On matters of level, a consensus can be present at the 'simple' level as a substantive agreement or at the 'meta' level as a thinner agreement over the legitimacy of positions that are in dispute. Thus, the foregoing taxonomy of consensus operates at the 'simple' level, as reference is made to a convergence of positions over values, belief systems or preferences. By contrast, the corresponding meta counterparts would have no convergence at this simple level. Instead, parties would perceive their positions to be in a zero-sum relationship, but would nevertheless be in mutual agreement that their disputed positions can rightfully form the basis of politics. In these terms: a *normative* meta-consensus would mean parties are holding divergent values but agreeing over the legitimacy of each other's values; an *epistemic* meta-consensus would mean parties are holding divergent worldviews but accepting the reasonableness of their disputed worldviews; and a *preference* meta-consensus would mean parties are diverging on what is the most appropriate way to act, but nevertheless accepting the range of disputed alternatives for action as being appropriate (Dryzek and Niemeyer 2006: 639–41).

The upshot of this typology is that any meaningful reference to consensus does not have to assume the discovery of agreement along all plains of social life. Instead of being an all or nothing phenomenon, consensus is available on a sliding scale of comprehensiveness, varying in scope and level across issue-domains and across actors with different kinds of stakes in different kinds of issues. Through this reconceptualisation, it becomes apparent that actors can approach a given policy issue with profoundly different values, but converge on the preferences they hold on how to act collectively. For example, Catholics value the traditional heterosexual family constituted by a gendered division of domestic labour, while radical feminists fiercely reject this ideal as the source of women's subordination. Nevertheless, both support bans or restrictions on pornography, seeing this policy option as supportive of their particular values.

Alternatively, we can appreciate that actors might approach a policy issue with the same values, but diverge profoundly on the desired choice of action. For example, classical Marxists and social democrats have overlapping egalitarian principles of justice focused on need. Nevertheless, a bitter rift has historically separated each camp based on their irreconcilable preferences for the realisation of their egalitarianism. Marxists have felt equality is best realised through the abolishment of the capitalist system that is deemed the source of labourers' exploitation, while social democrats believe equality is best served by renovating the capitalist system through distributive programmes and the expansion of worker's rights to give the system a more human face. In these examples, there is no universal consensus. But there is a consensus nevertheless, as agreement exists on some, though not all, aspects of these actors' identities.

The same point applies on matters of level. Where deep and impassioned conflicts divide populations, it may be an exercise in futility to search for consensus at the simple level, but not at the meta-level. Indeed, a meta-level consensus forms the basis of compromises, which are a ubiquitous form of conflict resolution and find expression in all spheres of human life: interethnic peace accords, international trade agreements, industrial relations agreements, commercial contracts, property settlements, native title acts, divorce settlements, are all relevant examples. On the face of it, a compromise seems like a simple level consensus over preferences in the sense of parties agreeing over what should be done. However, in actual fact, a compromise is a meta-consensus, as parties continue to have dissonant claims about what should be done, and have only come to agreement over how to manage those claims (Dryzek and Niemeyer 2006: 642). As Jones and O'Flynn (2013: 117, 128) point out, 'compromise entails regret', because 'each party makes concessions that he would prefer not to make', but makes nonetheless because such concessions are deemed a price worth paying in order to secure a resolution to the conflict. And yet, even though parties in a compromise retain, rather than dissolve, their conflicting claims, their relationship is defined by an element of consensus that was not present prior to their deliberations: in the course of argumentative exchange, parties have converged towards a mutually acceptable solution for the management of their disputed claims (meta-consensus) when such claims were previously an impediment to a cooperative relationship (meta-dissensus).

A meta-consensus is a less onerous objective. In comparison to a simple consensus, 'it makes fewer demands on partisans to compromise their first-order values, beliefs and preferences' (Dryzek and Niemeyer 2006: 642). This explains the greater frequency of its discovery, and why, as Dryzek and Niemeyer have argued, it is the less coercively fraught, and therefore normatively more favourable, mode of conflict resolution.

However, while the maintenance of modest conciliatory ambitions can guard against conformist zeal, this does not rule out the possibility or desirability of a simple level consensus. Reconciliation is not forever stuck at the meta-level: deep differences do dissolve at the substantive level of relationships. What is more, they do so in the absence of policing behaviour associated with assimilatory designs. To appreciate the legitimate place of these transformations in a normative theory of conflict resolution and to grasp how they are not necessarily bound up with unjust conformity pressures, we can build on the foregoing typology to incorporate an additional dimension of consensus, namely, that of consciousness.

Consciousness: active and passive consensus

A consensus can be an active or a passive agreement in the sense of people's awareness of the complementarities they have come to share and the roundness of the disclosure of those complementarities. An *active consensus* is the more familiar understanding of the two, and derives from what Alistair Johnston (2008: 25) would describe as an 'active assessment of the content of a particular message'. The changing of minds, opinions and attitudes towards convergence is a 'high intensity process of cognition, reflection and argument about the content of new information' (156). People come to agreement because they have systematically weighed evidence, puzzled through counterarguments, and as a consequence, been led to conclusions different to those with which they began. An active consensus is typically generated through a short timeframe of contact and high intensity of interaction. This interaction produces a strong sense of awareness that movement towards a shared position is taking place, and typically culminates with an explicit disclosure of the positive content of that shared position (either to oneself or externally).

By contrast, in a *passive consensus*, parties have non-reflectively undergone transformations towards convergence. Rather than being induced by deliberative flashes that trigger a sudden realisation that one was mistaken all along about one's deepest commitments, agreement arises through a low intensity process of cognition and assessment over values, beliefs or preferences. People drift towards a new interpretation of themselves and a rival, with the imagined disjuncture between them closing through an authorless process of identity change. This mode of reconciliation typically ensues over a prolonged period (often intergenerationally), and does not necessarily culminate with parties disclosing to one another or themselves what is held in common as distinct from what was formerly held apart. Rather, parties simply 'move on', either assigning diminishing weight to their disputed commitments, or where those commitments continue to be held as first-order, they have been reconstituted such that they are no longer perceived as diametrically oppositional.

The analytical distinction between a passive and active consensus can be further highlighted through a compact reformulation of the insights on conformity present in the social psychology literature (Checkel 2005: 811; Johnston 2008: 25): whereas an active consensus involves public conformity *with* conscious acceptance, a passive consensus involves public conformity *without* conscious acceptance. In the latter, agreement has a taken-for-granted quality, present as a non-calculative adherence to a common position, rather than resulting from any conscious act of persuasion. If individuals were invited to explain how they came to hold a position that is shared by an out-group, they would, upon reflection, respond by saying: 'I cannot identify a specific moment or reason. It's simply how things have come to be between us.'

This does not mean that a passive consensus is devoid of causal properties and represents only a coming together of random events we have no influence over. On the contrary, a social context can be nurtured that is conducive to its attainment, through, for example, the introduction of institutions that encourage the patterning of cooperative behaviour or the prevalence of discourses that break down prejudicial attitudes. However, relative to an active consensus, the actor transformations brought about by such interventions will be less consciously perceived.

While an active consensus implies a direct form of communication encompassing claim-making and reason-giving, a passive consensus implies communication that is indirect, but by no means less powerful in its transformative impact. One way of understanding the nature of this communication is through socialising experiences, whereby the exposure to discourses present in schools, the mass media, work, the family and friendship circles, among other formative environments, can subtly alter perceptions of values, beliefs and preferences towards convergence. It can also be understood from the complementary perspective of the public sphere. In this social space between individuals and the state, communication is subjectless and decentred, mediated among people dispersed in space and time (Young 2000: 167). Yet, despite its amorphous nature, this communication still leads to the consolidation of opinions, with these opinions being politically consequential to the point of having a bearing on policy making within the state. The opinion-formation that takes place through such deliberations is characteristic of a passive consensus whenever the convergent actor transformations underlying the process are not immediately apparent to those undergoing them.

Examples of active consensus

Some empirical examples will help to illustrate these points. Deliberative microcosms, such as deliberative polls and citizens' juries, are sites of preference convergence that embody an active consensus at both the meta and simple levels. These face-to-face deliberative arenas are cognition-rich settings, as participants receive carefully balanced information laying out the main policy options and the arguments for and against each, discussions are facilitated by trained moderators, and participants have the opportunity to ask competing partisans and policy experts questions (Fishkin and Luskin 2000: 19–20). When deliberative microcosms generate increased agreement, it represents an increase in active consensus at the simple level, as parties have come to support a course of action on which they previously had differing views through a process of reflective assent and after having thought long and hard about the implications of their own views.

An increase in simple level consensus is not the only notable form of reconciliation generated by deliberative microcosms. An increase in meta level consensus is also commonplace, for even when parties do not agree on proposals that have been subject to rigorous deliberation, they can come to accept the legitimacy of a wider sweep of proposals after gaining a more considered insight into why someone would support proposals different to their own. This increase in meta-consensus is also of the active kind, as shifts in attitudes are, once again, the result of systematic consideration and discussion of differing opinions, and parties are aware of the positive shift in attitude they have undergone, given that opinion changes are quantified and announced at the end of proceedings.

Such actor transformations have been documented in numerous deliberative microcosms covering a diverse range of policy issues. However, for the purposes of illustration, they can be noted here through a deliberative poll that was held in Omagh, Northern Ireland in 2007, which put to debate the deeply controversial issue of religious mixing in schools between Protestants and Catholics (Fishkin 2009; Luskin et al. 2014). Despite being limited to a single long day of deliberation, the poll demonstrated dramatically altered perceptions among the participants that were emblematic of an increase in active consensus. At the simple level, these shifts included a statistically significant rise in openness to change away from completely separate schooling systems and an openness to policies enabling partnering between neighbouring schools of a different religious composition for the delivery of new curricular standards. At the meta level, these shifts included a statistically significant rise in the proportion of each community's belief that the other is 'open to reason' and 'trustworthy' (Fishkin 2009: 167). In general, a greater percentage of participants came to believe they shared an interest in cooperating across religious lines in the cluster of policy matters that was put to deliberation.

An unlikely exemplar of active consensus at the simple level is peace negotiations to end political violence between states and their populations. Such negotiations follow a two-track structure, whereby a normative consensus must be established in the first track before second track negotiations can proceed to flesh out the finer details of a compromise agreement. The normative consensus entails an abstract principle of justice that belligerents jointly develop to denote what they expect from a fair outcome and is supposed to guide the give and take of positions in the course of negotiations so that parties avoid running afoul from their mutually shared idea of a fair outcome. The establishment of such a principle is integral to the success of peace negotiations, so much so that negotiations founder when parties fail to reach a mutually acceptable articulation of the principle (Zartman 2008: 68). Importantly, while the eventual peace agreement is a meta-consensus, the justice principle preceding it is a simple consensus: in the peace agreement, parties are agreeing over how to manage disputed assertions over practical arrangements, with this compromise agreement emerging through a degree of political horse-trading; in the justice principle, parties actually adhere to, rather than dispute, the values that should drive the negotiation process, with this adherence being 'not simply a matter of [compulsory] power, but of each side's calculations of acceptability' (Zartman 2008: 69). That is, it is reflective of the exchange of reasoned arguments constitutive of deliberative communication.

Thus, while successful negotiations more obviously produce an active meta-consensus over preferences (the actual peace agreement), they also produce an active consensus over values (the shared principle of justice) in order to guide negotiators to a shared endpoint. The normative agreement is an active, rather than passive, consensus because parties have come to jointly delineate the normative structure of their interaction through a process of assessment: that is, they have reflectively internalised a new understanding of what is a legitimate position to bargain over, what is off limits, and what is beyond the pale (Johnston 2008: 16).

This free-flow of arguments and openness to persuasion is uncanny for an environment typically associated with bargaining behaviour. However, it can be explained by the relative detachment of communications from the final decision moment of the peace talks as outlined in Chapter 5. That is, while preliminary negotiations do not directly determine the nature of the peace accord, the negotiations that follow do, making them what John Dryzek (2005: 229), following Archon Fung, would term 'hot' deliberative settings. In this higher-stakes environment, negotiators will be less open to reflection and changing their mind, given the high consequentiality of doing so. By contrast, the lower consequentiality of the preliminary negotiations takes the heat out of communications, freeing up negotiators to deliberate, and not simply bargain, their way to a common position.

Examples of passive consensus

Examples that illustrate a passive consensus at the simple level would include Arend Lijphart's (1969) archetypal consociations, the Netherlands, Austria, Switzerland and Belgium. Formerly, these societies were deeply divided along sectarian and class lines, with rival communities perceiving their identities to be profoundly incompatible and tolerable only through the maintenance of partitioned social institutions that sustained a parallel social existence. This system of voluntary social partition was known as pillarisation, and involved segmented and homogenous education systems, newspapers, broadcasting, trade unions, hospitals and leisure associations, all differentiated on the basis of membership in Catholic and Protestant faiths, or middle- and working-class communities. During this period of strongly pillarised self-perceptions, each society was held together by a meta-consensus consisting in political elites accepting the membership of each other's communities in the polity and committing themselves to across-pillar cooperation despite the deep antipathies that existed at the grass roots level. This elite-level cooperation became the basis of Lijphart's theory of consociational democracy.

However, beginning in the 1960s, these societies underwent a process of 'depillarisation' that led to the virtual (but not complete) disappearance of pillars within three decades (Dekker and Ester 1996: 326). In this period, the number of people with pillarised ideological and confessional self-perceptions significantly declined, with behavioural correlates such as party preference or associational membership being less obviously determined by membership in traditional communities and increasingly shaped by a growing heterogeneity of alternative cultural and ideological influences (Dekker and Ester 1996: 338–9). This transformation embodies a shift towards consensus at the simple level, as formerly divided communities began to perceive themselves as no longer embodying values and ways of life that were fundamentally at odds (increase in normative consensus), and, consequently, they began to no longer consider it imperative to wall themselves off from each other in every sphere of social life (increase in preference consensus). As Dekker and Ester (1996: 332) put it in the context of the Netherlands: 'Religious faith lives on, but its institutional pillarized consequences are rejected.' What is more, this transformation embodies a *passive* consensus, as the redefinition of identities in mutually compatible terms has occurred gradually and non-consciously, rather than through intentional action and active assessment.

Explanations for the causes of this dramatic social transformation are many and varied. Arend Lijphart has focused on the role of elites, contending their inter-pillar cooperation spilled over to the rest of society, proliferating 'cross-cutting cleavages' among ordinary citizens. Others have analysed the transformations through the broader lens of macro-processes, looking at the role of economic growth, technological change, rationalisation, urbanisation and increased mobility in exposing people to competing religious and ideological meaning systems. This functioned to break down the monopoly pillars possessed to socialise populations and narrowly shape identities (Dekker and Ester 1996: 330–1).

While multiple (though not necessarily competing) causal stories are advanced, they all highlight the non-calculative nature of reconciliation in these former consociations. The positive stimulation of perceptions of complementarity and the reduction in conflictual behaviour along plains of collective identification that formerly divided populations has occurred over a long and sustained period, lacking any immediate goal-directedness or purposive action. It has, moreover, unfolded in the absence of any plan between pillars to undertake the task of rearticulating their positions towards complementarity, even though this was the eventual outcome.

The EU offers another illustration of how a consensus can be passive in nature. Prior to the EU's inception shortly after the Second World War, the European territory was the site of intense interstate rivalries that periodically erupted into devastating wars. The defining impact of EU integration was to tame these rivalries, but also, to diminish the extent to which forms of authority below, above and across the nation-state were interpreted as predatory to each other. As Michael Keating (2004) has pointed out, conceptions of political authority and public action in Europe have undergone transformations towards 'post-sovereignty'. This does not mean that sovereignty has lost meaning, but rather, that it has undergone a shift in its meaning so that 'it is no longer monopolized by the state but becomes a claim to original authority, which can be advanced by various actors and institutions and is intrinsically divisible' (Keating 2004: 369).

Related back to the foregoing schema of consensus, postsovereignty embodies an epistemic consensus at the simple level, as it involves a convergence of beliefs over the impact of different assertions of sovereignty: whereas previously nationalists held a realist assumption that competition and the accrual of exclusive state sovereignty would further national interests, they have since come around to the Europeanist understanding that cooperation and the transferral of state sovereignty at the sub- and supranational level better advances national interests, and can do so to the overall benefit of all involved. Importantly, this convergence of belief has had consequences at the preference level, stimulating consensus on policy choices on the back of a shared faith in the potential for cooperation to advance everyone's interests better than competition.

This shift away from intractability towards mutual encompassment in perceptions of sovereignty can be illustrated at the various levels of institutionalised politics in the EU. Perhaps the most striking illustration at the level of the state is found in the dramatically altered relations between France and Germany. Prior to the Second World War, France and Germany were deemed 'hereditary enemies' who 'would never escape the security dilemma of two competing, neighbouring powers' (Diez et al. 2008: 4). Today, collaboration is perceived by these historical foes to advance national interests far better than rivalry, with each state perceiving the other to share political values common to its own. This was famously symbolised through French President Jacques Chirac's representation of Germany in the European Council in 2003 (Diez et al. 2008: 5).

At the regional or sub-state level, assertions of collective will were formerly considered a threat to the state's existence, and therefore best met with state suppression. Today, these identities have increasingly come to be perceived as complementary to the state, even though integration has weakened the authority of the state relative to the regions. This complementarity is evident through the growing trend of dual identification (for example, Catalan-Spanish) when formerly citizens felt impelled to choose between their regional or state identity (I am Catalan because I am not Spanish) (Guibernau 2007: 50–7). It is also evident in the trend towards devolution, whereby states increasingly accept assertions of political autonomy at the sub-state level (Guibernau 2007: 47–57), or in the opposite direction, the trend away from independence claims at the sub-state level, whereby minority nations increasingly seek to realise their aspirations for self-determination through asymmetrical federalism or insertion into 'Europe' (Keating 2004: 369–70).

At the supranational level, nationalists initially feared that a deepening of EU institutions would take away from the ability of states to self-govern and nations to be culturally distinct. Today, EU membership is regarded as constitutive of these and other national objectives among a broader section of the population, both inside the EU and outside it among those countries wishing to join (Vachudova 2014). For example, member and aspiring member states refer to the 'pooling' or 'sharing' of sovereignty, rather than its 'loss', in their characterisation of the transferral of authority to EU institutions. Furthermore, decades of EU integration has seen the rise of dual attachments, whereby citizens think of themselves as simultaneously national and European, rather than simply one or the other (Fligstein 2008: 250).

All this is not to suggest that the EU embodies a universal consensus. It clearly does not. Vocal Eurosceptics stand opposed to further integration and enlargement, and member states do not simply cooperate, but also pursue their interests as self-seeking competitors within the EU's intergovernmental institutions, sometimes quarrelling bitterly over critical policy issues.

Nevertheless, the EU has been more than an arena where conflicts are simply managed. It is also where conflicts have been dissolved, with sub-national, national and supranational actors coming to share common beliefs on the impact of European integration and, consequently, common policies in a range of domains that were previously sites of intense rivalry. Importantly, the epistemic consensus that has underpinned, but also been generated by, EU integration is *passive* in character. No decisive moment of deliberation to test and clarify cause and effect relations between the different assertions of sovereignty marks this epistemic convergence. Rather, it emerged gradually and non-reflectively in the course of expanding multi-level government, with historical experience revealing that this alternative paradigm of authority permitted, as opposed to took away from, economic development, cultural distinctiveness and geopolitical influence, among other traditionally defined national interests.

Passive consensus or non-conscious subjugation?

One objection to the concept of a passive consensus – particularly from agonistic quarters – might be that far from embodying the autonomy of action and thought one would expect from genuinely consenting parties, it resembles the subjugation and illusion of free will present in a Gramscian hegemony or Foucauldian disciplinary regime. After all, if people are not consciously reflecting on the norms they are internalising, then collective resonance towards a particular view is being attained through acquiescence that is subtle in nature and dominative in effect: that is to say, people are converging towards a particular form of consciousness because of the difficulty or impossibility in translating 'the outlook implicit in their experience into a conception of the world that will directly challenge the hegemonic culture' (Lears 1985: 569). Importantly, the constraints on agency imposed by the selective vocabulary within which people must think and act remain hidden from view, allowing a historically dominant segment of the population to claim with at least some plausibility its particular interests are those of society (Lears 1985: 571).

This objection maps onto an old ontological debate in social theory about the relation between action and the social structures that govern it. I do not wish to go into this debate in any detail other than to point to the one-sidedness of any account of human action that sees it as simply being eclipsed by the constraints of norms. While semantic rules are constraining in the sense that they oblige a speaker to adopt certain linguistic and grammatical forms, and while moral rules are constraining in the sense that they are associated with internal and external sanctions (Thompson 1994: 72), people can and do use their capacities to limit and reshape these constraints (Love 1989: 293). To the extent that this is so, the power of norms is not merely negative in the sense of subjugating and disciplining; it is also affirmative, in the sense of being implicated in the most radical processes of social change and self-creation (Love 1989: 291–3; Thompson 1994: 72).

Indeed, the possibility of independence from, and the ability to transform, social structures is entertained by the very theorists who have denied it. Norval (2004: 148), for example, argues 'there is no possibility of choice arising at all, for the nature of the philosophical enterprise is such that alternative possibilities are foreclosed and, as a consequence, are not visible as alternatives'. Under such circumstances, the best we can hope for is that deconstruction makes 'visible possibilities ruled out and not taken up' (148). However, such a conclusion actually assumes a possibility of choice, for the ability to be aware of what has been ruled out and not taken up implies an autonomy of thought that transcends the structural terrain on which one walks. Such transcendence is, after all, what is involved in the reflexive activity of deconstruction. Without it, there would be no thinking author capable of theoretical reflection, only a self who is, to use Benhabib's (1992: 216) apt metaphor, 'a ventriloquist for discourses operating through her or "mobilising" her'.

This insight provides a foundation for responding to the objection that a passive consensus is merely domination under camouflage. Non-conscious conformity does not mean non-conscious domination. It all depends on how this conformity is generated. Non-conscious conformity attained through the manipulation of socialisation processes and public sphere deliberations so that people are thwarted from gaining exposure to the full scope of views, beliefs and preferences relevant to their situation constitutes the type of ideological ruse associated with subjugation and hegemony. This is because a positive attitudinal conversion towards a particular position is being generated through the deceptive suppression of information that might encourage an alternative path of collective consciousness to arise.

Relevant examples would include citizenship education that discourages critical thought and promotes unreflective patriotism by glorifying past history and the current political system, while vilifying opponents of that history and system (Kymlicka 2001: 310); a captured media and accompanying information monopolies that lead to the circulation of historical myths and generate popular resonance towards a distorted image of the nation (Lake and Rothchild 1996: 54; Snyder and Ballentine 1996: 17–20); the withdrawal from education of children and women at an early age or the establishment of exclusive schooling systems by certain religious groups to suppress the development of a critical attitude towards inherited traditions and prevent exposure to alternative ways of life they might find attractive (Kymlicka 2001: 307); and the presence of protocols of style and decorum in public life that reproduce status inequalities and exclude the perspectives of subordinated groups (Fraser 1993). In all these situations, formative environments and the public sphere are captured by established and dominant identities, coercing people towards their narrow point of view. As such, one could rightly question the authenticity of any resultant consensus – passive or otherwise – that might be claimed.

By contrast, where a non-conscious conversion towards a common point arises against a formative and discursive backdrop that is open to the norms and actions of the multiplicity of groups present in society and embodies a critical attitude towards the standards underpinning the existing social order, then this conversion is emblematic of a passive consensus, and cannot simply be reduced to subjugation. While selfhood is being constructed non-reflectively, congeniality behind particular values and preferences, and resonance with particular interpretations of the world is being guided by a background discourse that creates clarity around the availability of social alternatives, permits freedom to take up these alternatives, and uncovers the contingency of all cultural standards informing people's desires. This discourse still determines what form of consciousness will be possible, and to this extent is not constraint free. But even so, it cannot be said to be merely dominative, as no single group's interests are being served by it at the expense of another subordinate group's, and there is no manipulative refashioning of this discourse to make some forms of experience readily available to consciousness at the expense of others (Lears 1985: 577). Institutional environments reflective of such non-coerciveness in the attainment of conformity would include public spheres that are welcoming of counter-discourses, particularly those discourses representing the identities, interests and needs of subordinated social groups (Fraser 1993: 14). They would also include contexts of socialisation that generate collective selfhood through broadmindedness, rather than vigilance, towards that which is strange, foreign or even obnoxious (Kymlicka 2001: 296).

Justifications for a norm of consensus

Having argued against an exclusive focus on absolute consensus as a measure of possibility, and having noted how a consensus can be available in varying quantities and qualities, several justifications can be stated explicitly in its defence.

As a starting point, it can be stressed that supporting a norm of consensus does not entail insisting on or enforcing the complete resolution of a conflict. As should be clear by now, such a heavy-handed application of the norm is neither feasible nor desirable. The imposition of an expectation that political communication *must* end in unanimous and absolute agreement introduces social pressures and sanctions that inhibit the free expression of opinions when they deviate from the prevailing point of view. While certain models of democracy, such as those influenced by republican tenets, maintain expectations of unanimity approaching this level of stringency, they represent merely one way among many that a norm of consensus can be incorporated into a dialogic forum. A consensually oriented democracy that was serious about showing deference to the expression of diversity would hold a much looser expectation of what argumentative dialogue should yield. The goal of unanimity would not trump the forum's constituent opinions. Rather, participants would be permitted, even encouraged, to conclude their deliberations without unanimous agreement where their exchanges revealed irreconcilable differences, and where their exchanges did not produce the transformations in values, beliefs or preferences necessary for those differences to be overcome (simple consensus) or even mutually accommodated through a compromise (meta-consensus).

Understood in this way, a norm of consensus signals a less demanding expectation that participants enter a political forum with a commitment to take each other's viewpoints seriously and reach an agreement, even where their preconceptions tell them they are unlikely to overcome their differences. However, where such encounters fail to achieve agreement because participants had good grounds to continue opposing each other, they would be free to leave the issue unresolved, deferring the search for a resolution for the time being, but anticipating a moment in the future when the dialogue can once again be reopened.

This non-compulsory formulation of consensus strikes an appropriate balance between, on the one hand, the freedom to hold firm convictions on one's own position when convinced of its merits, and on the other, the need for open-mindedness so that movement towards mutually acceptable positions becomes conceivable in a democracy. Both of these polar outcomes are possibilities when seeking agreement, given that a process of reflection does not automatically generate a convergence of positions, but can also reveal one has even stronger grounds for rejecting another's viewpoints. A norm of consensus understood as a disposition to seek (as opposed to compulsorily attain) outcomes acceptable to all sides leaves space for both, for it does not force people to compromise their convictions solely in the interest of agreement, but it does compel people to reflect on their convictions to determine the possibility of points of convergence with those of others (Gutmann and Thompson 1996: 84–5).

But why aim for consensus at all? We have noted that many conflicts are intractable to the point where they cannot be resolved without parties conceding something that is definitive of who they are. What justifies the search for common ground under such conditions? Would not the vitality of a democracy be better ensured by encouraging citizens to encounter one another as adversaries, unconstrained in their political endeavours by an expectation (non-obligatory or otherwise) that they aspire towards a common end-point that is for all intents and purposes elusive?

The answer is that societies have nowhere else to turn but to a norm of consensus if they wish to understand themselves as *communal* and *cooperative* enterprises. When problem-solving needs arise that are communal in nature, the processes of diagnosis and prescription at the centre of these needs rely on the pursuit of consensus in order to remain genuinely communal. At the level of diagnosis, collective consciousness of a problem implies some level of public acceptance of a particular interpretation of what is at fault or what is an issue. As Daniel Bray (2011: 161) points out through John Dewey's pragmatist insights, where there is no agreement on the existence or nature of a problem, there will be no shared consciousness of a problem-solving need, and no impetus for the appearance of a problem-solving public. The same point applies at the level of prescription, as authority around the most appropriate course of action implies a process of seeking its acceptance to those who must bear its consequences. In the words of Gerald Gaus, when '*something must be done* . . . we do not just want to do anything, but that which is best justified' (1997: 233; original emphasis).[2] Were there no sense of responsibility to justify the claims one is pressing on co-members, the 'jointness' is removed from problem solving. It becomes, instead, a solitary pursuit and authoritarian exercise of simply handing down private judgements and executing accompanying policies others must obey.

To uphold a norm of consensus is not to imply all political action must be governed by it. As I have articulated throughout this book, it can be legitimate to behave as an agonist under conditions of subordination, as disorderliness and civil disobedience may be the only way of nurturing the social changes that allow one to be treated as free and equal. Disruption calls to attention the unreasonableness of others (Young 2000: 49) and can make it politically costly for them to continue excluding from politics those with a stake in issues being debated. In this sense, the refusal to cooperate is a contribution to democracy, not least, because it can function as a motivational basis for inclusive political communication and decision making when inequalities in power leave some in a structurally privileged position to ignore the interests and opinions of others.

By the same token, while disruptive and offensive behaviour is not immediately associated with the search for consensus, its ultimate aim is still to achieve the conditions that make consensus more likely. After all, those who engage in civil disobedience to overcome their political exclusion do so with the aim of engaging others in a project of explaining and justifying their positions: in other words, their ultimate aim is to kick-start a process of persuasion (Young 2000: 50). To the extent that this is so, both agonistic and consensually oriented politics come to the service of democracy. Yet, agonistic politics is not justified for its own sake, but for the sake of enabling a conversation that has the potential to lead to some level of agreement.

Understood in these terms, a norm of consensus has several advantages over the non-teleological and adversarial mode of politics advocated by agonists. These advantages can be summarised as follows.

First, a norm of consensus is consistent with the just treatment of others. The process of reason giving to reach a joint decision embodies a reflexiveness that is at the heart of what it means to be attentive to others. By anticipating agreement, even if it is never attained, people weigh up each other's views and open themselves up to the possibility that a claim made by someone else has merit (Kingwell 1995: 47–8). Crucially, they are prepared to adjust their initial position in acknowledgement of this. This readiness to exercise curbs on one's preferences is important for anyone serious about justice, as the enjoyment of many shared goods will be zero-sum. Where the realisation of one's preferences takes away from the realisation of another's, justice presumes the mindset of self-limitation that goes with the search for solutions acceptable to all. People predisposed in this manner enter an encounter neither fully convinced of the rightness of their own positions nor determined to pursue their objectives unfettered by the concerns of those with whom they stand in relationships of interdependence. They are instead prepared to temper their desires when it becomes apparent that someone is harmed by them or has legitimate reasons to object to their position.

While agonists are at one with deliberative democrats in their wish to nurture an open, egalitarian and respectful society, it is difficult to see how these objectives can be met under their framework. The agonistic rejection of constraints on political action as illegitimate curbs on freedom implies an ideal citizen with a rigidity of disposition and a non-reflexive sense of entitlement. If constraint is always coercion, there can be no good reason for holding back on one's preferences. Any inhibitions on their expression can only amount to dominative force.

Aspirations towards boundless freedom may be desirable in an imagined other-worldly realm unburdened by scarcities in resources and incompatibilities in values. However, it is a moral liability when adopted as an aspiration in the earthly realm of society, where the exercise of political choice runs up against obstacles at every turn. Here, 'the benefits of one good may militate against the satisfaction of another, or limited resources mean more social support for some goods is less for others' (Bellamy 1999: 5). Under such conditions of finitude and value pluralism, expectations of untrammelled agency pave the way for the powerful to trammel the weak. Conflicts are left to be settled through a contest of countervailing wills, as human interaction is to avoid being obstructed by the check of dialogic norms, which can only amount to a hegemonic imposition. However well intended, the combative ideal of the agonistic citizen cannot plausibly protect the most vulnerable from the whims of the most powerful when it becomes the default position of politics. An ethos of self-restraint, for all its inhibitive drawbacks, appears the more promising route for establishing an open and accepting society, as it is how, in Mark Kingwell's (1995: 218) words, we rise above our own 'likes and dislikes, and come to consider those of others'.

A second justification for a norm of consensus is that the resolution of a conflict can be more advantageous to adversaries than its continuation. Indeed, the benefits of conflict resolution tend to go unnoticed by agonists, who characterise it simply as a matter of losing rather than gaining something. However, in reality, this pessimistic account is too sweeping, for adversaries can be better served by striving to make their peace with each other, even when this requires making concessions.

Take the practice of compromise. As we have noted, a compromise is a joint decision based on unmet realisations, as parties are giving ground to forge an agreement (meta-consensus) rather than embracing the agreement as the intrinsically best course of action (simple level consensus). And yet, even though parties are failing to meet their claims in full, and are instead making concessions they would ideally avoid, they nevertheless see it in their best interests to continue tying their own hands, as doing so is anticipated to bring some future gratification or at least avert a current deprivation (typically, by overcoming a mutually hurting stalemate). Indeed, were the total value of agreeing not perceived to be positive, there would be no motive for adversaries to search for, and come to, any agreement (Zartman 2008: 17–18, 37).

Finally, a norm of consensus opens up the political terrain to social learning. Social learning refers to the educative impact of deliberative interaction, whereby interlocutors learn something new as a result of placing themselves in each other's shoes and reflecting on each other's situations (Kanra 2005: 516–20). A benefit of social learning is that it allows compromises to be forged on the back of mutual understanding and an economy of disagreement where goals are not shared (Gutmann and Thompson 1996: 84–5). Through the process of ideal role-taking, participants come to understand the reasons for an opponent's position, and even respect those reasons, without necessarily agreeing with them (Warren 2002: 184). They also minimise the extent of disagreement by clarifying what is commonly shared and not simply what is commonly rejected.

Social learning is tied to a norm of consensus, as ideal role taking implies entering an encounter with the conviction to discover something acceptable about one's adversary. Indeed, social learning and its beneficial side-effects cannot emerge where behaviour is merely goal-oriented, as parties would not be seeking any insight into each other's positions, or at least not seeking it beyond any tactical advantage it brings. Under purely strategic behaviour, identity shifts can still be expected (Warren 2007: 284). But they would less reliably be of the relationship-building kind, as parties are not removing themselves from their own prejudices and pre-existing commitments in order to question them against the background of another's (Kingwell 1995: 26). The intent to win is subordinating the intent to learn, producing dynamics hostile to the attainment of mutual understanding.

Conclusion

Just because complete conflict resolution may appear out of reach does not mean we should do away with aspiring towards the resolution of conflict altogether. Conflict and coercion is everywhere, but so too is agreement and cooperation. Were this not true, there would be no foundation for constructive human relations and no basis for aspiring to transform conflicts in positive ways.

To see value in a norm of consensus is not to dismiss or trivialise its coercive potential. Assimilation, subjugation and marginalisation are very real perils of democratic practice geared towards unanimity in opinion, especially where the identities consolidating around a contested issue are strongly defined against one another. It is, however, important not to mistake closure in conflict as conceptually bound up with closure in democratic freedom. There is no logical basis for theorising a relationship of necessity between them. In this chapter, I have illustrated the subtle and beneficial ways a norm of consensus can inform democratic practice against arguments that it always subjugates and unjustifiably excludes. In doing so, I hope I have paved the way for an appreciation of the potential of consensus not only to limit democratic freedom, but also to serve as its very condition.

Notes

1. For a detailed analysis of how Mouffe and other agonists are reliant on consensus and foundational standpoints, despite criticising certain liberal and deliberative theories for this, see Dryzek and Niemeyer (2006: 644); Knops (2007: 116–17); and Erman (2009: 1044).
2. It should be stressed that Gaus would not share my conclusion that the normative imperative for justification should lead us to actually seek consensus in practice. In his view, public justification stands little chance of generating consensus in the face of deep disagreements, and given this, democratic decision making should ensue through 'adjudication': that is, an umpire hands down final decisions by striving to 'arrive at the best answer' (1997: 233). It is beyond the scope of this chapter to consider this proposal in full. Nevertheless, Gaus' response is not an intrinsic rejection of the need to seek consensus, but rather, arises in reference to the empirical obstacles to its generation, which in Gaus' view are excessive. I hope I have shown in the case study analysis above that his empirical assertion is perhaps overstated, given that consensus can be generated under specific institutional conditions. In addition, his proposal for an adjudicator is not mutually exclusive to having a place for a norm of consensus – both, in fact, will be necessary if adjudication is in some sense to remain tied to a process of accountability towards the adjudicated, rather than descend into authoritarianism.

Conclusion

What should be the nature of bonds between ethnically diverse citizens, and what kinds of interventions serve to bind divided populations are pressing questions that will always produce open answers rather than complete theoretical closure. Pinning down an ironclad formula for the expansion of solidarity is next to impossible, given the empirical variability in conditions that give rise to conflict and call for contextual variability in institutional responses. Moreover, to the extent that solidarity's core demands of answerability and autonomy sit together in tension, normative definitions of the phenomenon can only ever court controversy. Different individuals will pass different value judgements on the extent to which one constituent element of solidarity can legitimately encroach on the other, ensuring solidarity remains a topic of lively debate within academic and policy circles.

Nevertheless, this book has approached the study of solidarity with the view that certain generalisations can be made about the kinds of institutional arrangements conducive to cooperative and respectful relations, despite the empirical world's unwieldy nature. It has also taken it as given that universally valid suppositions can be made around the meaning of solidarity, even though trade-offs often arise between the demands of answerability to others on the one hand and autonomy over oneself on the other.

I have argued it is mistaken to assume the promotion of solidarity is dependent on the identification of supposedly inclusive national essences, and the expectation that ethnically diverse and divided populations bring their identities in line with those essences. Such a proposal offers an easy to grasp route to solidarity, and for this reason, is favoured by politicians in their rhetorical appeals for unity to a popular audience. Yet while offering a level prescriptive certainty that might be comforting to some, the notion that the internalisation of common national values and cultural traits is what brings diverse people to treat each other justly is simplistic and normatively spurious. Not only is such a programme of solidarity promotion inconsistent with respect for the integrity of individuals; it functions to intensify, rather than allay, antagonisms and divisions.

If any generalisations can be made around the nature and conditions of solidarity, it is that the phenomenon is dependent on the treatment of citizens as free, respected and materially secure. Each of these dimensions of human life is how a relation of attentiveness to another is expressed, given their core role in human well-being. Moreover, the expression of attentiveness along these dimensions of social existence has a self-fulfilling impact. People who feel others are making an effort to meet their concerns around freedom, respect and material security will be motivated to reciprocate this goodwill. Conversely, people who feel others are denying them such opportunities for self-realisation will be motivated to do the same in return.

This theoretical insight does not imply solidarity can always be generated. Across some identities it will be absent, as certain desires for freedom, respect and material security will clash irreconcilably and generate profound feelings of injustice. Nevertheless, the theoretical insight does identify what is necessary for a relationship of solidarity to be in existence, even though such relationships cannot be expected to always attain. In doing so, it offers a reference point for institutional designs seeking to pattern ties of obligation into the fabric of plural and divided societies.

Deliberative democracy was defended as the most suitable framework for meeting the normative demands of solidarity on the grounds that deliberative tenets call for a certain reflexivity in the pursuit of preferences. Deliberative exchanges emphasise reason giving and the justification of one's objectives to an affected constituency. For this reason, it entails a notion of collective organisation better reflecting the spirit of mutual obligation and reciprocity inherent to a relation of solidarity than do

competing models of multicultural coexistence with weak reflexivity demands.

By the same token, it was recognised that appeals to reason are
on their own insufficient for stimulating just institutional change
and attitudinal shifts reflective of solidarity when the starting
point of social interaction is inequality and disrespect. This is
because those occupying positions of privilege are not always
open to principled arguments and have the ability to withstand
pressure for change. As such, several non-deliberative proposals
were presented as legitimate counter-measures for the disruption
of circuits of domination where appeals to reason alone bear no
fruit. These proposals included acts of civil disobedience and
external influence, the intention of which is to make it excessively
costly for those in power to continue resisting principled demands
for reform. Other proposals that were defended as legitimate
included appeals to a speaker's authority, charisma and in-group
status during deliberations, the intention of which is to draw
attention to discredited arguments made by out-group members
and to generate a positive conversion of attitude towards their
identities.

While the promotion of national essences was regarded as
incompatible with solidarity, the pursuit of consensus was seen
as a constitutive element of the phenomenon. In opposition to
the assertion that aspirations to consensus can only ever diminish
opportunities for the expression of diversity, I argued it is actually
only when adversaries approach their disputes with a readiness
to find something valid about the other's position that collective
action becomes consistent with the just treatment of others. The
preparedness to be persuaded, but also to justify oneself to others,
serves as the very basis for the emergence of mutual understanding and communal association among equals, whether or not
consensus actually results from such interactions.

To some, the deliberatively oriented approach I have defended
throughout the book might come across as normatively arid
and too reactionary to offer a credible programme of progressive social change. If it is through practices of freedom, recognition and distribution that we enter into relationships of mutual
answerability, what then are the specific institutional arrange-

ments that enable us to cultivate solidarity? It seems that the empty proceduralism of deliberative theory can offer no guidance on this question. It only tells us how citizens should interact when pursuing their preferences and managing their disagreements. But it says nothing about what kinds of outcomes yielded by such interactions are most and least justifiable independently of how citizens interact. Everything is left to the democratic context, which might seem like a normatively weak response, especially when compared with *a priori* models of coexistence, such as Will Kymlicka's liberal theory of cultural rights explored in Chapter 2. These models specify upfront what kinds of group rights citizens can and cannot claim against each other, with the moral force of these specifications existing independently of what practical deliberation might have to say about them. In fact, the very point of *a priori* models is to provide institutional formulations that stand above practical deliberations. After all, if the objective is to determine what is right and what is wrong, it follows one must turn to philosophical reasoning for answers, rather than submit to what a community of citizens happens to be willing at a given moment, for the latter course can be disastrous for minorities subject to the caprices of majorities.

However, framing the problem as a stark choice between proceduralism on the one hand and *a priori* theorisation on the other sets up a false dichotomy, as each cannot do without the other. Proceduralism needs *a priori* theories to add philosophical grist and innovation to deliberations, while *a priori* models need inclusive deliberation to gain popular legitimacy and to be tailored to the specificities of a society. This co-dependency has gained increasing acknowledgement in theoretical debates formerly treating questions of justice as a choice between one approach or the other. For example, although advocating a procedurally oriented approach centred on 'dialogic contestation' to deal with disagreements over recognition, James Tully cautions against treating this as a final solution, as dialogic contestation too is 'always fraught with imperfections, injustices and irreducible disagreements' (Tully 2004: 101). While he still favours a 'dialogic' approach over a 'monologic' one to process competing claims for recognition, he also insists the latter plays 'an important yet non-sovereign counter-balancing role' on the former, given the former's propensity to run awry under majoritarian decision-making rules and asymmetries in power.

Similarly, although Kymlicka offers a set of upfront solutions to disagreements over the accommodation of diversity, he is also open to the view that some level of deliberation will be necessary in grounding his solutions. In his view, legal norms expressing minority rights must be targeted, rather than generic, in order to better reflect the considerable variation in characteristics existing between minorities and state structures around the world. This legal tailoring of rights, he asserts, would ideally come about collaboratively, through an international and inter-disciplinary conversation between academics, and state and non-state actors (Kymlicka 2007a: 298–303), pointing to the necessity of inclusive deliberation.

In light of this co-dependency, a more adequate reframing of the dilemma would be to ask how procedural or how *a prioristic* ideal theories of coexistence must be in order to remain consistent with solidarity. For reasons I will now identify, my view is they must be more procedural than *a prioristic*, explaining the book's preference for a deliberative approach to questions of diversity.

Turning first to *a priori* theorisation, its indispensability lies with the role it plays in initiating, feeding and enriching deliberations over institutional designs. *A priori* models supply deliberators with novel ideas, philosophically sound content and innovative solutions around impasses. As such, pre-deliberative formulations add to the quality and fairness of formulations that end up being developed and endorsed by a deliberating public. Indeed, were it not for the multicultural turn in political philosophy beginning in the 1980s, the empirical world would be much the worse for it, as philosophy's interest in questions of diversity spawned a bourgeoning body of normative literature that has influenced how partisans and lay people interpret the rightness or wrongness of their actions in relation to the most vulnerable members of society. It is therefore no exaggeration to say that advances we have witnessed in the rights and non-discrimination of cultural minorities, racial groups, women, gay, lesbian and transgender people, among others, cannot be understood in isolation of philosophical work contemplating the ethics of policies and laws directed at ending the mistreatment of these historically marginalised actors.

Nevertheless, inasmuch as *a priori* theorisation supplies the broader public with the epistemic and philosophical input necessary for sound judgement and just behaviour, it is also true that *a priori* thinking cannot do without the reflexive input of the broader public, for it is by undergoing the check of democratic deliberation that philosophically derived modes of being deliver on their promises of inclusion and emancipation. The point here is not simply that the authorship of affected actors in the design of their societies enables a better fit between philosophical content and empirical concerns, but more fundamentally, that permitting people to decide for themselves what their governing institutions should look like is the very essence of how they are treated as free and equal (Tully 2002; O'Flynn 2006: 48–50). If such popular involvement were not an integral condition of freedom and if the appropriateness of proposals could be surmised outside their intended empirical contexts, we would have no qualms leaving institutional design to philosophers, and no qualms doing away with the notion of popular consent. We would be consoled by the Platonic view that philosophers know what is in our best interests, and that questions of right and wrong are therefore best left to them. The reason we recoil from such moral perfectionism today is that we perceive it to be bound up in the very acts of domination and imperialism that philosophy hopes to eradicate. Our understanding of ourselves as free and equal is guided by the intuition that the laws and governing institutions with which we must comply have in some sense been shaped by us, approved by us, or sufficiently justified to us by those who enact them. For this reason, solidarity and questions of justice will always be reliant on deliberative practice and cannot be resolved through philosophical contemplation alone.

Bibliography

Abizadeh, Arash (2002), 'Does liberal democracy presuppose a cultural nation? Four arguments', *American Political Science Review*, 96: 3, 495–509.

Abizadeh, Arash (2005), 'Does collective identity presuppose an Other? On the alleged incoherence of global solidarity', *American Political Science Review*, 99: 1, 45–60.

Acharya, Amitav (2004), 'How ideas spread: Whose norms matter? Norm localization and institutional change in Asian regionalism', *International Organization*, 58: 239–75.

Amstutz, Mark R. (2005), *The Healing of Nations: The Promise and Limits of Political Forgiveness*, Oxford: Rowman & Littlefield.

Anderson, Benedict (1983), *Imagined Communities*, London: Verso.

Bächtiger, André, Markus Spörndli, Marco R. Steenbergen and Jürg Steiner (2007), 'Deliberation in legislatures: Antecedents and outcomes', in S. W. Rosenberg (ed.), *Deliberation, Participation, and Democracy: Can the People Govern?*, New York: Palgrave Macmillan, pp. 82–100.

Bakker, Edwin (2003), 'Roma policies in Eastern Europe. Success and its side-effect', *Helsinki Monitor*, 2: 161–72.

Balkan Insight (2008), 'Athens: No Macedonian minority in Greece', *Balkan Insight*, 16 July, <http://www.balkaninsight.com/en/article/athens-no-macedonian-minority-in-greece> (last accessed 5 February 2015).

Bauböck, Rainer (2001), 'Public culture in societies of immigration', *Willy Brandt Series of Working Papers in International Migration and Ethnic Relations*, 1: 01.

Bauböck, Rainer (2002), 'Farewell to multiculturalism? Sharing values and identities in societies of immigration', *Journal of International Migration and Integration*, 3: 1, 1–16.

BBC (2005), 'Writer repeats Turk deaths claim', *BBC*, 17 September,

<http://news.bbc.co.uk/2/hi/europe/4369562.stm> (last accessed 5 February 2015).

Bell, Daniel A. (1999), 'Democratic deliberation: The problem of implementation', in S. Macedo (ed.), *Deliberative Politics*, Oxford: Oxford University Press, pp. 70–87.

Bellamy, Richard (1999), *Liberalism and Pluralism: Towards a Politics of Compromise*, London: Routledge.

Benhabib, Seyla (1992), *Situating the Self: Gender, Community and Postmodernism in Contemporary Ethics*, Cambridge: Polity Press.

Benhabib, Seyla (1996), 'Toward a deliberative model of democratic legitimacy', in S. Benhabib (ed.), *Democracy and Difference: Contesting the Boundaries of the Political*, Princeton: Princeton University Press, pp. 67–94.

Benhabib, Seyla (2002), *The Claims of Culture: Equality and Diversity in the Global Era*, Princeton: Princeton University Press.

Berlin, Isaiah (1969), *Four Essays on Liberty*, Oxford: Oxford University Press.

Bieber, Florian (2006), 'After Dayton, Dayton? The evolution of an unpopular peace', *Ethnopolitics*, 5: 1, 15–31.

Bieber, Florian (2008), 'Power-sharing and the implementation of the Ohrid Framework Agreement', in S. Dehnert and R. Sulejmani (eds), *Power-Sharing and the Implementation of the Ohrid Framework Agreement*, Skopje: Friedrich-Ebert Stiftung, pp. 7–40.

Black, David (1999), 'The long and winding road: International norms and domestic political change in South Africa', in T. Risse, S. C. Ropp and K. Sikkink (eds), *The Power of Human Rights: International Norms and Domestic Change*, Cambridge: Cambridge University Press, pp. 78–108.

Bohman, James (1996), *Public Deliberation: Pluralism, Complexity, and Democracy*, Cambridge, MA: The MIT Press.

Boulden, Jane and Will Kymlicka (2015 forthcoming), 'Introduction', in J. Boulden and W. Kymlicka (eds), *International Approaches to Governing Ethnic Diversity*, Oxford: Oxford University Press.

Bray, Daniel (2011), *Pragmatic Cosmopolitanism: Representation and Leadership in Transnational Democracy*, New York: Palgrave Macmillan.

Brown, David (1994), *The State and Ethnic Politics in Southeast Asia*, New York: Routledge.

Brusis, Martin (2003), 'The European Union and interethnic power-sharing arrangements in accession countries', *JEMIE*, 1, 1–22.

Bukovansky, Mlada, Ian Clark, Robyn Eckersley, Richard Price,

Christian Reus-Smit and Nicholas Wheeler (2012), *Special Responsibilities*, New York: Cambridge University Press.

Butler, Judith (2004), *Precarious Life*, London: Verso.

Calvert, Aubin (2013), 'Politicizing deliberative democracy: Strategic speech in deliberative systems', PhD Dissertation, University of British Columbia.

Canovan, Margaret (2000), 'Patriotism is not enough', in C. McKinnon and I. Hampshire-Monk (eds), *The Demands of Citizenship*, London: Continuum, pp. 276–97.

Chambers, Simone (2003), 'Deliberative democratic theory', *Annual Review of Political Science*, 6, 307–26.

Chambers, Simone (2009), 'Rhetoric and the public sphere: Has deliberative democracy abandoned mass democracy?', *Political Theory*, 37: 3, 323–50.

Chambers, Simone and Jeffrey Kopstein (2001), 'Bad civil society', *Political Theory*, 29: 6, 837–65.

Checkel, Jeffrey T. (2005), 'International institutions and socialization in Europe: Introduction and framework', *International Organization*, 59: 801–26.

Chee-Beng, Tan (2002), *Chinese Minority in a Malay State: The Case of Terengganu in Malaysia*, Singapore: Eastern Universities Press.

Chen, Yu-Wen (2012), 'A comparative qualitative analysis of the international activism of ethnopolitical groups in Europe', *Ethnopolitics*, 11: 1, 43–65.

Chesterman, John (2005), *Civil Rights: How Indigenous Australians Won Formal Equality*, St Lucia: University of Queensland Press.

Chrisafis, Angelique (2011), 'Eurozone crisis forces Belgium to finally form a government', *The Guardian*, 2 December, <http://www.guardian.co.uk/world/2011/dec/01/eurozone-crisis-forces-belgium-government> (last accessed 6 February 2014).

Chua, Amy (2003), *World on Fire: How Exporting Free Market Democracy Breeds Ethnic Hatred and Global Instability*, London: Arrow Books.

Císař, Ondřej and Kateřina Vráblíková (2012), 'Transnational activism of social movement organizations: The effect of European Union funding on local groups in the Czech Republic', *European Union Politics*, 14: 1, 140–60.

Clark, Phil (2005), 'When the killers go home: Local justice in Rwanda', *Dissent*, Summer, 14–21.

Clifford, Bob (2002), 'Political process theory and transnational movements: Dialectics of protest among Nigeria's Ogoni minority', *Social Problems*, 49: 3, 395–415.

Collins, Barry E. (1970), *Social Psychology: Social Influence, Attitude Change, Group Processes and Prejudice*, Reading, MA: Addison-Wesley.

Dekker, Paul and Peter Ester (1996), 'Depillarization, deconfessionalization, and de-ideologization: Empirical trends in Dutch society 1958–1992', *Review of Religious Research*, 37: 4, 325–41.

Derrida, Jacques (1976), *Of Grammatology*, Baltimore: John Hopkins University Press.

Deveaux, Monique (2003), 'A deliberative approach to conflicts of culture', *Political Theory*, 31: 6, 780–807.

Diez, Thomas, Stephan Stetter and Mathias Albert (2008), 'Introduction', in T. Diez, M. Albert and S. Stetter (eds), *The European Union and Border Conflicts*, Cambridge: Cambridge University Press, pp. 1–12.

Dryzek, John (1990), *Discursive Democracy: Politics, Policy, and Political Science*, Cambridge: Cambridge University Press.

Dryzek, John (2000), *Deliberative Democracy and Beyond: Liberals, Critics, Contestations*, New York: Oxford University Press.

Dryzek, John (2005), 'Deliberative democracy in divided societies: Alternatives to agonism and analgesia', *Political Theory*, 33: 2, 218–42.

Dryzek, John (2007), 'Theory, evidence, and the tasks of deliberation', in S. W. Rosenberg (ed.), *Deliberation, Participation and Democracy: Can the People Govern?*, New York: Palgrave Macmillan, pp. 237–50.

Dryzek, John (2009), 'Democratization as deliberative capacity building', *Comparative Political Studies*, 42: 11, 1379–402.

Dryzek, John and Simon Niemeyer (2006), 'Reconciling pluralism and consensus as political ideals', *American Journal of Political Science*, 50: 3, 634–49.

Eckersley, Robyn (2000), 'Deliberative democracy, ecological representation and risk', in M. Saward (ed.), *Democratic Innovation: Deliberation, Representation and Association*, New York: Routledge, pp. 117–32.

Ercan, Selen A. (2011), 'The deliberative politics of cultural diversity: Beyond interest and identity politics?', in F. Monsouri and M. Lobo (eds), *Migration, Citizenship and Intercultural Relations: Looking through the Lens of Social Inclusion*, Farnham: Ashgate, pp. 75–88.

Ercan, Selen A. and Carolyn M. Hendriks (2013), 'The democratic challenges and potential of localism: Insights from deliberative democracy', *Policy Studies*, 34: 4, 422–40.

Eriksen, Thomas Hylland (2003), *Ethnicity and Nationalism*, 2nd edn, London: Pluto Press.

Erman, Eva (2009), 'What is wrong with agonistic pluralism?: Reflections on conflict in democratic theory', *Philosophy and Social Criticism*, 35: 9, 1039–62.

Festenstein, Matthew (2000), 'Cultural diversity and the limits of liberalism', in N. O'Sullivan (ed.), *Political Theory in Transition*, London: Routledge, pp. 70–89.

Festenstein, Matthew (2005), *Negotiating Diversity: Culture, Deliberation, Trust*, Cambridge: Polity.

Fishkin, James S. (2009), *When the People Speak*, Oxford: Oxford University Press.

Fishkin, James S. and Robert C. Luskin (2000), 'The quest for deliberative democracy', in M. Saward (ed.), *Democratic Innovation: Deliberation, Representation and Association*, New York: Routledge, pp. 17–28.

Fligstein, Neil (2008), *Euroclash: The EU, European Identity, and the Future of Europe*, Oxford: Oxford University Press.

Fraser, Nancy (1993), 'Rethinking the public sphere: A contribution to the critique of actually existing democracy', in B. Robbins (ed.), *The Phantom Public Sphere*, Minneapolis: University of Minnesota Press, pp. 1–32.

Fraser, Nancy (1995), 'From redistribution to recognition? Dilemmas of justice in a "post-socialist" age', *New Left Review*, 212, 68–93.

Fraser, Nancy (1997a), *Justice Interruptus: Critical Reflections on the 'Postsocialist' Condition*, New York: Routledge.

Fraser, Nancy (1997b), 'The public sphere: Models and boundaries', in C. Calhoun (ed.), *Habermas and the Public Sphere*, Cambridge, MA: The MIT Press, pp. 109–42.

Fraser, Nancy (2000), 'Rethinking recognition', *New Left Review*, 3, 107–20.

Freedman, Amy L. (2000), *Political Participation and Ethnic Minorities: Chinese Overseas in Malaysia, Indonesia, and the United States*, New York: Routledge.

Frost, Brian (1998), *Struggling to Forgive: Nelson Mandela and South Africa's Search for Reconciliation*, London: HarperCollins.

Gargarella, Roberto (1998), 'Full representation, deliberation, and impartiality', in J. Elster (ed.), *Deliberative Democracy*, Cambridge: Cambridge University Press, pp. 260–79.

Gaus, Gerald F. (1997), 'Reason, justification, and consensus', in

James Bohman and William Rehg (eds), *Deliberative Democracy: Essays on Reason and Politics*, Cambridge, MA: The MIT Press, pp. 205–42.

Geddes, Andrew (2000), 'Lobbying for migrant inclusion in the European Union: New opportunities for transnational advocacy?', *Journal of European Public Policy*, 7: 4, 632–49.

Gellner, Ernest (1983), *Nations and Nationalism*, London: Basil Blackwell.

Geyer, Robert (2003), 'Beyond the Third Way: The science of complexity and the politics of choice', *British Journal of Politics and International Relations*, 5: 2, 237–57.

Goodwin, June and Ben Schiff (1995), *Heart of Whiteness: Afrikaaners Face Black Rule in the New South Africa*, New York: Scribner.

Gordy, Eric D. (2005), 'What does it mean to break with the past?', in F. Bieber and C. Wieland (eds), *Facing the Past, Facing the Future: Confronting Ethnicity and Conflict in Bosnia and Former Yugoslavia*, Ravenna: Longo Editore, pp. 85–101.

Gourevitch, Philip (2009), 'People's hearts and minds need time to heal', *The Observer Magazine*, 8 November.

Gozdecka, Dorota A., Selen A. Ercan and Magdalena Kmak (2014), 'From multiculturalism to post-multiculturalism: Trends and paradoxes', *Journal of Sociology*, 50: 1, 51–64.

Greek Helsinki Monitor and Minority Rights Group – Greece (1998), 'Greece against its Macedonian minority: The Rainbow trial', Athens: ETEPE.

Green, Leslie (1995), 'Internal minorities and their rights', in W. Kymlicka (ed.), *The Rights of Minority Cultures*, Oxford: Oxford University Press, pp. 257–72.

Guelke, Adrian (2012), *Politics in Deeply Divided Societies*, Cambridge: Polity Press.

Guibernau, Montserrat (2007), *The Identity of Nations*, Cambridge: Polity Press.

Gutmann, Amy and Dennis Thompson (1996), *Democracy and Disagreement*, Cambridge, MA: Belknap Press of Harvard University Press.

Guy, Will (2011), 'Roma inclusion at the crossroads: Can the lessons from PHARE be learned?', *Roma Rights*, December, 7–17.

Habermas, Jürgen (1984), *The Theory of Communicative Action*, London: Heinemann Educational.

Habermas, Jürgen (1994), *Justification and Application: Remarks on Discourse Ethics*, Cambridge, MA: The MIT Press.

Habermas, Jürgen (1996), *Between Facts and Norms*, Cambridge: Polity Press.

Habermas, Jürgen (1998), *The Inclusion of the Other: Studies in Political Theory*, Cambridge, MA: The MIT Press.

Habermas, Jürgen (2001),'The postnational constellation and the future of democracy', in M. Pensky (ed.), *The Postnational Constellation: Political Essays*, Cambridge: Polity Press.

Hage, Ghassan (1998), *White Nation: Fantasies of White Supremacy in a Multicultural Society*, Sydney: Pluto Press.

Hassanpour, Amir (1992), *Nationalism and Language in Kurdistan 1918–1985*, Lewiston: Mellen University Press.

Hays, Allen (2012), 'Policing in Northern Ireland: Community control, community policing, and the search for legitimacy', *Urban Affairs Review*, 49: 4, 557–92.

Hendriks, Carolyn M., John Dryzek and Christian Hunold (2007), 'Turning up the heat: Partisanship in deliberative innovation', *Political Studies*, 55: 362–83.

Honneth, Axel (1992), 'Integrity and disrespect: Principles of a conception of morality based on the theory of recognition', *Political Theory*, 20: 2, 187–201.

Horowitz, Donald L. (1985), *Ethnic Groups in Conflict*, Berkeley: University of California Press.

Horowitz, Donald L. (2004), 'The alternative vote and interethnic moderation: A reply to Fraenkel and Grofman', *Public Choice*, 121: 507–16.

Human Rights Watch (1994), 'Denying ethnic identity: The Macedonians of Greece', New York: Human Rights Watch.

Humphrey, Michael (2009), 'Securitisation and domestication of diaspora Muslims and Islam: Turkish immigrants in Germany and Australia', *International Journal on Multicultural Studies*, 11: 2, 136–54.

ICG (2009), 'Bosnia: A test of political maturity in Mostar', *Europe Briefing Report, No. 54*, 27 July, Sarajevo and Brussels: International Crisis Group.

Illievski, Zoran and Dane Taleski (2009), 'Was the EU's role in conflict management in Macedonia a success?', *Ethnopolitics*, 8: 3–4.

James, Michael R. (2004), *Deliberative Democracy and the Plural Polity*, Lawrence, KA: University Press of Kansas.

Jarstad, Anna K. (2008a), 'Dilemmas of war-to-democracy transitions: Theories and concepts', in A. K. Jarstad and T. D. Sisk (eds), *From War to Democracy: Dilemmas of Peacebuilding*, Cambridge: Cambridge University Press, pp. 17–36.

Jarstad, Anna K. (2008b), 'Power sharing: Former enemies in joint government', in A. K. Jarstad and T. D. Sisk (eds), *From War to Democracy: Dilemmas of Peacebuilding*, Cambridge: Cambridge University Press, pp. 105–33.

Johnston, Alastair Iain (2005), 'Conclusions and extensions: Toward mid-range theorizing and beyond Europe', *International Organization*, 59, 1013–44.

Johnston, Alastair Iain (2008), *Social States: China in International Institutions, 1980–2000*, Princeton: Princeton University Press.

Jones, Peter and Ian O'Flynn (2013), 'Can a compromise be fair?', *Politics, Philosophy & Economics*, 12: 2, 115–35.

Kanra, Bora (2005), 'Democracy, Islam and dialogue: The case of Turkey', *Government and Opposition*, 40: 4, 515–40.

Karpowitz, Christopher, Chad Raphael and Allen S. Hammond (2009), 'Deliberative democracy and inequality: Two cheers for enclave deliberation among the disempowered', *Politics and Society*, 37: 4, 576–615.

Keating, Michael (2004), 'European integration and the nationalities question', *Politics and Society*, 32: 3, 367–88.

Keck, Margaret E. and Kathryn Sikkink (1998), *Activist Beyond Borders: Advocacy Networks in International Politics*, Ithaca: Cornell University Press.

Kelley, Judith (2004), 'International actors on the domestic scene: Membership conditionality and socialization by international institutions', *International Organization*, 58, 425–57.

Kingwell, Mark (1995), *A Civil Tongue: Justice, Dialogue, and the Politics of Pluralism*, University Park: Pennsylvania State University Press.

Knops, Andrew (2007), 'Debate: Agonism as deliberation – on Mouffe's theory of democracy', *The Journal of Political Philosophy*, 15: 1, 115–26.

Koinova, Maria (2008), 'Kinstate intervention in ethnic conflicts: Albania and Turkey compared', *Ethnopolitics*, 7: 4, 373–90.

Krog, Antjie (2008), '"This thing called reconciliation . . ." Forgiveness as part of an interconnectedness-towards-wholeness', *South African Journal of Philosophy*, 27: 4, 353–66.

Kymlicka, Will (1995), *Multicultural Citizenship: A Liberal Theory of Minority Rights*, Oxford: Oxford University Press.

Kymlicka, Will (2001), *Politics in the Vernacular: Nationalism, Multiculturalism and Citizenship*, Oxford: Oxford University Press.

Kymlicka, Will (2007a), *Multicultural Odysseys: Navigating the New International Politics of Diversity*, Oxford: Oxford University Press.

Kymlicka, Will (2007b), 'The new debate on minority rights (and postscript)', in A. Laden and D. Owen (eds), *Multiculturalism and Political Theory*, Cambridge: Cambridge University Press, pp. 23–59.

Kymlicka, Will and Magda Opalski (eds) (2001), *Can Liberalism Be Exported? Western Political Theory and Ethnic Relations in Eastern Europe*, Oxford: Oxford University Press.

Laclau, Ernesto (1996), *Emancipation(s)*, London: Verso.

Laclau, Ernesto and Chantal Mouffe (1985), *Hegemony and Socialist Strategy: Towards a Radical Democratic Politics*, London: Verso.

Laden, Anthony (2000), *Reasonably Radical: Deliberative Liberalism and the Politics of Identity*, Ithaca: Cornell University Press.

Lake, David A. and Donald Rothchild (1996), 'Containing fear: The origins and management of ethnic conflict', *International Security*, 21: 2, 41–75.

Lears, T. J. Jackson (1985), 'The concept of cultural hegemony: Problems and possibilities', *The American Historical Review*, 90: 3, 567–93.

Lijphart, Arend (1969), 'Consociational democracy', *World Politics*, 21: 2, 207–25.

Lijphart, Arend (1977), *Democracy in Plural Societies: A Comparative Exploration*, New Haven, CT: Yale University Press.

Lijphart, Arend (1997), 'Self-determination versus pre-determination of ethnic minorities in power-sharing systems', in W. Kymlicka and I. Shapiro (eds), *Ethnicity and Group Rights*, New York: New York University Press, pp. 275–87.

Lijphart, Arend (1998), 'Consensus and consensus democracy: Cultural, structural, functional, and rational-choice explanations', *Scandinavian Political Studies*, 21: 2, 98–108.

Little, Adrian (2003), 'The problems of antagonism: Applying liberal political theory to conflict in Northern Ireland', *British Journal of Politics and International Relations*, 5: 3, 373–92.

Little, Adrian (2012), 'Political action, error and failure: The epistemological limits of complexity', *Political Studies*, 60: 1, 3–19.

Love, Nancy (1989), 'Foucault & Habermas on discourse & democracy', *Polity*, 22: 2, 269–93.

Luskin, Robert C., Ian O'Flynn, James S. Fishkin and David Russell (2014), 'Deliberating across deep divides', *Political Studies*, 62: 1, 116–35.

McAleese, Deborah (2007), 'Yob Ulster: Hit and run victim ordered to sing Sash before being beaten', *Belfast Telegraph*, 7 August, <http://www.

belfasttelegraph.co.uk/news/local-national/yob-ulster-hitandrun-vic tim-ordered-to-sing-sash-before-being-beaten-13465222.html> (last accessed 5 February 2015).

McClure, Kirstie (1992), 'On the subject of rights: Pluralism, plurality and political identity', in C. Mouffe (ed.), *Dimensions of Radical Democracy: Pluralism, Citizenship, Community*, London: Verso, pp. 108–27.

McDougall, Gay (2009), 'Report of the independent expert on minority issues, Gay McDougall: Addendum: Mission to Greece (8–16 September 2008)', UN Human Rights Council, <http://www.unhcr. org/refworld/docid/49b7b2e52.html> (last accessed 5 February 2015).

McGarry, John and Brendan O'Leary (1994), 'The political regulation of national and ethnic conflict', *Parliamentary Affairs*, 47: 1, 94–115.

McGarry, John and Brendan O'Leary (2006), 'Consociational theory, Northern Ireland's conflict, and its agreement. Part 1: What consociationalists can learn from Northern Ireland', *Government and Opposition*, 41: 1, 43–63.

McGarry, John and Brendan O'Leary (2009), 'Must pluri-national federations fail?', *Ethnopolitics*, 8: 1, 5–25.

Mansbridge, Jane, James Bohman, Simone Chambers, Thomas Christiano, Archon Fung, John Parkinson, Dennis Thompson and Mark Warren (2012), 'A systemic approach to deliberative democracy', in J. Parkinson and J. Mansbridge (eds), *Deliberative Systems: Deliberative Democracy at the Large Scale*, Cambridge: Cambridge University Press, pp. 1–26.

Markell, Patchen (1997), 'Contesting consensus: Rereading Habermas on the public sphere', *Constellations*, 3: 3, 377–400.

Markell, Patchen (2003), *Bound by Recognition*, Princeton: Princeton University Press.

Martinez-Torres, Maria Elena (2001), 'Civil society, the internet, and the Zapatistas', *Peace Review: A Journal of Social Justice*, 13: 3, 347–55.

Marusic, Sinisa-Jakov (2012), 'Macedonia protests pass off without bloodshed', *Balkan Insight*, 11 May, <http://www.balkaninsight. com/en/article/macedonia-protests-tense-with-minor-incidents> (last accessed 5 February 2015).

Mead, George Herbert (1934), *Mind, Self, and Society from the Stand-Point of a Social Behaviorist*, Chicago: University of Chicago Press.

Michas, Takis (2008), 'Why critics of Greece's Macedonia policy keep silent', *BIRN*, 17 September, <http://www.balkaninsight.com/en/

article/why-critics-of-greece-s-macedonia-policy-keep-silent> (last accessed 5 February 2015).

Mill, John Stuart (2003), 'Bentham', in *Utilitarianism; and, On Liberty*, ed. M. Warnock, Malden: Blackwell Publishing, pp. 52–87.

Miller, David (1995), *On Nationality*, Oxford: Oxford University Press.

Miller, David (2000), *Citizenship and National Identity*, Malden: Blackwell Publishers.

Modood, Tariq (1998), 'Anti-essentialism, multiculturalism and the recognition of religious groups', *The Journal of Political Philosophy*, 6: 4, 378–99.

Montague, James (2009), 'Lebanese season ends amid violence and political intrigue', *The Guardian*, 30 April, <http://www.guardian.co.uk/football/blog/2009/apr/30/lebanon-football-league-hezbollah-sectarianism> (last accessed 5 February 2015).

Moore, Alfred (2014), 'Deference in numbers: Consensus, dissent and judgement in Mill's account of authority', *Political Studies*, 62: 1, 187–201.

Mouffe, Chantal (2000), *The Democratic Paradox*, London: Verso.

Norval, Aletta J. (2004), 'Hegemony after deconstruction: The consequences of undecidability', *Journal of Ideologies*, 9: 2, 139–57.

Ober, Josiah (1989), *Mass and Elite in Democratic Athens*, Princeton: Princeton University Press.

O'Flynn, Ian (2006), *Deliberative Democracy and Divided Societies*, Edinburgh: Edinburgh University Press.

O'Flynn, Ian (2009), 'Deliberative democracy, the public interest and the consociational model', *Political Studies*, 58: 572–89.

O'Neill, Shane (2002), 'Democratic deliberation and cultural rights: The Orange Order march at Drumcree', in M. P. d'Entrèves (ed.), *Democracy as Public Deliberation*, Manchester: Manchester University Press, pp. 178–200.

Parekh, Bhikhu (2006), 'Europe, liberalism and the "Muslim question"', in T. Modood, A. Triandafyllidou and R. Zapata-Barrero (eds), *Multiculturalism, Muslims and Citizenship: A European Approach*, London: Routledge, pp. 179–203.

Pettit, Philip (1997), *Republicanism: A Theory of Freedom and Government*, Oxford: Oxford University Press.

Pettit, Philip (2005), 'In reply to Bader and Vatter', in M. S. Williams and S. Macedo (eds), *Political Exclusion and Domination*, New York: New York University Press, pp. 182–8.

Pevnick, Ryan (2009), 'Social trust and the ethics of immigration policy', *The Journal of Political Philosophy*, 17: 2, 147–67.

Phillips, Anne (1995), *The Politics of Presence*, Oxford: Oxford University Press.

Phillips, Anne (1999), *Which Equalities Matter?*, Malden: Polity Press.

Pitkin, Hanna (1972), *The Concept of Representation*, 2nd edn, Berkeley: UCLA Press.

Price, Robert M. (1991), *The Apartheid State in Crisis: Political Transformation in South Africa, 1975–1990*, Oxford: Oxford University Press.

Przeworski, Adam (1998), 'Deliberation and ideological domination', in J. Elster (ed.), *Deliberative Democracy*, Cambridge: Cambridge University Press, pp. 140–60.

Putnam, Robert D. (2000), *Bowling Alone: The Collapse and Revival of American Community*, New York: Simon and Schuster.

Putnam, Robert D. (2007), '*E pluribus unum*: Diversity and community in the twenty-first century', *Scandinavian Political Studies*, 30: 2, 137–74.

Rawls, John (1997), 'The idea of public reason', in J. Bohman and W. Rehg (eds), *Essays on Reason and Politics: Deliberative Democracy*, Cambridge, MA: The MIT Press, pp. 93–131.

Reilly, Benjamin (2001), *Democracy in Divided Societies: Electoral Engineering for Conflict Management*, Cambridge: Cambridge University Press.

Reynolds, Andrew (2002), *The Architecture of Democracy: Constitutional Design, Conflict Management, and Democracy*, Oxford: Oxford University Press.

Risse, Thomas (2000), '"Let's argue!": Communicative action in world politics', *International Organization*, 59, 1–39.

Risse, Thomas and Kathryn Sikkink (1999), 'The socialization of international human rights norms into domestic practices: Introduction', in T. Risse, S. C. Ropp and K. Sikkink (eds), *The Power of Human Rights: International Norms and Domestic Change*, Cambridge: Cambridge University Press, pp. 1–38.

Roeder, Philip G. (2005), 'Power dividing as an alternative to ethnic power sharing', in P. G. Roeder and D. Rothchild (eds), *Sustainable Peace: Power and Democracy after Civil Wars*, Ithaca: Cornell University Press, pp. 51–82.

Roeder, Philip G. (2009), 'Ethnofederalism and the mismanagement of conflicting nationalisms', *Regional and Federal Studies*, 19: 2, 203–19.

Rothchild, Donald and Philip G. Roeder (2005a), 'Dilemmas of state-building in divided societies', in P. G. Roeder and D. Rothchild (eds), *Sustainable Peace: Power and Democracy after Civil Wars*, Ithaca: Cornell University Press, pp. 1–25.

Rothchild, Donald and Philip G. Roeder (2005b), 'Power Sharing as an impediment to peace and democracy', in P. G. Roeder and D. Rothchild (eds), *Sustainable Peace: Power and Democracy after Civil Wars*, Ithaca: Cornell University Press, pp. 29–50.

Sandel, Michael (1984), 'The procedural republic and the unencumbered self', *Political Theory*, 12: 1, 81–96.

Sandel, Michael (1996), *Democracy's Discontent: America in Search of a Public Philosophy*, Cambridge: Belknap Press of Harvard University Press.

Schaap, Andrew (2004), 'Political reconciliation through a struggle for recognition', *Social and Legal Studies*, 13: 4, 523–40.

Schaap, Andrew (2006), 'Agonism in divided societies', *Philosophy and Social Criticism*, 32: 2, 255–77.

Schimmelfennig, Frank (2005), 'Strategic calculation and international socialization: Membership incentives, party constellations, and sustained compliance in Central and Eastern Europe', *International Organization*, 59: 827–33.

Schimmelfennig, Frank and Hanno Scholtz (2007), 'EU democracy promotion in the European neighbourhood: Political conditionality, economic development, and transnational exchange', Working Paper no. 9.

Shapiro, Ian (1996), *Democracy's Place*, Ithaca: Cornell University Press.

Shapiro, Ian (1999), 'Enough of deliberation: Politics is about interests and power', in S. Macedo (ed.), *Deliberative Politics*, Oxford: Oxford University Press, pp. 28–38.

Sharples, R. W. (1994), 'Plato on democracy and expertise', *Greece & Rome*, 41: 1, 49–56.

Smooha, Sammy (2001), 'The tenability of partition as a mode of conflict regulation: Comparing Ireland with Palestine-Land of Israel', in J. McGarry (ed.), *Northern Ireland and the Divided World: The Northern Ireland Conflict and the Good Friday Agreement in Comparative Perspective*, Oxford: Oxford University Press, pp. 309–35.

Snyder, Jack and Karen Ballentine (1996), 'Nationalism and the marketplace of ideas', *International Security*, 21: 2, 5–40.

Staub, Ervin (2006), 'Reconciliation after genocide, mass killing, or intractable conflict: Understanding the roots of violence, psychological recovery, and steps toward a general theory', *Political Psychology*, 27: 6, 867–94.

Stokes, Susan C. (1998), 'Pathologies of deliberation', in J. Elster (ed.), *Deliberative Democracy*, Cambridge: Cambridge University Press, pp. 123–39.

Sunstein, Cass R. (2001), *Designing Democracies: What Constitutions Do*, Oxford: Oxford University Press.

Sunstein, Cass R. (2002), 'The law of group polarization', *The Journal of Political Philosophy*, 10: 2, 175–95.

Svensson, Isak (2007), 'Mediation with muscles or minds? Exploring power mediators and pure mediators in Civil Wars', *International Negotiation*, 12: 229–48.

Tamir, Yael (1993), *Liberal Nationalism*, Princeton: Princeton University Press.

Thompson, John B. (1994), 'The theory of structuration', in D. Held and J. B. Thompson (eds), *Social Theory of Modern Societies: Anthony Giddens and His Critics*, Cambridge: Cambridge University Press, pp. 56–76.

Thompson, Simon (2006), *The Political Theory of Recognition: A Critical Introduction*, Cambridge: Polity Press.

Tucker, Robert C. (1995), *Politics as Leadership*, Columbia: University of Missouri Press.

Tully, James (2000), 'The challenge of reimagining citizenship and belonging in multicultural and multinational societies', in C. McKinnon and I. Hampshire-Monk (eds), *The Demands of Citizenship*, New York: Continuum, pp. 212–34.

Tully, James (2002), 'The unfreedom of the moderns in comparison to their ideals of constitutional democray', *The Modern Law Review*, 65: 2, 204–28.

Tully, James (2004), 'Recognition and dialogue: The emergence of a new field', *Critical Review of International Social and Political Philosophy*, 7: 3, 84–106.

Uslaner, Eric M. (1999), 'Democracy and social capital', in M. E. Warren (ed.), *Democracy and Trust*, Cambridge: Cambridge University Press, pp. 121–50.

Vachudova, Milada Anna (2005), *Europe Undivided: Democracy, Leverage and Integration after Communism*, Oxford: Oxford University Press.

Vachudova, Milada Anna (2014), 'EU leverage and national interests in the Balkans: The puzzles of enlargement ten years on', *Journal of Common Market Studies*, 52: 1, 122–38.

Valadez, Jorge M. (2001), *Deliberative Democracy, Political Legitimacy, and Self-Determination in Multicultural Societies*, Boulder, CO: Westview Press.

Valentine, Jeremy (2001), 'The hegemony of hegemony', *History of the Human Sciences*, 14: 1, 88–104.

Vasilev, George (2011), 'EU conditionality and ethnic coexistence in the Balkans: Macedonia and Bosnia in a comparative perspective', *Ethnopolitics*, 10: 1, 51–76.

Vasilev, George (2013), 'Multiculturalism in post-Ohrid Macedonia: Some philosophical reflections', *East European Politics and Societies*, 27: 4, 685–708.

Walsh, Katherine Cramer (2007), 'The democratic potential of civil dialogue', in S. W. Rosenberg (ed.), *Deliberation, Participation and Democracy: Can the People Govern?*, New York: Palgrave Macmillan, pp. 45–63.

Walzer, Michael (1977), *Just and Unjust Wars: A Moral Argument with Historical Illustrations*, New York: Basic Books.

Walzer, Michael (1983), *Spheres of Justice: A Defense of Pluralism and Equality*, New York: Basic Books.

Walzer, Michael (2006), 'Nation and universe', in B. Haddock, R. Peri and P. Sutch (eds), *Principles and Political Order: The Challenge of Diversity*, London: Routledge, pp. 10–41.

Warren, Mark E. (2002), 'Deliberative democracy', in A. Carter and G. Stokes (eds), *Democratic Theory Today: Challenges for the 21st Century*, Malden: Polity Press, pp. 173–201.

Warren, Mark E. (2007), 'Institutionalising deliberative democracy', in S. W. Rosenberg (ed.), *Deliberation, Participation and Democracy: Can the People Govern?*, New York: Palgrave Macmillan, pp. 272–88.

Waterbury, Myra A. (2008), 'Uncertain norms, unintended consequences: The effects of European Union integration on kin-state politics in Eastern Europe', *Ethnopolitics*, 7: 2–3, 217–38.

Weymans, Wim (2005), 'Freedom through political representation: Lefort, Gauchet and Rosanvallon on the relationship between state and society', *European Journal of Political Theory*, 4: 3, 263–82.

Wild, Leni (2006), 'Strengthening global civil society', London: Institute for Public Policy Research.

Williams, Melissa S. (2000), 'The uneasy alliance of group representation and deliberative democracy', in W. Kymlicka and W. Norman (eds), *Citizenship in Diverse Societies*, Oxford: Oxford University Press, pp. 124–52.

Wimmer, Andreas (2013), *Waves of War: Nationalism, State Formation, and Ethnic Exclusion in the Modern World*, Cambridge: Cambridge University Press.

Wolff, Stefan (2006), *Ethnic Conflict: A Global Perspective*, Oxford: Oxford University Press.

Young, Iris Marion (1990), *Justice and the Politics of Difference*, Princeton: Princeton University Press.

Young, Iris Marion (2000), *Inclusion and Democracy*, New York: Oxford University Press.

Zaller, John R. (1992), *The Nature and Origins of Mass Opinion*, Cambridge: Cambridge University Press.

Zartman, William (2001), 'The timing of peace initiatives: Hurting stalemates and ripe moments', *Ethnopolitics*, 1: 1, 8–18.

Zartman, William (2008), *Negotiation and Conflict: Essays on Theory and Practice*, New York: Routledge.

Index

EU representative:
Easy Access System Europe
Mustamäe tee 50, 10621 Tallinn, Estonia
Gpsr.requests@easproject.com

www.ingramcontent.com/pod-product-compliance
Lightning Source LLC
Chambersburg PA
CBHW070755240726
48654CB00007B/93